MW01193762

"With meticulous researc
a well-deserved tribute tc
pioneering Black sportsw
this compelling book does... .... _....
of Black newspapers and Negro League baseball, and a testament to everything that was gained—and lost—with the integration of American sports
and media."

Mark Whitaker, author of *Smoketown: The Untold Story of the
Other Great Black Renaissance* and *Saying It Loud: 1966-The
Year Black Power Challenged the Civil Rights Movement*

"I stand on the notebooks of Sam Lacy and Wendell Smith. Though working
for competing Black publications, they conspired—unintentionally most
likely—to shame and shatter baseball's race barrier, opening the gates for
myriad Black players to excel in the majors. Make no mistake: 'Baseball'
did not eliminate its color barrier, Lacy and Smith did. They also cleared
the path for generations of Black journalists to not just "cover" sports but
challenge its racist ways—challenge it to change, and change America."

Roy S. Johnson, co-author of *Magic's Touch* with Earvin Johnson,
Outrageous! with Charles Barkley, and *Aspire Higher* with
Avery Johnson

"This is like a major stage production. Wayne Dawkins presents us with
overlapping tales from early-to-late 20th-century Black journalism, and
sports is the backdrop, with an early focus on the crass racism of 'America's
favorite pastime,' baseball. Key characters in the book are Sam Lacy and
Wendell Smith, now deceased Black journalists who displayed singular
courage and talents over the past century. Dawkins' well researched accounts can bring one to tears even as they inspire hope."

Ron Howell, retired Brooklyn College Associate Professor,
veteran journalist, and author of *King Al: How Sharpton Took the
Throne* (2021); *Boss of Black Brooklyn: The Life and Times of
Bertram L. Baker* (2019); and *One Hundred Jobs: A Panorama
of Work in the American City* (2000)

Sam Lacy and Wendell Smith

This dual biography highlights the transformative influence of Sam Lacy and Wendell Smith, two journalists who changed American sport and society through their calls to desegregate Major League Baseball and recognize Black baseball players.

In a decade-long battle, Lacy and Smith tirelessly advocated for the inclusion of Black players in the major leagues, reporting in the *Baltimore Afro-American* and *Pittsburgh Courier*, respectively. Both sports writers covered players in the Negro Leagues, following off-season games in places like Mexico, Cuba, and the Dominican Republic. In 1947, Lacy's and Smith's work helped break through MLB's racial barriers when Jackie Robinson joined the Brooklyn Dodgers. Over the coming years, Lacy and Smith, on individual career trajectories but sharing a common goal, would report on the dissolution of the Negro Leagues and future MVPs such as Willie Mays, Hank Aaron, and Elston Howard. The book considers the lasting legacies of these sports journalists, both recognized in the writers' wing of the Baseball Hall of Fame.

Through its thoughtful analysis of Lacy and Smith's groundbreaking impact on America's pastime, this book will appeal to students and general readers interested in sports history and journalism and Afro-American history.

Wayne Dawkins is a professor of professional practice at Morgan State University in Baltimore. He is the author of biographies of politician Emanuel Celler and voting rights activist Andrew W. Cooper. Dawkins was a journalist at four daily newspapers for a quarter century before transitioning to academia two decades ago.

ROUTLEDGE HISTORICAL AMERICANS

SERIES EDITOR: PAUL FINKELMAN

Routledge Historical Americans is a series of short, vibrant biographies that illuminate the lives of Americans who have had an impact on the world. Each book includes a short overview of the person's life and puts that person into historical context through essential primary documents, written both by the subjects and about them. A series website supports the books, containing extra images and documents, links to further research, and where possible, multi-media sources on the subjects. Perfect for including in any course on American History, the books in the Routledge Historical Americans series show the impact everyday people can have on the course of history.

Theodore Roosevelt: A Manly President's Gendered Personal and Political Transformations
Neil H. Cogan

Elie Wiesel: Humanist Messenger for Peace
Alan L. Berger

Clare Boothe Luce: American Renaissance Woman
Philip Nash

Sam Lacy and Wendell Smith: The Dynamic Duo that Desegregated American Sports
Wayne J. Dawkins

Sam Lacy and Wendell Smith

The Dynamic Duo that Desegregated American Sports

WAYNE DAWKINS

Dear Connie,

Thanks for the generously kind words!

Enjoy.

Wayne J. Dawkins

2025

Routledge
Taylor & Francis Group

NEW YORK AND LONDON

Designed cover image: National Baseball Hall of Fame and Museum

First published 2025
by Routledge
605 Third Avenue, New York, NY 10158

and by Routledge
4 Park Square, Milton Park, Abingdon, Oxon, OX14 4RN

Routledge is an imprint of the Taylor & Francis Group, an informa business

ISBN: 978-1-032-25566-8 (hbk)
ISBN: 978-1-032-23386-4 (pbk)
ISBN: 978-1-003-28392-8 (ebk)

DOI: 10.4324/9781003283928

Typeset in Times New Roman
by KnowledgeWorks Global Ltd.

To Horace E. Shuman and Joseph Dorinson

CONTENTS

PART II
Documents

PREFACE

Baseball, an iconic American pastime, infiltrated society more than a century ago. As America transitioned from an agrarian to mostly urban society because of the Industrial Revolution, the sport kept pace with the historical evolution of the country, influencing U.S. culture, and continues to do so. America's 20th-century pastime was enjoyed by its Black citizens too. However, its sportsmen were banned during Jim Crow segregation in the early 1900s.

A curious psychological game followed. Judge Kennesaw Mountain Landis, who became Commissioner of Baseball in November 1920, said in March 1933 that he was not opposed to Blacks playing Major League Baseball if the league's team owners were OK with the practice. After a dozen years of silence Landis' position was relayed via Leslie O'Conner, secretary-treasurer of MLB, in response to a handful of Black Press commentaries, wrote Chris Lamb in his book "Conspiracy of Silence."

The baseball team owners smacked Landis' metaphorical ball back, saying it was the commissioner who tied their hands and forbade the hiring of Blacks. While the owners of White baseball teams engaged in these sophistries, Negro League professional baseball sprouted and flourished for decades in Chicago, Kansas City, Missouri, Birmingham, Alabama, Newark, New Jersey, and New York City.

SAM LACY and WENDELL SMITH, both sports journalists working in the Black-owned press, each campaigned to convince Major League Baseball to desegregate their teams. Lacy of the Baltimore *Afro-American*, and Smith of the *Pittsburgh Courier*, operated on parallel tracks focused on the same mission: To reason, ridicule, and report to owners and the commissioner that Black ballplayers deserved to compete on Major League Baseball teams.

Lacy and Smith covered Black talent in the Negro Leagues and followed them out of the United States to Mexico, Cuba, and Santa Domingo (Dominican Republic), where players traveled to play off-season ball, often for better pay and for relief from aggressive racism.

By 1947, Lacy and Smith's reporting helped change minds: Jackie Robinson, a four-sport college varsity athlete from California and commissioned Army officer, broke through with the Brooklyn Dodgers.

Lacy and Smith's lifelong journalism work transformed American Society. Baseball touched many branches of America including its folklore, politics, and culture. Because of their impact, like the third and fourth hitters on a baseball team, these men are deserving of a joint biography.

Smith's strategic writing about Jackie Robinson – celebratory, indignant, or conciliatory depending on situations – wrote Andrew Schall in 2011, was the media playbook for the emerging civil rights movement. Smith exerted soft power over public opinion.

Lacy and Smith were transformative influencers of American society crying out for wider recognition. Smith's role in the integration of baseball has reached the level of popular culture. In 2013, Andre Holland played the role of Wendell Smith in "42" a successful biopic of Jackie Robinson with Chadwick Boseman in the starring role as Robinson. Harrison Ford of "Indiana Jones" and "Star Wars" fame portrayed Brooklyn Dodger's general manager and part-owner Branch Rickey.

Lacy and Smith's careers and lives were opposites. Except for a brief stint at the *Chicago Defender*, the third trident of the great, Black-owned early 20th-century newspapers, Lacy worked at the Baltimore *Afro-American* from the 1930s through the early 21st century. He lived well into his nineties. Smith worked most of his career at the Black-owned *Pittsburgh Courier*, then made the leap to daily, White-majority owned journalism at the *Chicago American*, where he excelled. Smith leaped again to the new medium, television, at WGN-Chicago. Smith, in 1968, also co-wrote a biography about the inventor of automotive power steering.

Unlike Lacy, Smith's life was brief. He lived into his late fifties and died in 1972.

I was introduced to Lacy's work in 1985 when I attended the National Association of Black Journalists convention in Baltimore. During the awards ceremony at the Morris Mechanic Theatre, Lacy the local hero was celebrated. There I learned that Black sports journalists for decades lobbied and eventually helped make Robinson's breakthrough possible.

More importantly, perhaps, the reporting of Smith and Lacy also helped make Robinson's breakthrough successful. Both were instrumental in bringing his skills, and the issues Robinson faced, to the American public.

Finally, just as Robinson integrated baseball, Smith and Lacy integrated American sports writing.

In 2013, Smith received a posthumous induction into the NABJ Hall of Fame. I was tasked to write the article that introduced Smith and his accomplishments. Meanwhile, Smith's profile grew because of Andre Holland's portrayal of him as Robinson's chaperon/ghost writer in the movie "42."

While lobbying relentlessly to break baseball's color line, Smith and Lacy shattered barriers too. Wendell Smith was inducted into the writer's wing of the Baseball Hall of Fame. Lacy followed him into the hallowed hall years later.

When Jackie Robinson integrated baseball, both writers were banned from press boxes. Smith routinely sat in the ballpark seats with the fans, his typewriter on his lap. There were times when Lacy was barred from the ballpark seats but was allowed to sit on the edge of a team's dugout. Once, Lacy sat on the roof of a ballpark to work. White sportswriters left the press box and joined him in a rare show of solidarity.

Lacy and Smith did more than cover baseball. They were versatile journalists, whether they had to fill in as editors on the news desks, or whether they covered other sports, especially boxing, tennis, and football, with the same insight, authority and oftentimes wry humor, or irony. Late in their careers, Lacy and Smith covered the dissolution of the Negro Leagues and the remarkable flow of superstar talent from the Negro Leagues, including future winners of the Most Valuable Player (MVP) award Willie Mays, Hank Aaron, and Elston Howard, who followed pacesetters, Robinson, Larry Doby, Don Newcombe, Satchel Paige, and Roy Campanella into the majors. Newcombe by the way was an MVP and Rookie of the Year.

Twenty-first century Major League Baseball became less Black after the 1970s as the National Football League and National Basketball Association became the major attractions for emerging Black athletes. There was a remarkable moment in 1979 when the Pittsburgh Pirates fielded an all-Black starting nine, a veritable all-Western Hemisphere team of players from the United States, Central America, and the Caribbean. That year the Pirates won the World Series.

In the 2020s, Black professional athletes are millionaires and at times at odds with overwhelmingly White billionaire sports team owners – specifically the NFL – who engage in "re-tread" hiring of mediocre-to-losing White coaches rather than hire Black coaches despite some accomplishing winning records or at least coaching up God-awful teams to competitiveness. Struggles for access and opportunity continued even in the transformed 21st century.

A tip of the hat to Sam Lacy and Wendell Smith, the winning combination whose influences profoundly changed American sport and society.

ACKNOWLEDGMENTS

An author's name is presented in big, bold type on a book cover and its spine; however, many hands are responsible for making the book possible. Again, that's the case here.

Paul Finkelman, my editor. He invited me to write this biography, first offering Sam Lacy, then me counter offering to write about Lacy and peer Wendell Smith. Finkelman accepted. As an editor, he was equal parts blunt and nurturing, as well as trustworthy. Even in my anxious moments, Finkelman assured me, "this is going to be a great book," or "you're in the last mile of a 26-mile marathon." When I raced to make the contractual deadline, he slowed me down. Take a little more time if necessary to tell the story well, he counseled. Thank you.

Our mutual colleague Candace Jackson Gray is appreciated for long talks about the process of research and writing. We were mutual support systems for my book and for her doctoral dissertation.

DeWayne Wickham, emeritus and founding dean of the Morgan State University School of Global Journalism and Communication where I am a faculty member, recalled minor league Baltimore Orioles baseball of the 1940s when Jackie Robinson came to town with the Montreal Royals. Wickham read parts of the draft that dealt with Baltimore and provided valuable feedback. Praises too to his successor, Jackie Jones, who supported me immensely, specifically by covering travel and lodging for my research trip to Cooperstown, New York, in June 2022.

Thank you to the editors at Routledge, Allison Sambucini, editorial assistant, and Kimberley Smith, senior editor, History of the Americas, for guiding my manuscript through proposal, acceptance, and production.

Alex Holt, a student at the University of Maryland, in June 2022, shared audio recordings he made to interview Tim Lacy, Sam's octogenarian son. Karen Turner, associate professor at Temple University, Philadelphia, alerted me about the May 2022 symposium about the Negro Leagues/Jackie Robinson in which Branch Rickey Jr. participated.

Gregory Lee and David Squires, both members of the National Association of Black Journalists Sports Task Force, enthusiastically read early drafts of the manuscript. Hamil Harris invited me to Howard University, where he was teaching in February 2023, so I could interview him about his experiences in working for Sam Lacy in the late 1980s.

John Horne of the Baseball Hall of Fame, Cooperstown, sent photographs of Jackie Robinson, Sam Lacy, Wendell Smith, and others to illustrate this book. Thanks also to the researchers at Baseball Hall of Fame, who assisted me during my research trip in June 2022.

Campus and public librarians. I appreciated their helpfulness – universally done with cheer – in assisting me with research. Thanks to the help at Morgan State University Richardson Library, Norfolk State University Library, Howard University, Washington, DC, and its new Black Press Archives, Christopher Newport University Library, George Mason University Law Library, Fairfax, Virginia, the New York Public Library, SOHO/Village, Arlington, Virginia, Public Library, and the North Suffolk, Virginia, Public Library; College of William and Mary Law School Wolf Library, Slover Library, Norfolk, Virginia. Also, the Library of Congress Madison Wing, Washington, DC.

Milton Kent and Edward Robinson Jr., fellow faculty at Morgan State University SGJC, read and did vacuum cleaner copy editing to early chapters of the manuscript, which was much appreciated.

Special thanks to my blended family of adult children, Faith, and Roger Wynn, and Carmen Dawkins, for their thoughtful Father's Day gifts – writing supplies – that immediately supported my work.

Todd S. Burroughs, collaborator, and alter ego on my 2012 and 2020 biographies proffered valuable advice: bury myself in the library microfilm rooms and read Sam Lacy's "A to Z" columns, loaded with revealing nuggets.

Olivia Chipepo, Morelys Urbano, Brianna Washington, Kameron Hobbs, all of them students in my 200-level (sophomore-junior) spring 2023 Information Gathering and Research class, answered my challenge. I asked each of them to read several chapters of books then write book reports and submit them to me. I was on a tight submission deadline. My scheme was to compress some reading time. Chipepo, Urbano, Washington, and Hobbs were engaging and high-performing students in that 30-member class, and I pitched to them. I made the right choices. Also, Melanie Battle and Reginald Allen, both Morgan State University 2023 graduates, jumped in when I asked to transcribe audiotape.

Thank you to Michael Scott Pifer and Michael Marsh, co-authors of *The Wendell Smith Reader*, which was published in April 2023. Pifer, editor of the anthology, reached out to me before publication and sent an advance copy of the book. The resource helped me immensely in cutting research time.

Thank you to Justice Hill and Ricky Clemons. They both put me in touch with Bob Kendrick of the Negro League Baseball Museum in Kansas City. Kendrick generously provided valuable insight about the golden era of Negro League baseball, right at the time when Jackie Robinson made his leap to the Dodgers organization.

Because Earl Caldwell proudly wore a Pittsburgh Pirates ballcap, I asked him if he remembered Wendell Smith and the *Pittsburgh Courier*. Caldwell surely did. The Central Pennsylvania native read the *Courier* voraciously during his youth. He gave me an interview. Caldwell told me about the time he and his sibling came face-to-face with Jackie Robinson after a game at Forbes Field.

Inside the Jackie Robinson Museum on Varick Street in lower Manhattan, I studied artifacts and took copious notes. I noticed another man at my side scribbling as feverishly. I introduced myself. He answered, Lee Loenfish. I smiled. When my editor urged me to track down a book to cite a small, precise detail, it was Loenfish's 2010 book about baseball and labor. He was at the museum, like me, to do research on his next baseball book. We promised to keep in touch and support each other's work. Loenfish also asked if I knew Joseph Dorinson, which brought another smile. Dorinson, who taught history at Long Island University-Brooklyn, was my favorite professor when I was his student in the 1970s. Dorinson, 90, is retired. It was a thrill to purchase a copy of his 2022 book about African American sports heroes and get the book autographed. It was also a blessing to have dinner with Dorinson and other LIU sports alumni last June in New York.

Thanks to a search on Facebook, I connected in May 2023 with Ryan Cuffee, granddaughter of John Wendell Smith, the sportswriter's son. Smith Jr. had a recording career, supported by Sara Wright Smith, his mother, who was Wendell Smith's ex-wife. Cuffee sent an image of the record disc "Puddin' Pie," one of Smith's songs.

Thanks to Lorenz Finison and Carmen Fields for sending articles about champion Black bicyclist Major Taylor that Wendell Smith wrote about in August 1971 for the Tuesday at Home magazine supplement in the *Cleveland Plain Dealer.*

Finally, gratitude to Claudia Cox Dawkins, my wife and trusted confidante. She consoled and protected me when I felt blue or bruised, and she needled me when she believed I needed to get in gear. "It's time to wrap it up," said Claudia, as in stop collecting more research and write the ending. She read my late drafts. I handed Claudia red pens to mark up my hard copy. She was candid, cheering me on for pages she thought were well crafted, or clumsy, or needed to be cut back. Her candor anchored me.

PART I

SAM LACY AND WENDELL SMITH

CHAPTER 1

COMING OF AGE

Sam Lacy and Wendell Smith

For this dual biography of crusading Black Press sports journalists, we begin with Sam Lacy, because of his age, and conveniently because of alphabetical order. Wendell Smith's early life will be subject of the second half of the chapter.

Samuel Harold Lacy was born October 23, 1903, Washington, DC. Many written accounts – including Lacy's autobiography *Fighting for Fairness* – report he was born in 1903 in Mystic, Connecticut, and that the Lacy family moved from the seaport New England town to Washington, DC when Sam was two years old. However, census record shows he was actually born in Washington, DC in 1905. His mother Rose (Bell) was a member of the Shinnecock Tribe which is part of the Mohawk nation.[1] His father Samuel Erskine Lacy was a public notary. As an adult he recalled attending the funeral service for his paternal grandfather Henry Erskine Lacy when he was six years old. In 1893 his grandfather became the first Black detective – and (later a) sergeant – to serve in the Washington Metropolitan Police Department.[2]

The extended family lived in the northwest section of the city. Edward Kennedy "Duke" Ellington, the future American music icon, lived nearby. During Sam's high school years his classmates included Charlies Drew, the future physician and blood plasma specialist, William Hastie, the first African-American federal judge, and Allison Davis, who as an anthropologist at the University of Chicago, would become only the second African-American professor at a major elite university.[3]

The nation's capital was a segregated Southern town during Lacy's childhood. He initially attended Paul Lawrence Dunbar, one of the most

DOI: 10.4324/9781003283928-2

important segregated public high schools to serve African Americans in the United States (and in the early 1900s a rare public college-prep institution that served Blacks), then Lacy transferred to Armstrong (Technical) High School.[4]

Schoolboy Sam was too young to know; however, his introduction to a six-decade-long newspaper career began as a preschooler who watched his father read newspapers and then save them. The newsprint was used to stuff the worn-out shoes handed down from older siblings.

Sam's father also stacked old newspapers in a woodshed. One day four-year-old Sam was making mudpies near the shed. He also played with matches. Sam asked his older sister for a glass of water, then another, and then another.

"What are you doing with all of this water?" asked Rosina. She soon found out. The shed burst into flames. Rosina yelled out to her sister Evelyn to help put out the flames. Getting no response, Rosina battled the fire. Fire engines were racing to the scene. Evelyn did not hear Rosina's yelling because she was at the piano inside the house practicing her piano lesson.[5]

Though too young at the time to imagine a career in journalism, as a schoolboy Sam was blessed with a superior skill, handwriting. His style was unconventional. Sam held his pencil between the third and fourth fingers instead of the thumb and index fingers. Mrs. Payne, Sam's first-grade teacher at Garnet Elementary, admonished him for not holding his pencil her way. Angrily Payne cracked Sam's knuckles with a ruler to make him grip the instrument "properly." The next morning, Sam's mother accompanied him to school. Rose Lacy told Payne, "This child writes better than anyone in the room, including the woman in charge." Sam was immediately transferred to Miss Beason's first-grade class.[6]

In 1909, when Sam was six years old, 47 Whites and six Blacks founded the National Association for the Advancement of Colored People. Sixty-nine Blacks were reported lynched that year. Two years later three other organizations merged and formed the National Urban League largely to assist southern Blacks migrating to the urban north.[7]

Sam's first job, at age eight, was as a printer's helper at a shop two blocks from the family home. He learned to set type and run a rotary press. Sam was paid $2 a week ($62 in 2013 dollars). As a grade-school boy and later high school teenager, Sam engaged in numerous entrepreneurial – his euphemism for dishonesty – schemes that nearly placed him on the path to being a jailbird instead of a journalist. At home Sam demanded bribes from his older sisters, so he wouldn't interrupt when boyfriends came courting.

Then there was this bartering scheme: An elderly woman, "Aunt Susie," began living in his family's house as a boarder. Sam and his pals met Mr. Turner, an old bachelor who agreed to sew the horsehide covers back on baseballs the boys scavenged in a vacant lot. As compensation, Sam would sneak into "Aunt Susie's" room and pour Old Orchard liquor into a thimble to give Mr. Turner.

Schoolboy pranks escalated to teenage petty crime. Sam became addicted to betting on horses, then a leading American sport along with boxing and baseball. Sam passed some bad $10 and $20 checks, until he came to his senses, paid his debts, and stopped dodging the police.[8]

Sam's family had a professional breadwinner, his dad was a notary public and researcher for a Washington, DC law firm, and his mom espoused middle-class values. Sam began at college prep-oriented Dunbar High School; however, he rebelled against the rules at the class-conscious institution. "Actually, I have been considered anti-establishment," Lacy wrote in his autobiography. "Maybe stubborn and impulsive would be a better description. I resented authority figures who behaved in an autocratic fashion."[9]

Sam's temperament was tested during his sophomore year when he made first sergeant on the school's prestigious drill team. Sports-loving Sam was caught avoiding drill practice so he could play baseball and the school principal took away his stripes. Angered over his demotion, Sam transferred to crosstown rival Armstrong Technical High School, previously known as Armstrong Manual Training School. There Sam played football, basketball, and baseball, earning acclaim for his pitching prowess. "Sam Lacy, the high school hurling ace," crowed one sportswriter, who said the short, slim, and wiry teenager struck out the side of freshmen Howard University batters and preserved a win for Armstrong Tech.[10] Sam was also praised for helping defeat intercity rival Baltimore High School. Most of all he took pride and vengeance in striking out 17 Dunbar hitters: "[I] got a kick out of beating Dunbar when the two teams squared off."[11]

Sam wrote about sports for his high school newspaper yet did not envision turning that activity into a career. He grew up mere blocks from Griffith Stadium, home of the Washington Senators (which fans also called the Nationals, like their 21st-century team name).

Sam and several neighborhood boys were allowed inside the ballpark to shag fly balls during Senators batting practice. Up close with some of the Senators, Sam was friendly with pitching legend Walter Johnson, and he also ran errands for other players. Furthermore, young Sam, 18 at the time, made extra money as a vendor and sold merchandise in the stands at Griffith Stadium. He was so embedded that Senators management rewarded him for his pregame work by giving him the most lucrative items to sell, coffee in the spring, cold drinks by summer, and scorecards in 1924 when the Senators beat the New York Giants in the World Series.[12]

These contacts were exceptions to the rule and reality that Washington, DC was a Jim Crow city. On Memorial Day, (May 30) 1922, at the dedication of the Lincoln Memorial, District police were positioned to maintain racially segregated seating at the National Mall. Robert R. Moton, a Black educator and disciple of Booker T. Washington, was censored by the Lincoln Memorial Commission and forbidden from uttering a critique that the memorial honoring the Great Emancipator was a hollow gesture contradicting racial inequality that flourished across America.

Sam Lacy attended Senators games but could only watch from the "colored" section in right field. His friendly interactions with big-league players did not matter; he was a second-class citizen.[13] In addition to Walter Johnson, Sam Lacy watched baseball immortals Babe Ruth and Ty Cobb and Negro League all-stars Oscar Charleston and John Henry Lloyd because the Pittsburgh-based Homestead Grays played at the ballpark in 1921, and in 1940 rented the stadium to play home games. "I was in a position to make some comparisons," Lacy remembered in 1990, "and it seemed to me that those Black players were good enough to play in the big leagues. There was of course, no talk then of that ever happening. When I was growing up, there was no real opportunity for Blacks in any sport." Among other ways to earn summer money, Sam served as a caddy at the all-White Columbia Country Club in Chevy Chase, Maryland. Senators' secretary-treasurer Ed Eynon was among those golfers.

While in high school, Sam landed a job at the District of Columbia's largest Black newspaper, the *Washington Tribune*. He earned 25 cents per column inch reporting on high school sports as a stringer. Sam's sports editor was Louis Lautier, a future barrier-breaking Black Press White House correspondent in the 1940s and 1950s.[14]

Lacy graduated from Armstrong Tech High School in 1922.[15] He wanted full-time work in sports. He imagined coaching a basketball team or competing and serving as player/manager with a semipro baseball team. For two years Lacy played for the Black, semipro Washington Black Sox, and the (Atlantic City) Bachrach Giants.[16]

Lacy was able to compete against John Henry Lloyd, Oscar Charleston, and Martin Dihigo, who would later be elected to the Baseball Hall of Fame for their accomplishments in the Negro Leagues. At the time Lacy was only 17-years-old, and he later said he stopped playing professional baseball because of the culture it created. "When the games ended all of the players would go back to the boarding houses and smoke and drink and have women in their company." He recalled, "I went once and said this is not my life."[17] But, while on the Black teams Lacy played infrequently and with mediocre results. The existing statistics from his playing days are incomplete, but show he was not a great player.

Pressed by his mother to go to college, Lacy spent a year at Howard University but never went back.[18] In 1927 and about age 23, Lacy married Alberta Robinson.[19] Their son Samuel Howe "Tim" Lacy was born on February 8, 1938.

In 1934 Sam Lacy started his professional journalism career writing about sports for the city's major Black paper, the *Washington Tribune*. Lacy covered local teams and wrote a column called "Looking 'Em Over with the Tribune." That year he was promoted to sports editor. More than reporting on box scores and chronicling wins and losses, Lacy possessed a platform to comment on social trends, especially on discrimination against Black athletes.

For example, in 1934 Lacy opined that White public school students often were given new and modern athletic facilities, while DC-area Black student-athletes had to accept outdated and inadequate gymnasiums and equipment. Lacy also critiqued how Black people were depicted on the new medium radio, and notably admonished comedian Will Rogers for uttering "nigger" during a network radio skit.[20]

Samuel Lacy Sr. was an enthusiastic *Washington Senators* fan. Sam's father attended games regularly. A Senator's tradition was to walk in a parade to Griffith Stadium for the first game of the season. In 1923, Lacy Sr. who was in his fifties stood in the parade route cheering the team as it passed. He wore a white ribbon with the inscription, "I saw Walter Pitch His First Game – 1907," which referenced revered pitcher Walter Johnson.

"And then," said son Sam Lacy, "this guy spits right in this old man's face." The man was Nick Altrock, a Senators pitcher, who after retiring, coached the team for 40 years. Sam's father nevertheless continued to go to games until Opening Day April 1945 when he stopped in protest. The Senators signed Bert Shepard, a war hero, who was a one-legged pitcher. Lacy's father, age 77 at the time, explained his boycott in a letter to owner Griffith: "I found a one-legged man on the team and no colored given a tryout."[21]

By this time Sam was an emerging sports journalist who was fine-tuned to answer insults of Black sports. Washington radio announcer Arch McDonald plugged a game between Black baseball teams and said, "these are funny things, these colored ball games." McDonald pretended to be informed but was clueless, and Lacy suspected that the announcer did not know that annual games were played between the Baltimore Black Sox and White Major League all-stars. Lacy's response:

> I dare say a WJSV sports announcer would laugh in your face if you attempted to tell him that a colored baseball team played "ring-around-the-rosey" with an outfit composed of Lefty Grove, Hack Wilson, Joe Hauser, Kiki Cuyler, Monte Weaver, and a host of others. But Arch says, "They will keep you laughing, these colored ball games." Haw, haw, haw …[22]

In May 1934, Lacy, at age 31, reasoned that during the Depression Black inclusion in professional baseball could be also good for the game and the bottom line.[23]

Yet maintaining rigid segregation of baseball was relentless. Four months later in September, Lacy's *Tribune* reported that the Springfield, Massachusetts entry in the American League Junior Baseball Tournament was withdrawn because the Gaston, North Carolina hotel where reservations had been made would not accept the African American pitcher-outfielder Ernest Taliaferro of Springfield.[24]

Lacy's first *Washington Tribune* column was published in August 1935. He asked, "Why not give baseball a little color?" He prophesized that integration would increase attendance in Major League ballparks. The Great Depression was crippling America. In 1934, US unemployment was 21.7%. Hobos, unemployed men, and runaway children stowed away on railroad cars, moving from town to town.

It was a time of breadlines. Economic pain also spread around the globe.[25] Still, even the poorest couples saved nickels and dimes in order to go out on weekends where for a few hours they could escape from the poverty and dreariness and dance to America's popular music, orchestral jazz. Ballgames were another form of cheap entertainment.

In 1937, Lacy had a two-and-half-hour discussion with Washington Senators owner Clark Griffith about the integration of Major League Baseball. Lacy had shagged flies with Homestead Grays stars that included Josh Gibson and Buck Leonard. Seeing those players up close like the White stars on the same Griffith Stadium field, only on different days, convinced Lacy they were as talented or possibly more talented than White major league stars.

"This was not the right time and integration would kill Black organized baseball," Griffith told Lacy. The sports journalist pushed back. If you don't try there will never be a good time to change. Griffith countered that integration would put "Four hundred colored guys out of work." Lacy volleyed, "When Abe Lincoln ended slavery, he put 400,000 [Negroes] out of work." Still Griffith would not budge. However, the owner added that he supported setting up a league of eight bona fide clubs of Black players."[26]

Some Negro League players at that time expressed doubt or resignation that breaking the barrier was worth it. Jud Wilson of the Grays told Lacy when baseball finally accepted Black players those men would be segregated when it came to hotels housing them and "we will be madder than we are now." Felton Snow, manager of the Baltimore Elite Giants, 1939 Negro National League champions, told Lacy that summer that major league moguls might pick the wrong player or players to enter their league and the result would be "the opposition forces would have strong support for their disapproval of colored baseball talent."[27]

As a sportswriter Lacy wrestled with the conflicting, see-sawing attitudes of White Major League Baseball owners and Black (Negro) baseball players. Lacy did have an unwavering criticism: It seemed Major League Baseball was willing to include anybody, as long as they were not Black. Lacy wrote:

> There have been Italians, Jews, Germans, Frenchmen, Irishmen, Indians, Spaniards, Mexicans, Slavs, name-what-you-want-and-you-can-get-'em, wearing the uniforms of major league teams within the past decade. But no colored.

Lacy also wrote:

> Baseball has given employment to known epileptics, kleptomaniacs, and a generous scattering of saints and sinners. A man who is totally lacking in character has turned out to be a star in baseball. A man whose skin is white or red or yellow has been acceptable. But a man whose character may be of the highest and whose ability may be Ruthian has been barred completely from the sport because he is colored.[28]

***

At the time Lacy began crusading for Blacks to be allowed to play professional baseball, Black athletes were already popular American champions in boxing and track and field. Joe Louis was "the Brown Bomber" and became world heavyweight champion in 1937. The year before, sprinter Jesse Owens was the multi-gold medal Olympic runner, along with a number of other Black gold medal winners, including Mack Robinson and Ralph Metchalfe.[29] With these achievers on display Lacy wrote that Joe Louis did not need distractions such as entertainer Bill "Bojangles" Robinson, who turned up in Louis' entourage. Lacy noted that Louis' managers did a good job of polishing the champ's images as a wholesome, humble bruiser, unlike the previous Black champion Jack Johnson who was a cocky, carousing chap who antagonized Whites in the early decade of Jim Crow America. Bojangles, Lacy wrote, was tied to the Jack Johnson era and should be avoided:

> [They are] ... different types. Robinson belongs to the minstrel world. Louis is part of our athletic life, a life we are anxious to raise from the slough of burnt-cork performance.

Lacy referenced Bojangles's chair dance in front of Dr. W.A. Goodloe's home, and his tapdancing atop a table, and the dancer's moss-covered joke at an Elks event that honored Louis and Owens. The joke Lacy wrote was pleasant as a decayed tooth. The criticism drew a rebuke from Fannie S. Clay Robinson, Bojangles' wife, manager, and co-founder of the Negro Actors Guild of America. As for the "burnt cork" reference, Mrs. Robinson said her husband was pleased to be linked with Al Jolson, Eddie Cantor, and others. Burnt cork was applied to perform in blackface, a conventionalized comic travesty of Blacks. She told Lacy, "He should be pitied instead of censured" for what he wrote. Lacy published her letter in the *Tribune* without comment, except to reprint his original comments "for those who tuned in late."[30] Lacy did not dislike "Bojangles" or deny he was a talented entertainer. The sportswriter did believe that "Bojangles" minstrelsy was a distraction to Joe Louis, who was projected as a clean-cut sports hero deserving of respect. Yet Lacy was demeaning to a rare Black star who was able to navigate a cruel and discriminatory America. Bojangles Robinson smiled and danced his way into mainstream America's hearts and was successful artistically and financially. He was charitable with his wealth, which earned Robinson grace with Blacks who felt he pandered to Whites.[31] It remains mystifying why Lacy was so nasty.

***

On October 23, 1937, Lacy broke news that a Syracuse University football player advertised as the only Hindu in college football was actually a Black teenager, quarterback Wilmeth Sidat-Singh. Sidat-Singh rebuffed school public relations suggestions that he wear East Indian attire. Syracuse was to play at the University of Maryland. "Negro to play U. of Maryland: Boy called Hindu by Papers" (in Baltimore, Washington, DC, and New York) was the headline on Lacy's *Washington Tribune* column.

No White college in Dixie hosted a game against a team with Black players because of a "gentleman's agreement" to exclude Blacks. That record remained intact. Syracuse lost 13-0 to Maryland without Sidat-Singh, who was benched by his school.[32]

Lacy pursued the story to expose racism in college sports plus hypocrisy practiced by some college athletic conferences. The expose prevented Sidat-Singh from playing and handicapped the Syracuse team. Lacy took flak from critics who said he should have kept quiet about the Hindu scam and allowed Sidat-Singh to play. Lacy was unrepentant in print: "This writer does not concur in the opinion that waiting until after the boy had played would have been a better 'joke' on Maryland University." The last laugh occurred the following year. In a rematch at Syracuse in upstate New York, Sidat-Singh played, and Syracuse beat Maryland 53-0. That win persuaded Maryland's Southern Conference rival, Duke University, to rescind its racial exclusion before its game with Syracuse.[33] Lacy was too self-righteous. He could have been silent about Sidat-Singh's true ethnicity before the first University of Maryland match. That choice would be more than a mere "joke." Instead, it could have been a heavyweight blow to segregationist attitudes.

The student-athlete was born Wilmeth Webb in Washington, DC to Black parents. After Wilmeth's biological father died, reported Lacy, the widow married Samuel Sidat-Singh, an immigrant from Trinidad of South Asian descent and a Howard University-trained physician with a practice in Harlem. The stepfather legally adopted Wilmeth and changed his last name. The son would become Lieutenant Sidat-Singh during World War II. Sidat-Singh became a Tuskegee Airman with the 332nd Fighter Group, 100th Fighter Squadron. Weeks after graduating from Tuskegee Airfield Academy in Alabama in March 1943, Sidat-Singh was sent to flight training in Michigan. During a flight, he experienced engine trouble and parachuted, landing in Lake Huron. A search for the pilot was unsuccessful. After 49 days a Coast Guard patrol found the body offshore. Sidat-Singh was wrapped in his parachute and had drowned near East Tawas, Michigan. His body was brought to Washington, DC for burial at Arlington National Cemetery.[34] The buried include 3,000 Civil War "contrabands," Civil War US Colored Troops, and Sgt. Medgar Evers, a World War II veteran and later civil rights martyr. [35]

***

In the final weeks of 1937 Lacy left the *Washington Tribune* where he was sports editor/managing editor for the competing *Washington Afro-American*. He was a sports editor and stayed until 1939. Lacy departed because of a conflict of interest. Lacy acknowledged that while serving as the *Afro's* sports editor, he was also coaching the Washington Bruins professional basketball team that played Sunday games at Turner's Arena. Lacy's team included Black college basketball stars Tarzan Cooper, who once played for the New York Renaissance (Rens), and Soup Campbell, former captain of the historically Black Virginia Union University CIAA championship team. *Washington Afro* editor Ralph Matthews told Lacy he did not approve of him sponsoring and promoting a team while working for the paper as a sports journalist.

In addition to coaching the Bruins, Lacy handled team business affairs that included paying the players and rent to play in the arena. Lacy resisted Matthews' order to set aside coaching because he believed he could not abandon his players. But the journalism field established a code of ethics. SPJ – the Society of Professional Journalists – in 1926 established its code by borrowing language from the American Society of Newspaper Editors.[36]

Lacy had to be aware he was violating professional rules, and now another newspaper was about to expose his bad judgment. On February 19, 1941, the *Washington Daily News* reported that Lacy was coaching the Bruins. A news hook was his team was about to play the Heurich Brewers of the Whites-only Industrial League. Lacy was on the verge of becoming a sports barrier breaker: The Bruins was about to become the first Black team to join the American Basketball League that included the Heurich club.

Carl Murphy, publisher of the *Afro-American* chain and Matthew's (and Lacy's) boss, summoned Lacy to Baltimore to discuss the conflict. Murphy told Lacy, "I like to have my editors responsible. So, suppose you disassociate yourself from the *Afro-American* until such time as the season is over. When your season is over, you come back and see me." Lacy complied, and he transferred to the *Afro's* Baltimore office in 1941.

But his stint at the Baltimore *Afro-American* was brief and contentious. Art Carter, a friend of Lacy, was sports editor, so Lacy was tasked with other assignments. One of the assignments was a July 1941 article about an aircraft manufacturer's plan to ignore President Franklin D. Roosevelt's new anti-discrimination executive order. Lacy did not like reporting so-called hard news and wanted to resume sports writing. However, there was no opportunity at that time in Baltimore. Lacy's editor was Elizabeth "Bettye" Murphy Phillips, one of his publisher's five daughters. While driving along Orleans Street (Route 40) for an assignment that in Lacy's opinion made no sense, he swung the car into a U-turn then disappeared. The next time someone from the *Afro* heard from Lacy he was in Chicago.[37]

After working at a few short-term jobs, Lacy visited Lucius Harper of the Black-owned *Chicago Defender*, among the trio of leading, nationally distributed newspapers along with the Baltimore *Afro-American* and the *Pittsburgh Courier*. Lacy did not go to the *Defender* initially he said because he left the rival *Afro* and might not be looked upon favorably in that orbit of Black media workers. Yet John Sengstacke, nephew of founding publisher of the *Defender* Robert S. Abbott, accepted Harper's recommendation and hired Lacy as a desk editor.[38]

He did not cover sports at the *Defender*. Frank A. "Fay" Young was a sports editor, and at that time the first dean of Black baseball writers.[39] Young, who arrived at the *Defender* not long after its 1905 launch, was "Medium sized, bespectacled, always immaculately dressed and sometimes caustic of tongue," wrote A.C. Doc Young (not related) in a 1970 *Ebony* magazine profile. The writer added, "He [Fay Young] was justifiably proud of his position, if unwisely selfish in the operation of his department."[40] Lacy often clashed with Young, and while both men had forceful personalities, Young had the last word: Lacy would not be covering sports for the *Defender*.[41]

Still, Lacy thought often about baseball, and he realized he was in the same city with Major League Baseball Commissioner Kennesaw Mountain Landis, who had been a federal judge before becoming commissioner. Lacy reached out to Landis in the 1930s when he worked at the *Washington Tribune* and a second time when he moved to the Washington *Afro-American*.

Now in Chicago, Lacy tried to schedule a meeting with Landis. "Judge Landis did everything possible to avoid meeting with me or anyone to talk about the segregation issue," said Lacy, adding, "I sent him a note that said I would meet with him any hour of any day of any week, any week of any year, any time of time." He received no response.[42]

In the fall of 1943, Landis answered, "OK, you can talk. You can come in." After writing about allowing Blacks to play professional baseball with Whites in 1935 and engaging in a lengthy conversation with Washington Senators owner Griffith in 1937, Lacy anticipated the long-desired opportunity to make his pitch directly to the baseball commissioner and American and National League owners.

Lacy assumed that because he connected with Landis, he would be allowed to attend the baseball owners meeting from November 29 to December 3 in New York City. Landis invited internationally famed singer-actor Paul Robeson, and three leading Negro Newspaper Publishers Association members, Ira F. Lewis of the *Pittsburgh Courier,* John Sengstacke of the *Chicago Defender,* and Howard Murphy of the Baltimore *Afro-American.* Lacy, who helped arrange the meeting, was not invited. Despite his absence Lacy's work made a difference. For the first time Black people spoke face-to-face with the leaders of organized baseball about integration.

Before the four Black men spoke, Landis read a joint American League-National League statement that said, "There is no rule, formal or informal, or any understanding – unwritten, subterranean or sub-anything – against the hiring of Negro players by the teams of organized baseball."[43] Ira Lewis of the *Pittsburgh Courier* pushed back against the commissioner's claim: "We believe that there is a tacit understanding, there is a gentleman's agreement that no Negro players be hired." Lewis' reply angered Landis, but the assertion silenced the room and appeared to draw the approval of the owners. Those owners met privately on December 3, then returned to tell the Black delegation: "Each club is entirely free to employ Negro players to any and all extent it pleases. The matter is solely for each club's decision, without restriction whatsoever."[44] Howard Murphy of the Baltimore *Afro-American* voiced four recommendations: Immediate steps to be taken to accept Negro players into the framework of organized baseball; the process for promotion and elevation in baseball be applied without prejudice; same system for selection of players be used, and a joint statement be made by the leagues.

Lacy's work, communication with Landis that resulted in talks among Black publishers and Robeson, the commissioner, and the baseball owners, was a breakthrough. For nearly 25 years Landis succeeded in stifling any discussion of integrating professional baseball. But in December 1943, Major League Baseball went on the record they could consider allowing Blacks to play the national pastime.

Still, Lacy was humiliated because he was not allowed to participate in the summit he helped facilitate. Wendell Smith however was at the meeting and reported for the *Pittsburgh Courier*.[45] Lacy came home to Washington for Christmas to celebrate with family. He also did fence-mending with his former employer. Lacy dropped by the Washington office of the *Baltimore Afro-American* to see friends William "Scottie" Scott and John H. Murphy III. Publisher Carl Murphy was there too.

He asked, "What are you doing in Washington Sam?" Lacy replied, "Looking for a job."

"Are you?" said Murphy. The publisher led Lacy into an anteroom then said, "Are you serious?" There was an opportunity to work at the *Baltimore Afro-American*. Lacy said, "I can't come back at the same salary, and I can't come back working under your daughter."

Murphy answered, "That's all right. When can you start?"[46]

Lacy was allowed time to give notice to the *Chicago Defender* and he returned to the *Afro-American* for good on January 4, 1944. Art Carter, Lacy's friend and the paper's sports editor, was overseas in Europe as an *Afro's* World War II correspondent.[47] Lacy resumed covering sports again. His column – like the *Washington Tribune* days – was called "Looking 'Em Over." His initial offering was what Lacy called the real story of the Cleveland meeting of Negro Publishers, Robeson, and Landis.

The *Afro-American* did publish Lacy's story, given that Murphy was in the room. It showed that the publisher respected Lacy and his journalistic instincts. Lacy wrote:

> The major league club owners are almost fanatical in their dislike of communism. Robeson's presence on the occasion under discussion and at the [insistence] of Landis, reminds me of a cartoon I once saw of a man extending his right hand in a gesture of friendship while clenching a long knife in a left hand concealed behind his back.

In other words, by this clever little maneuver, Landis told the gullible colored folks, "Here's how I feel. This is your chance to put it squarely up to the men who control the purse strings of the game. I'm with you, now go to it."

But on the other hand, he said to his owners, "Use your own judgment in this matter, but remember, here's a communist influence along with the torchbearers."[48]

Lacy was 40 years old when he returned to the *Afro-American* in 1944. Lacy dropped anchor and covered sports from that base for the rest of the 20th century and for the early years of the 21st century. His defining story would be the erasure of the baseball color line.[49]

***

Wendell Smith grew up in Detroit. His father was the chef for Henry Ford Sr. In high school, Smith outpitched a rival, however scouts pursued the White athlete and passed him over. Smith also played basketball at West Virginia State College. He pursued a journalism career in the late 1930s.

Unlike most Blacks of his generation, Smith grew up around Whites. Born in Detroit on June 27, 1914, John Wendell Smith was named after his father, who was raised on a farm in Dresden, Ontario, Canada.[50] In 1911, Wendell Sr. migrated to Detroit as a Great Lakes ship kitchen hand. He also cooked for Canadian and American railroads. In 1912 Smith married Detroit native Lena Gertrude Thompson, who did not work outside the home but was a member of three volunteer groups connected with St. Matthews Episcopal Church, a Black congregation that existed for 170-plus years.[51]

Eventually, the elder Wendell became the personal chef to Henry Ford. The auto tycoon started inviting the elder Smith to functions at his Dearborn, Michigan mansion, and at the age of ten Wendell began to tag along. He became friends with Ford's son Edsel, and during the summers he invited Wendell over to play ball.

"He's a fine-looking boy," Henry Ford once remarked to John Smith as they observed the children. "What does he want to be when he grows up?" John answered that Wendell dreamed of being a major league pitcher. The father, who spent much of his life in Canada, didn't understand yet that playing professional baseball wasn't possible for a Negro boy in America.

Young Wendell grew up on the East Side, a predominantly White, working-class neighborhood. He attended predominantly White Southeastern High School. Wendell played basketball for the Detroit Athletic Association at Central Community Center.

"With Wendell Smith, a 17-year-old forward pacing the way with seven baskets and three foul shots," wrote sportswriter Russell J. Cowan in 1932, "the Detroit Athletic Association basketball team crushed the highly touted Cincinnati Lion Tamers 62-22 Saturday night." Cowans continued, "Smith was a thorn in the side of the Cincinnati outfit. He might have increased his point total but numerous times he passed to a teammate with an easier shot near the basket."[52]

Neighbor Martin Hogan said teenage Wendell experienced many good times, yet experienced racial problems. He was not allowed to play on sports teams at Southeastern High School. "I know it was hard for him," said Hogan. "I don't know what the policy was." Wendell Smith however did play American Legion baseball. Initially, league officials removed him from the team, but auto magnate Ford, interceded on behalf of his chef's son, and the teenager was reinstated.[53]

At age 19, Smith experienced racial discrimination the emotionally hard way. He pitched for an American Legion team, and in the playoff that year he hurled a 1-0 shutout. Wish Egan, a top scout for the Detroit Tigers, was in the stands. Afterward, Egan offered contracts to the opposing pitcher and to Wendell's catcher, Mike Tresh, who went on to have a 12-year major league career. "I wish I could sign you too, kid," Egan told Smith. "But I can't." That night, Wendell cried harder than he ever had before. "That broke me up," he recalled to sportswriter Jerome Holtzman years later. "It was then that I made the vow that I would dedicate myself and do something on behalf of the Negro ballplayers."

Wendell was stung, yet he wasn't naïve. He knew professional baseball was segregated. Wendell went to Negro League baseball games at Mack Park, a single-decked, wooden stadium near his home, said Hogan, to watch the Detroit Stars, led by outfielder Turkey Stearnes.[54]

Higher education was a way to make good on that mission to challenge segregated sports. Smith enrolled at historically Black West Virginia State College in 1933 and majored in physical education. Smith's higher education was not confined to classrooms or even the campus. As an adolescent he learned a lot about human relations in railroad cars. Smith frequently rode the train from Detroit to West Virginia. The train would pass briefly through Kentucky and the conductor would enforce the segregated seating laws of that state. Smith would have to move to the segregated care and would return to his original seat after the train exited Kentucky. Smith befriended a White conductor. Perceptively, teenage Smith was able to separate the conductor's behavior from his soul. Smith was able to build a bridge to a reasonable White man. Smith consistently repeated the behavior throughout his professional career.[55]

He played varsity baseball and basketball for the Yellow Jackets. On Christmas Day 1933, Smith and his teammates faced the Detroit Athletic Association, Smith's former team, which was rebranded as the Central Big Five. Smith scored nine points, however his school lost 28-19.[56]

Smith developed his media skills by serving as a publicist for the football team, keeping professional sports writers informed about the Yellow Jackets' progress. Smith also wrote a sports column for the *Yellow Jacket* campus newspaper. At the Institute campus, Smith's roommate was Will Robinson, a four-sport letterman.[57]

Smith also met Sara Wright, a music major. They married sometime in the late 1930s.

When Smith graduated from West Virginia State College in 1937, he accepted a reporter job at the *Pittsburgh Courier*, among the big three nationally circulated Black-owned weekly newspapers. Their competitors were the *Chicago Defender* and Baltimore *Afro-American*. Smith's new job paid $17 a week ($340 in 2022 dollars). He wrote photo captions and covered high school sports. A year later, at age 24, Smith was named sports editor and began to write a column, called "Smitty's Sport Spurts," which he turned into his personal soapbox on the subject of race and baseball.

Seeing how the *Courier's* crusades – from boxer Joe Louis to war, Italy's ruthless conquest of Ethiopia – roused readers and drove sales, Wendell proposed a new one. "I suggested a campaign for the admittance, the inclusion of Negro ballplayers in the big leagues," he recalled. Smith's 1938 column, "A Strange Tribe" launched his crusade to erase MLB's color line. He criticized Blacks for enabling MLB segregation:

> They're real troupers, these guys who risk their money and devote their lives to Negro baseball. We Black folk offer no encouragement and don't even seem to care if they make a go of it or not. We literally ignore them completely. With our noses high and our hands deep in our pockets, squeezing the same dollar that we hand to the White players, we walk past their ballparks and go to the major league game. Nuts – that's what we are. Just plain nuts![58]

***

The year 1939 was consequential because of events that blasted bigger holes in metaphorical brick walls that blocked access to Black professional baseball players, wrote "Baseball's Tipping Point" author Talmadge Boston. That year Marian Anderson was barred from singing at Constitution Hall in Washington by the Daughters of the American Revolution (DAR), which owned the building. The DAR was a patriotic organization of female descendants of Revolutionary War soldiers, but only allowed

White members, despite the thousands of Black men who fought against the British. In the search for an alternative venue the DC. Board of Education spurned a request to move the Anderson concert to its Central High School auditorium. The Constitution Hall rejection elicited mild public protest, however the Board of Education blockage resulted in louder protests, angry letters by Blacks to newspapers, and a petition signed by hundreds of DC schoolteachers asking the school board to reverse itself. When first lady Eleanor Roosevelt canceled her DAR membership in protest, her action put the conflict on the front pages of daily newspapers. The first lady intervened to get the National Park Service to offer Anderson space. She performed on April 9, Easter Sunday, in the district at the Lincoln Memorial.[59]

Also, that year, Wendell Smith interviewed National League President Ford Frick on February 9, 1939, face to face in the lobby of the William Penn Hotel in Pittsburgh. Smith asked why were there no Blacks playing big league baseball. Frick answered that there was a misunderstanding; the big leagues wanted Blacks but could not add them until society became more tolerant. "The general public," said Frick, "has not been educated to the point where they will accept them on the same standard as they do the White player."[60] Smith pressed on: was there a formal policy barring Blacks from baseball? Frick said there was not. Segregation represented the attitudes of fans and players, but not the attitudes of managers, team owners, and other baseball executives.

Smith's Frick interview was published February 25 on page one of the *Pittsburgh Courier.*[61] Over a few months Smith interviewed 40 White players and all eight National League managers at the Schenley Hotel in Pittsburgh. It was the reporter's chance to corroborate or contradict Frick's narrative. Smith conducted the interviews at a nearby hotel because the Baseball Writers Association of America denied him access inside Forbes Field, the Pirates' stadium.[62] The association denied Wendell's application for a press card on the grounds that he covered sports other than baseball.[63] A reasonable assumption was most of Smith's sports journalism in the 1940s was baseball, however it was Negro League baseball, with frequent critiquing of Major League Baseball. Yet in 1947, Jackie Robinson's rookie season, Smith covered the Dodgers full time as staff of the *Pittsburgh Courier* but was rejected for BBWAA membership. [64]

So instead, Smith went to the Schenley Hotel, where the visiting teams stayed, and as National League teams passed through Pittsburgh to play the Pirates, Smith polled their players and managers about their views on integration.

"Have you ever seen any Negro ballplayers who you think could play in the major leagues?"

Smith asked everyone he interviewed. Every week for more than a month, the results were splashed across the *Courier's* sports pages. Twenty percent of the baseball men he interviewed opposed integration, Wendell estimated. Five percent ventured no opinion. But 75% voiced support for opening pro baseball's doors. That list included such All-Stars as Dizzy Dean, Honus Wagner, Mel Ott, Carl Hubbell, and Pepper Martin. Except for Wagner, all these men were born and raised in segregating Southern states.[65]

"I have seen at least 25 colored players who could have made the grade," said Cincinnati Reds manager Bill McKechnie. "Some of the greatest ball players I have seen were Negroes."[66]

Johnny Vander Meer, a Reds player, and New Jerseyan, told Smith, "I don't see why they [Negroes] are barred."[67]

On July 22, Smith said he called New York Giants manager Bill Terry from the hotel lobby and identified himself. Smith asked to do an interview. Terry, a Tennessean from Memphis answered "No, absolutely no!" and hung up. Smith persisted and waited for Terry outside Forbes Field. Smith was allowed inside the clubhouse and was told to wait until Terry was through talking with Pittsburgh manager "Pie" Traynor. After waiting an hour, Smith and Terry came face to face. The latter said, "I know, as well as everybody else does, that there are a number of Negroes who have the ability to play in the major leagues." But "No, I do not think Negro players will ever be admitted to the majors."

Wendell Smith said he was not surprised by the manager's take because he was a "dyed-in-the-wool conservative. He is neither liberal nor sympathetic." Terry said Black inclusion was not possible because Blacks and Whites would be required to travel together and share trains and hotels. However, by 1939, a cohort of Black entertainers professionally and socially interacted with White entertainers, managers, and promoters. Ella Fitzgerald, Louis Armstrong, Duke Ellington, and Lena Horne were in that small circle. Still, Terry and others may have been wary because the US military, a more representative sample, was still segregated. On the other hand, Black schoolchildren integrated northern public schools, albeit in small numbers. Professional baseball integration at that time was not impossible, but improbable.

At that time rail service was the preferred method of travel, flying was still new, rare, and expensive. Still, despite the golden age of Jim Crow, there were rare exceptions.[68] Blacks and Whites in the entertainment business sometimes traveled together without incident, Smith told Terry, who realized that the manager was not going to budge. "I think they [Negroes] can be more successful with a league of their own."[69] Terry was immovable because of doubts that the American majority would accept integration.

Giants slugger Mel Ott, whom Wendell Smith described as the "Louisiana Lasher," said he too had seen Black players who were good enough for the major leagues, however, Ott could not remember their names. Smith moved on to teammate Carl Hubbell, among the greatest pitchers in major league history. Famously quiet, Hubbell would have nothing to say, Terry told Smith. But this time Hubbell spoke up: He began talking about Josh Gibson and called the Homestead Grays star one of the greatest catchers "in the history of baseball." Hubbell praised Satchell Paige too. "I'll say this," said Hubbell, "that the players I've named, and some of the names I can't remember at the present time, would have been in the majors had their skins been White. Only their color kept them out of big-league baseball."[70]

Philadelphia Phillies manager James "Doc" Prothro told Smith on July 29 that he played in a series of exhibition games in California where he saw at least six Black players possessing big-league ability. Paige particularly was "one of the greatest pitchers in baseball," said the manager who worked during off-seasons as a dentist in Memphis. Smith asked Prothro if given permission would he sign Black players. Answer: "I certainly would. If given permission, I would jump at the opportunity to sign up a good Negro ball player." When? "That's up to the owners and league officials, not the managers. I can't say just when that will happen. Maybe sometime soon, maybe never."

Phillies catcher Virgil "Spud" Davis of Alabama told Smith he did not object to Blacks playing professional baseball. "Well, I suppose some of them [white players] would object. Some of the players from the South might kick, but I wouldn't say for sure. If a good Negro player was signed by a club that was having a difficult time and the fans took to him, I don't suppose it would make much difference who kicked."[71]

On August 26, Smith quoted Boston Braves manager Casey Stengel who told Smith, "Most Negro players are what we call naturals. They can hit, run, and throw exceptionally well. They seem to take to the game naturally and play it with all their heart and soul."

Leo Durocher, the garrulous Dodgers skipper, said, "I've seen plenty of colored boys who could make the grade in the majors – hell, I've seen a million." Durocher eight years later would be Jackie Robinson's manager when he first entered Major League Baseball.

So did Stengel, the future Yankees manager, think the time was near for Blacks to get the opportunity to play big-league baseball? He told Smith, "That is solely up to the owners."

Major League owners expressed concerns that if they let Blacks into their ballparks, those fans would bring their alleged rowdy behavior and offend White consumers.

Smith and like-minded integration advocates knocked down those arguments. First, White fans were not going to stop coming to games because Blacks were playing. The reverse would happen, argued Smith: "Club owners could put a few Black players in their lineups and pack their parks. Can you imagine Satchel Paige pitching against Lefty Grove in an empty stadium? Neither can the club owners."[72]

Furthermore, some Black press sportswriters countered by questioning why the Negro Leagues allowed White Major League Baseball owners to make so much money off of its enterprises. Lucious Harper of the *Chicago Defender* wrote that Negro League owners paid $8,000 ($171,344 in 2022 dollars) in order to rent Comiskey Park for the 1939 East-West All-Star classic and incredibly did not receive any revenue from the hot dogs, peanuts, and Cracker Jacks sold at the concession stands. Harper advised that money from that game should go toward building a ballpark "with the idea that someday we may play the game there and not forever in the other fellow's yard at unreasonable rentals."

MLB owners leased their other ballparks to Negro League teams at exorbitant rates because Blacks did not own their stadiums. There was an exception. In the 1930s, Gus Greenlee, owner of the Pittsburgh Crawfords, built and operated Greenlee Field in "Little Harlem," Pittsburgh's Hill District. However, that venture was shaky because Greenlee feuded with crosstown rival and Negro baseball owner Cumberland "Cum" Posey, of the Homestead Grays. Then in 1938 a federal housing project was approved on land that included the Greenlee field site. Greenlee reluctantly accepted a $38,000 settlement or he would lose his property to eminent domain.[73]

A Black baseball alternative that was suggested by a reader of Wendell Smith's series was why not insert a complete Negro League team into the MLB minor leagues, which could mean the big-league teams could buy players from Negro League teams?[74] White *and* Black executives did not want Negro baseball teams absorbed into the big leagues. Black players were divided on whether to be absorbed into Major Leagues, wrote Sam Lacy.[75] Jud Wilson of the Philadelphia Stars said integration was a nonstarter because of strong Southern influence of White ballplayers plus segregation laws in those states. Black players, wrote Lacy, gave little thought to playing in the big leagues because it seemed improbable and simply accepted segregation: "It was like saying, 'How would you like to be a millionaire?'"[76]

Smith's series concluded on September 2. It was not a scientific sample. Some sources probably did not mean what they said. Nevertheless, dozens of White men were on the record that they were confident Blacks were qualified to play MLB. Most said they would not stop Black inclusion; the decision was up to the owners and the baseball commissioner.[77]

The *Chicago Defender* praised White writer Jimmy Powers of the New York *Daily News* when he wrote that Josh Gibson would be worth $25,000 a year to any big-league team. Powers also urged readers to attend Negro League games when they played at Yankee Stadium because "I have personally seen at least ten colored ball players I know are big leaguers but are barred from play by the Jim Crow law that Frick of the National League insists does not exist." The *Defender's* writer did not credit the rival and peer *Pittsburgh Courier* for Smith's series. It was one thing for a Black paper to argue for integration; another for major White baseball writer in one of the most important papers in the country to say it. That *was* news.

Smith's series meanwhile was praised by the communist *Daily Worker* newspaper. For weeks the *Daily Worker* quoted liberally from Smith's dispatches and emphasized to its readers that players and managers supported integration.[78]

Smith's investigative series was a big hit with readers. His bosses at the *Pittsburgh Courier* rewarded Smith with a raise.[79]

Days after Smith's series ended, events across the Atlantic rattled onlookers in the United States. Nazi Germany led by Adolf Hitler, invaded Poland on September 1, 1939. England and France declared war on Germany and World War II was officially underway. Americans observed from afar, praying that they would not have to get involved and that the Atlantic Ocean would serve as a buffer against trouble. But reality set in and engagement occurred two years later.

In early 1940, months after the baseball series, Smith was promoted to city editor. Soon after that he became sports editor and succeeded Chester "Ches" Washington.[80]

Wendell Smith's ascension to the chair previously occupied by Washington signaled a change in editorial tone. Moderately measured was replaced by militant. In 1933 when Washington in print praised the candor of baseball executives, years later Smith was blunt in his criticism of the White establishment's hide-the-ball-from-Blacks tricks: "According to Mr. Frick's theory, the American public doesn't mind seeing a Cuban third baseman throw out a Greek base runner, or a Russian outfielder catch a high fly hit by a Japanese batter. But this 'land of the free' will not stand to see a black man do anything on a major league club but sweep out the locker room."[81]

When the Cincinnati Reds manager told Smith that other managers had long been interested in Black players, Washington in a column pointed out that New York Giants manager John McGraw tried to hire Charlie Grant. McGraw's successor Bill Terry told Smith he doubted that Blacks would ever get to play big-league baseball. The attempted hiring of Charlie Grant failed because McGraw tried in 1901 to pass Grant, an unambiguous complexioned man of color, off as an American Indian.

Smith, like all other men his age, was required to register for the draft under the Selective Service Act of September 16, 1940. The first peacetime inductees were called up in November 1940. By this time Smith was the 26-year-old city editor of the *Courier*. Smith's height and weight were 6-feet tall and 173 pounds. Smith filled out his draft card on October 16, 1940.[82] At 26 he was available for military service, but few men that age were drafted, and most men with children were not drafted as well. His son was born in 1940.

Gender and workplace assignments were another change that defined Smith's arrival as city editor. Before 1940, *Courier* female writers were confined to the newspaper women's section. Edna Chappell did not want to be pigeonholed. She complained to Smith. He listened, then offered to give her assignments beyond that part of the paper. One day, Chappell was in a foul mood over having to cover yet another wedding party. Chappell gathered up her typewriter, pens, and notepad and carried them to a large round table at the other end of the newsroom.

Bill Nunn charged out of the office and confronted her. "What are you doing?" the managing editor asked. "I'm moving over to the city desk," Chappelle said, tears streaming down the dark cheeks behind her thick glasses. "I'm not going to work over here anymore. I'm sick of it."

"Who said you could move?" Nunn demanded. "Well, Wendell said I could work for him, so I'm moving," replied Chappell.[83]

***

L'Affaire Jake Powell in 1938, then in 1939 Marian Anderson's-rejection-turned-to-triumph concert performance, and Wendell Smith's investigative series that broke the silence of talking openly about big-league baseball and race may have planted seeds for a future harvest of talent. At that time Black baseball players when asked thought the suggestion that some of them might soon play big-league baseball was improbable. Yet America and the world was changing. That year, 1939, the first commercial-use television set was introduced at the World's Fair in New York City. In a decade American consumers would be able to watch baseball on television in addition to listening on the radio or reading about games in the newspapers.

And improbably, several Western European countries – Spain, Italy, and Germany – kindled or ignited a world war. Aggressors' war aims largely involved racism and ethnic cleansing, whether the targets were Jews, gypsies, or other people deemed undesirable. In two years when

America joined the fight it would face its internal racial conflicts and contradictions, even when the White majority ignored the grievances and the Black minority answered with indictments.

Sam Lacy and Wendell Smith from competing newspapers led the charge to destroy the baseball barrier stonewalling Black Americans. Lacy in 1943 convinced Commissioner Kennesaw Landis, the steely gatekeeper, to allow major league baseball owners to meet face-to-face with Black publishers who were advocating for inclusion. At about the same time Wendell Smith polled White major league players and their bosses. Most of the on-the-record replies were if there were Black players of comparable talent and industry, then yes, they should be competing with them in professional baseball. It was remarkable that Smith began his campaign to integrate professional baseball and eight years later would succeed when Jackie Robinson broke in with the Montreal Royals one year after World War II ended in Europe.

As World War II momentum swung optimistically to the United States and its allies, pivotal social change through baseball was imminent too. Baseball often was called a child's game played by adults, yet the sport that was the national pastime would become the defining instrument of the race debate in the next decade.

NOTES

1. Snyder, Brad, "Beyond the Shadow of the Senators: The Untold Story of the Homestead Grays and the Integration of Baseball," New York, Contemporary Books, 2003, p 7, p 307 n35. Society of American Baseball Research reported when Sam learned his mom's ethnicity.

2. Lacy, Sam, Newson, Moses J., "Fighting for Freedom: The Life Story of Hall of Fame Sportswriter Sam Lacy," Centreville, Maryland, Tidewater Publishers, 1998, p 15. dcmetropolicecollector.com/mpd-african-american http://www.dcmetropolicecollector. com/MPD-African-American-Officers.html Via Chuck Gallagher, Black Sheep Productions, 2009.

3. Lacy, "Fighting for Freedom," p 16.

4. Notable Dunbar High School graduates included sculptor and artist Elizabeth Catlett; jazz pianist Billy Taylor; US Sen. Edward Brooke; delegate to Congress Eleanor Holmes Norton; Wesley A. Brown, first Black graduate of the US Naval Academy; surgeon and discoverer of blood plasma Charles R. Drew, and Allison Davis, University of Chicago anthropology professor.

5. Lacy, "Fighting for Freedom," p 15.

6. Lacy, "Fighting for Freedom," pp 19–20. The first names of Lacy's school teachers were not available. (Lacy's unique handwriting saved him when he suffered a baseball injury as a teenager and again in 1978 when an automobile accident with injury made Lacy give up the typewriter for writing his copy longhand), pp 21–22.

7. Bennett, Lerone Jr., "Before the Mayflower: A History of Black America," New Millennium Edition, 2003, pp 546, 548.

8. Lacy, "Fighting for Freedom," pp 16–17, 18–19.

9. Snyder, "Beyond the Shadow of the Senators," p 9.
10. Halper, Donna L., Society of American Baseball Research #7.
11. Snyder, "Beyond the Shadow of the Senators," p 10.
12. Snyder, "Beyond the Shadow of the Senators," pp ix, 1.
13. Society for American Baseball Research #8.
14. "CBS Weekend," May 28, 2022.
15. English, J. Douglas, Morgan State University, Prentice-Hall.
16. Lacy "Fighting for Freedom," p 24.
17. Peterson, "Only the Ball was White," p 63. The Bacharach Giants originally was the Duvall Giants, a rare, entire team of Black players who migrated from Jacksonville, Florida. "I had this job in a grocery store, but I wanted to be a ball player," said first baseman Napoleon Cummings. "In 1916 Tom Jackson and Henry Tucker – they were a couple of politicians around here in Atlantic City – brought us up here."
18. Morgan State University, Prentice-Hall ("This is not my life").
19. Society for American Baseball Research #13.
20. Lacy, "Fighting for Fairness," p 27. Prentis Hall said in 1928 Lacy in 1953 married Barbara Robinson, after his 1952 divorce from the former (Roberta) Alberta Robinson.
21. Society for American Baseball Research #15 … Lacy, "Fighting for Fairness," p 31. Snyder, "Beyond the Shadow of the Senators," p 216. Shepard, a left-hander who lost his right leg, pitched August 4 against the Boston Red Sox with an artificial leg. He allowed three hits and one run in five and one third innings. Weintraub, Robert, "The Victory Season: The End of World War II and the Birth of Baseball's Gold Age," New York, Little, Brown, and Company, 2013, pp 137–138.
22. "Conspiracy of Silence," p 58; "Fighting for Fairness," p 25. In Lacy's autobiography, in a column account he said Altrock, a heralded clown, threw a dirty wet towel in Sam Lacy Sr.'s face.
23. Lacy, "Fighting for Fairness," p 31.
24. Lacy, "Fighting for Fairness," p 31.
25. Lacy, "Fighting for Fairness," p 31.
26. Lacy, "Fighting for Fairness," p 32; Klingaman, Mike, "Hall of Fame Opens Doors for Writer," Baltimore Sun, July 26, 1998. As for 400 Blacks losing jobs, Griffith did not want to lose the rent Negro league teams played to use his stadium
27. Lamb, "Conspiracy of Silence," p 59.
28. Lacy, "Fighting for Fairness," p 39. Both references are undated, however Lacy most likely wrote these comments in 1939 in response to Clark Griffith's resistance and the Negro League Baltimore Elite Giants manager's reluctance. There were no Asians playing in the major leagues at that time. Lacy exaggerated.
29. Mack Robinson was Jackie Robinson's older brother. Ralph Metcalfe would later serve in Congress as a four-term Democrat from Illinois. "Ralph Metcalfe dead: Congressman, 68, climbed the ranks," Chicago Tribune, October 11, 1978, p 1.
30. Lacy, "Fighting for Fairness," pp 32–34.
31. Haskins, Jim, Mitgang, N.R., "Mr. Bojangles: The Biography of Bill Robinson," New York, William Morrow and Company, Inc., 1988, pp 9–11.
32. Lacy, "Fighting for Fairness," pp 37–38; McKenna, Dave, "The Syracuse Walking Dream," Washington City Paper, May 23, 2008.
33. McKenna, Dave, Washington City Paper, May 23, 2008.
34. cafriseabove.org/wilmeth-sidat-singh (stories of the Tuskegee Airmen and WASP) + US Census, 1930, NARA microfilm publication T626 (2002), roll 1563, FHL microfilm 2,341,298.
35. Arlington National Cemetery, Prominent African Americans.
36. SPJ Code of Ethics https://www.spj.org/ethicscode.asp
37. Society for American Baseball Research, pp 5, n31–32, Lacy, "Fighting for Fairness, p 37.

38. Lacy, "Fighting for Fairness," p 43, Snyder, "Beyond the Shadow of the Senators," p 104.
39. Reisler, Jim, *Black Writers/Black Baseball*, pp 15–16.
40. Lacy, "Fighting for Fairness," p 44.
41. Reisler, "Black Writers/Black Baseball," p 61.
42. Society for American Baseball Research, p 5.
43. Wiggins, David K., "Wendell Smith, the Pittsburgh Courier and the Campaign to Include Blacks in Organized Baseball, 1933–1945," Journal of Sports History 10, No. 2, 1983, p 21.
44. Drebinger, John, "Cox Retracts Admissions on Betting, Gets New Hearing Before Landis Today," New York Times, December 4, 1943, p 17.
45. There is a photo of Wendell Smith interviewing Robeson and several baseball owners during a break in the meeting. The image is at the Jackie Robinson Museum in Manhattan. Credit, Bettman Archive, Getty Images.
46. Lamb, "Conspiracy of Silence," pp 79–80.
47. Snyder, "In the Shadow of the Senators," pp 104–105. At the time Lacy left Washington for Chicago, the Negro league Grays who played home games in the district hired Art Carter as their publicity agent. Carter succeeded in helping the Grays transition from Pittsburgh's team to Washington's team. Carter was a Lacy protégé. In 1935 Carter joined Lacy's *Washington Tribune* sports staff as a college and high school sports reporter. After two years Carter moved to the *Afro-American*. In 1939, two more years later, Lacy joined his former protégé at the *Afro*.
48. Lacy, "Fighting for Fairness," pp 45–46.
49. Lacy, "Fighting for Fairness," p 46.
50. Date of birth stated on the draft card Smith completed during World War II. Other sources reported March 23 as Smith's date of birth.
51. Detroit Free Press, October 1, 1970, pp 17-C. Now known as St. Matthew's and St. Joseph's Episcopal Church. The volunteer groups were Willing Workers, King's Daughters, and the Dorcas Society. McCaughan, Pat, "Detroit's Historically Black St. Matthews added to 'Freedom Network,'" Episcopal News Service, February 25, 2016. https://www. episcopalnewsservice.org/2016/02/25/detroits-historically-black-st-matthews-added-to-freedom-network/
52. Cowans, Russell J., "Detroit Nips Cincinnati 5," Chicago Defender, January 16, 1932.
53. After graduating in 1937, Robinson coached Pershing High School in Detroit and won a 1967 state basketball title with a team led by Spencer Haywood, Olympic champion, and NBA star. Robinson also became the first Black scout for an NFL team (Detroit Lions) and first Black head basketball coach for NCAA Division I school Illinois State University. There he coached future NBA players and head coach Doug Collins, reported Michael Marsh of Society for American Baseball Research.
54. Michigan Chronicle, July 9, 1966, p A-1.
55. Pifer, Michael Scott, Marsh, Michael, "The Wendell Smith Reader: Selected Writings on Sports, Civil Rights and Black History," Jefferson, North Carolina, McFarland & Company, Inc., Publishers, 2023, pp 55. "There was nothing wrong with that man," Smith decades later told Will Leonard of the Chicago Tribune. "He was doing something stupid that he'd been ordered to do."
56. Bak, Richard, "Turkey Stearnes and the Detroit Stars: The Negro Leagues in Detroit, 1919–1933," Detroit, Wayne State University Press, 1995, p 58.
57. Cowans, Russell J., "Detroit team defeats West Virginia 28-19," The Tribune Independent, December 30, 1933.
58. Smith, Wendell, "Smitty's Sports Spurts," Pittsburgh Courier, May 14, 1938, p 17.
59. "Eleanor Roosevelt and Marian Anderson," Franklin D. Roosevelt Presidential Library and Museum, https://www.fdrlibrary.org/anderson Lamb, Conspiracy of Silence," pp 133–134.
60. Lamb, "Conspiracy of Silence," p 135.

61. Lamb, "Conspiracy of Silence," pp 137, 138–147.

62. Holtzman, p 315.

63. Article IV of the modern Baseball Writers' Association of America constitution reads as follows, Section 1: "Membership in this association shall be classified as Active and Honorary." Section 2: "Active membership in this Association shall be reserved for professional journalists whose primary responsibility is the coverage of Major League Baseball."

64. "Writers who worked for non-daily publications, regardless of skin tone, were ineligible for membership," said Jack O'Connell, BBWAA secretary-treasurer, in an August 2023 email reply. He also said the Sam Lacy was not listed on a membership roster until 1958. Lacy in his autobiography said he was sponsored by writers from the New York Daily Mirror and New York World-Telegram and was accepted as a member in April 1948. Wendell Smith followed him later that year.

65. Lamb, "Conspiracy of Silence," p 139.

66. Lamb, "Conspiracy of Silence," p 140.

67. Lamb, "Conspiracy of Silence," p 141.

68. Reisner, Alex, "Baseball Geography and Transportation," Baseball Research Journal, 2006, Vol. 35. On June 8, 1934, the Cincinnati Reds flew 19 of its players to Chicago for a series against the Cubs. A dozen years later in 1946, the New York Yankees became the first team to fly its players on a regular basis, chartering a Douglas DC-4 dubbed the "Yankee Mainliner."

69. Lamb, "Conspiracy of Silence," p 141.

70. Lamb, "Conspiracy of Silence," p 142.

71. Lamb, "Conspiracy of Silence," pp 147–148.

72. Ibid., RE 1939 prices vs. 2022.

73. Whitaker, "Smoketown," pp 89–91, 119, 121.

74. Lamb, "Conspiracy of Silence," p 149.

75. Lamb, "Conspiracy of Silence," pp 148–149.

76. Lamb, "Conspiracy of Silence," p 149.

77. Lamb, "Conspiracy of Silence," p 149.

78. Lamb, "Conspiracy of Silence," p 152.

79. Holtzman, N-9.

80. Lamb, "Conspiracy of Silence," p 155.

81. Lamb, "Conspiracy of Silence," pp 137–139.

82. Lamb, "Conspiracy of Silence," p 137.

83. Whitaker, "Smoketown," p 272.

CHAPTER 2

NEGRO LEAGUES

A Response to the MLB Lockout

In 1884, Moses Fleetwood "Fleet" Walker debuted as a major league baseball (MLB)player, more than a half-century before Jackie Robinson broke the modern MLB color barrier in 1947. Walker shattered carefully framed assumptions about Black physical and intellectual inferiority and upset or enraged some White competitors and spectators. Other Whites accepted the college-educated athlete. By 1892, Walker and fellow Black baseball players were banished from grass and dirt diamonds of all major league and minor league teams. During the next century a decade of lobbying by Black sports journalists, especially Sam Lacy and Wendell Smith, helped remove the barrier preventing Blacks from playing in MLB. Walker, a catcher, competed with and against Whites as a member of the Toledo Blue Stockings of the American Association, which would eventually merge into the National League.

Walker, described by several biographers as a mulatto, competed as a self-identified Black man. At the time, people who appeared to have African (or Negro) ancestry were considered Black, without regard to any other ancestry they might have. William Edward White, another man of mixed ancestry, preceded Walker as a color-line breaker. However, as John R. Husman wrote, White was able to "pass" as a White person and lived his life accordingly.[1] Furthermore, Bud Fowler in 1878 joined a minor league team in Lynn, Massachusetts making him the first African American to play professional baseball. In 2022, Fowler who grew up in Cooperstown, New York, was inducted into the Baseball Hall of Fame, along with major leaguers Gil Hodges, Jim Kaat, and Minnie Minoso, an Afro-Cuban who was the first Afro-Hispanic to play in the major leagues

DOI: 10.4324/9781003283928-3

in 1949 after playing for New York Cubans in the Negro National League (NNL) for three years.[2]

Walker, meanwhile, was repeatedly reminded about his hue by opponents. In 1881, while playing for a semipro team in Cleveland, the opponents balked at playing because of his skin color. Walker was benched. The hometown *Toledo Blade* newspaper covered Walker sympathetically; the *Sporting News* condemned overt and sometimes savage racial denigration of Walker.[3]

Internally, Walker was undermined by some of his teammates. Pitcher Tony Mullane said he disliked Walker and would not cooperate with him on the field. Mullane would defy Walker's signals and throw curve balls when asked to throw fastballs and vice versa, choices that could seriously injure catchers, who in early baseball wore scant protective gear, unlike the face mask, chest protector, and shin guards, worn today.

"I had it in for him. He was the best catcher I ever worked with, but I disliked a Negro and whenever I had to pitch to him, I used to pitch anything I wanted without looking at his signals," Mullane confessed to *New York Age* reporter Dave Young on January 11, 1919.[4]

"One day he signaled me for a curve, and I shot a fastball at him. He caught it and walked down to me. 'Mr. Mullane, I'll catch you without signals, but I won't catch you if you are going to cross me when I give you a signal.'" Mullane told Young, "And all the rest of the season he caught me and caught anything I pitched without knowing what was coming." Mullane's intransigence resulted in a league-leading 63 wild pitches that season. Outfielder Curt Welch, another Walker teammate, was an open, ardent segregationist.[5] Welch grew up in East Liverpool, Ohio, across the river from Virginia, an area of Ohio sympathetic to the Confederate cause during the Civil War. Mullane, an Irish immigrant, landed in Chicago at a time when Irish Americans believed they were in competition with Blacks.

Another Walker tormentor was future Baseball Hall of Fame player turned manager Adrian "Cap" Anson. He relentlessly protested Walker competing against his Chicago White Stockings team.[6] In 1883, Anson tried to bar Walker from playing against the White Stockings (the future American League White Sox) at a game in Toledo. Toledo manager Charlie Morton said that Walker would play or there would be no game. Anson chose to play and not risk losing his share of the gate receipts. Walker did not play because of a sore hand. His team successfully bluffed.[7]

Yet banishment mattered because of the role that baseball played in the American psyche.[8] The 1880s- and 1890s-era White professional baseball players who stridently rejected playing or posing for photographs with Black teammates were influenced by majority American attitudes. Blacks who excelled in other sports were also forced out. At that time Black jockeys dominated horse racing, notably Isaac Murphy, winner of the Kentucky Derby in 1884, 1890, and 1891. After Black jockey Oliver Lewis rode Aristides to the first Kentucky Derby win in 1875, 14 of the next 27 winners were Black riders.[9] However, White resentment of such success took hold, forcing out Black riders. In 1894, Whites created the Jockey Club in order to license riders. The club systematically denied the relisting of Black riders.[10] Furthermore, on the track, White jockeys ganged up and maimed Black jockeys and their horses and physically forced them off the tracks.[11] This growing discrimination against Black athletes occurred during a rise of segregation, reinforced by major US Supreme Court decisions supporting segregation in the *Civil Rights Cases* (1883) and *Plessy v. Ferguson* (1896).

By the 1890s the nation's pastime, freighted with ideological overtones, had taken a mythic cast. Many saw sport – especially baseball – as a metaphor for American democracy, where a gritty meritocracy trumped class and nationality. Sons of European immigrants proved their merit to become Americans by showing their athletic mettle. African Americans, however, were barred from the major leagues and most Whites thought their absence was due to inherent athletic inferiority. They concluded that Blacks were unable to compete in sport, and by extension, unworthy.[12]

***

"Only the ball was White," was a refrain about the Negro Leagues, Black America's answer to MLB's denial that it excluded Black ball players. Oscar Charleston, Josh Gibson, Buck Leonard, Judy Johnson, and Ray Dandridge were among the superb players who brought star power and showmanship to Black baseball. None of them played in the traditionally all-White major leagues, but all of them and others are today in the National Baseball Hall of Fame in Cooperstown. Others like Satchel Paige, Monte Irvin, and Willard Brown, who played briefly in the major leagues, were elected to the Hall of Fame based on their Negro League careers.

By 1910, Negro professional baseball was centered in the industrialized, urban American North despite 90% of America's Black population, nearly nine million people, living in the mostly rural South. Nine Negro professional baseball teams competed within 100 miles of Philadelphia and each of them bore the name "Giants."[13]

Between 1900 and 1920, more Black teams emerged, including: The Chicago American Giants, Lincoln Giants of New York, Bacharach Giants of Atlantic City, which came north by way of Jacksonville, Florida, and were the former Duval Giants. Other teams were the Hilldale Club of Darby, Pennsylvania, Indianapolis ABCs, and Homestead Grays of Greater Pittsburgh.[14]

In 1920, Andrew "Rube" Foster launched the modern Negro League, one year after MLB's Black Sox scandal.[15] Foster was a talented pitcher from Texas who played on Black teams in his home state. Foster shrugged off his father's disapproval in 1897 when he was 18 and joined the barnstorming Waco Yellow Jackets team. Later that year Foster moved to Chicago at age 19 and continued to pitch.

Foster was warned by manager Frank C. Leland of the Chicago Union Giants that he would be put to severe tests because his new team intended to play all of the good White ball clubs. "If you play the best clubs in the land, White clubs as you say, it will be a case of Greek meeting Greek," Foster told Leland. "I fear nobody." Foster, who stood at 6-feet 4-inches and weighed more than 200 pounds, arrived packing a pistol in brash Texas tradition.[16] Foster pitched a shutout in his debut but was inconsistent thereafter. After moving to the Chicago Leland Giants, he jumped to a White semipro team in Otsego, Michigan, then later the Black Cuban X Giants of Zanesville, Ohio. In 1903, Foster pitched the Cuban X Giants to the colored championship, beating the Philadelphia Giants in 1903.[17] Rube Foster played on a Chicago team that won 133 of 154 games in 1904. One of Foster's teammates was Jack Johnson, the future heavyweight boxing champion, who played first base.

Foster rejoined Frank Leland in 1907. Leland allowed Foster to do the booking and secure a larger percentage of the gate for fellow players. Foster also pitched three times against the Chicago Cubs and lost all three times. When his pitching skill declined, he played first base and then became a player-manager. Foster took over as manager of the Leland Giants in 1910. That season the team record was 123 wins and 6 losses. In 1911, Foster became co-owner of the team with John Schorling.[18]

Once Foster left the playing field, he was a committed game-changer. In 1915, Foster unsuccessfully challenged the White Federal League to integrate its teams. The Federal League was an upstart that took on MLB.[19] The year 1919 brought the "Red Summer" riots and lynching that targeted Black people in multiple cities. The mayhem also reinforced a White gentleman's agreement to ban Blacks from organized baseball.[20]

Undeterred, Foster took another path. He observed that many Black ballplayers jumped from team to team and did not honor contracts or obligations. Too many club owners were enablers who tolerated such double-dealing. In February 1920, Foster convened a meeting of owners hoping he could bring order to the chaos. The NNL included his Chicago American Giants and mostly Midwest teams from Indianapolis, Cleveland, and Detroit.

The NNL began competition on May 2, 1920, when the Indianapolis ABCs beat the Chicago Giants at home before 8,000 spectators.[21] The league functioned with a shortage of trustworthy umpires and not enough parity among the clubs. Owners were wary that they were at the mercy of White booking agents, particularly Nat Strong, who scheduled games.

Foster, unlike most of his peer owners, had control of a field in Chicago in which to host games. He split a share of the gate receipts and concessions with White partner John M. Schorling, a tavern owner who had previously managed sandlot clubs. Their agreement was based on a handshake, not a written contract.[22]

The year 1923 was good for the NNL. Total attendance was 402,436, an average of 1,650 spectators per game. Total receipts were $197,218 ($3.4 million in 2022 dollars) and from that total player, salaries amounted to $101,000. Other expenses were railroad travel ($25, 212) and $7,965 spent on baseballs at $23 per dozen.[23] As for MLB attendance that year, five of sixteen teams each attracted at least 500,000 spectators and averaged 7,200 attendees per game. The New York Yankees led all of baseball, with 1 million spectators and an average of 13,250 at each game. The Boston Braves ranked last with 227,800 total attendees and 2,958 average game attendance.

The NNL was not the only Black baseball league. In March 1920, the Southern Negro League (SNL) was formed. The circuit included the Chattanooga Black Lookouts, New Orleans Black Pelicans, Birmingham Black Barons, Atlanta Black Crackers, Jacksonville Red Caps, and Nashville Elite Giants. The SNL kept a separate record of games played among themselves, however, the league agreed to play against non-SNL teams.[24]

In 1925, Foster asked each NNL owner for 5% of their gate receipts as compensation for serving as commissioner and manager of the league. Foster also fired five umpires that year.[25] Rival owners were suspicious of Foster's motives. For example, was he going to make a power move and control booking? Foster surprised the owners when he presented a written plan to propose offering MLB Negro teams to compete in their league. This plan was far-fetched yet visionary. Foster paid attention to a court decision, *Federal Baseball Club of Baltimore v. National League,* that gave MLB (and the NNL) an exemption from anti-trust laws.[26] In that case, Justice Oliver Wendell Holmes, Jr., speaking for a unanimous Court, concluded that baseball was not interstate commerce as related to the Sherman Act. For a century, baseball had been the only sports league with such an antitrust exemption.[27]

In 1926, Foster at about age 48, had a nervous breakdown and relinquished his leadership role of NNL baseball. At the time of Foster's illness, his son Earl said that his father met with New York baseball Giants manager John McGraw and American League President Ban Johnson to concoct an agreement in which the American Giants would play any major league club – the hometown White Sox or Cubs, or visiting teams – which had an off day in Chicago.

The plan collapsed when Foster was committed to a state mental hospital, where he spent the last four years of his life, dying on December 9, 1930, at age 51.[28]

His successors staggered along. In the 1930s during the Great Depression, Black baseball clearly lacked the uniformity and consistency of the White major leagues and their minor league farm system. Yet the Negro Leagues continued to function. The umpiring of Negro baseball too often was uneven, whether the arbiters were White, or later Black, and there were times when umpires were assaulted by players with no backing from the league office. By 1930, the Midwest-oriented NNL circuit faced competition from an upstart eastern Black league that included teams from Philadelphia, Atlantic City, New York, and elsewhere.

There were periods of player raids which resulted in a lack of uniformity. Some teams did not get to play a full season of games because of cancellations and forfeits. When players were paid skimpily, or not at all, they jumped to teams with better monetary terms or just refused to play. Players signed contracts, like in White professional baseball, but too often the contracts were not enforced. The Black leagues lacked commissioners who could enforce rules, when necessary, as were the conventions of MLB, with its strong and famous commissioner, Judge Landis. Black baseball needed management enforcement especially when ballplayers jumped from team to team, ignoring contracts in search of better pay.

Some teams made small profits while others did not. For example, from 1920 to 1925, the Kansas City Monarchs averaged $41,000 profit per year from its games and Foster's Chicago American Giants had an average profit of $85,000 per year. The remaining teams did not fare as well, averaging from $10,000 to $15,000 in annual profits.[29] The weak teams often operated barely even or at losses.

Indeed, Black baseball had its flaws, but the overall product was good, and in many areas it was excellent. Judy Johnson and Walter F. (Buck) Leonard said that compared to White professional rosters, Negro League teams usually matched evenly or better against the first six out of nine players on the field, which meant the remaining three players were of semipro-level skill. Sam Lacy, who was an adolescent and emerging journalist once pitched for the East Coast Bacharach Giants and fit the description of the semi-pro skilled players.

The star assessors also said that their teams were Triple-A quality, just short of major league skill. For example, pitching rotations could go about three deep and head-to-head with White professional pitchers, meaning two pitchers were "Sockmayocks," said slugger Buck Leonard. That meant those second-rate hurlers were saved for semipro games because of their lesser skills.[30] Leonard's career spanned the 1930s and 1940s which was the second, golden era of Black baseball leagues. Today, he is in the Baseball Hall of Fame.[31]

The most identifiable Negro baseball star of the mid-20th century was Leroy "Satchel" Paige. At age 18, Paige began his pitching career with the Mobile Tigers. By 1926, Paige earned between $50 and $200 per month when he pitched for the Chattanooga Black Lookouts and after that the New Orleans Black Pelicans.[32] At that time Paige did not play with NNL or Eastern Colored League (ECL) teams. Yet the mention of Paige's name guaranteed sold-out ballgames nationwide. "Paige struck out 18 of us at three o'clock in the afternoon," said Newt Allen, an opponent and premier second baseman. "His arms were so long. He'd raise up that big foot and next thing you'd know the ball was by ya."[33]

***

Leading Black-owned press sports journalists began a decade-long crusade during the 1930s to 1940s to desegregate America's pastime. One reason was the fiction that White major and minor leaguers were superior to Black baseball players was exposed. During the off-season, barnstorming Negro League players competed against White teams that often included its superstars. In 167 games between Blacks and "all-star" White barnstorming teams during the 1930s, reported John Holway, the White barnstormers won less than one-third of the contests.[34] Much of small-town America witnessed those games, unlike the limited audiences in 16 major league cities concentrated in seven northern and midwestern states and the District of Columbia.[35]

Negro sports heroes in other sports – notably heavyweight boxing champion Joe Louis and Olympic runner Jesse Owens – applied pressure on MLB because of their spectacular triumphs during the 1930s.

Black soldiers who proved their patriotism, loyalty, and bravery on foreign battlefields were returning home to fight and win another war against American apartheid. For the first half of the 20th century, baseball reflected the racism of American society, wrote author Jules Tygiel, author of *Baseball's Great Experiment: Jackie Robinson and His Legacy*. It was time for that institution to change.[36]

When the *Sporting News* learned the Philadelphia Athletics had teammates who were violent Ku Klux Klan (KKK) members, an editorial said, "In organized baseball there has been no distinction raised except the tacit understanding that a player of Ethiopian descent [Black] is ineligible. The wisdom of which we will not discuss except to say that by such a rule some of the greatest players the game has ever known have been denied their opportunity."[37] Rogers Hornsby and "Gabby" Street told sportswriter Fred Lieb that they were Klansmen. Philadelphia Athletics pitcher Robert Hastie, a Klansman, was arrested in 1923 for flogging a Black man and woman in Georgia. Hastie was exonerated by an all-White jury. The KKK was violently anti-Jewish and anti-Catholic as well.[38]

Yet about a decade before Landis became baseball commissioner Clark Griffith, then manager with the Cincinnati Reds, in 1911, allowed some olive-skinned Afro-Cubans to pass as White and play big-league ball. Clark found the talent thanks to Joe Cambria, his primary scout. Most Cubans were aware they had some African blood coursing through their bodies. When American soldiers arrived in Cuba in 1898 to fight the Spanish-American War, they were stunned to see Black, White, and Brown natives together fighting against the Spanish colonizers. Then and in the 21st century, if Cubans were ethnically categorized like Americans, the island nation would be at least half to two-thirds Black.

Baseball owners named Landis commissioner in 1920, in the wake of the previous year's "Black Sox" scandal where eight Chicago White Sox teammates conspired to fix World Series games. To some, Landis was seen as a progressive on racial issues. William Clarence Matthews, a Black former Harvard infielder who became an assistant US attorney general in Washington, DC, wrote to Landis and asked that he erased the baseball color line: "Why keep the Negro out if he can play the same grade of baseball demanded by other groups?"

There was no record of Landis responding to Matthews.[39] In nearly a quarter century as commissioner (1920–1944) Landis usually responded to the question of Blacks in baseball with silence. He ordered an end to off-season barnstorming exhibitions between Major League and Negro League teams. Landis also ignored letters and telegrams from Black sportswriters, notably Lacy and Smith, and other activists who wanted to discuss the issue as noted in Chapter 1.[40]

***

His first and middle name equaled a phrase that honored his father, a Northern Civil War soldier who was wounded at the battle of Kennesaw Mountain near Atlanta, Georgia in 1864. In 1905, President Theodore Roosevelt nominated Kennesaw Mountain Landis to serve as a federal district judge in Chicago. In January 1915, Landis heard a complaint from the Federal (baseball) League, an upstart that charged MLB engaged in monopolistic tactics. Landis reserved judgment. Many months passed. In December, the parties reached a settlement and the Federal League disbanded.[41]

Landis was personally passionate about baseball. At 5 feet, 6 inches tall, and 130 pounds, at times he was dismissed as unsuitable for athletics or physical work. Landis proved critics wrong. He played first base for the Goosetown, Indiana semipro club. Landis supposedly turned down a minor league contract, explaining that he played "merely for sport and the love of the game." At age 17, he became manager of the Goosetown team.[42]

Landis' reputation was that of a Roosevelt-leaning trustbuster. In 1907, he fined John D. Rockefeller and Standard Oil Co. $29.2 million for taking illegal rebates from a railroad company. But in the baseball case before him, Landis was reluctant to engage in such antitrust zeal. That case was settled before Landis could issue a ruling.

Baseball and Landis would be linked again. In fall 1919, the Chicago White Sox were accused of throwing the World Series in exchange for bribes. The "Black Sox" scandal resulted in Landis banning eight players from the game for life, despite the teammates' acquittals in a Chicago trial. A year later in November 1920, MLB owners visited Landis' courtroom to offer him the job of baseball commissioner. Landis admonished the owners for disrupting his courtroom during a bribery trial. When the judge learned the owners' reason for visiting, he had them escorted to his chambers where they waited for 45 minutes. Landis was offered the commissioner's job for $50,000.[43] The owners wanted a leader who would clean up the sport following the championship scandal. The judge accepted on the condition they reduce the offer by the $7,500 and match what he was making as a federal judge.

But in saying "yes" Landis ignited a personal scandal. He did not resign as a federal judge and some members of Congress threatened to impeach the judge for conflict of interest. "Let the boys lather themselves good," said Landis. "Why I'm no more interested in this than I am in the appointment of the bellhop in that hotel across the street."

A House committee dropped the impeachment effort: however, the American Bar Association in a September 1921 resolution concluded Landis' double dipping "meets our unqualified condemnation as conduct unworthy of the office of the judge, derogatory to the dignity of the bench and undermining public confidence in the independence of the judiciary." Five months later in February 1922, Landis announced he would resign from the bench to serve exclusively as baseball commissioner.

***

In winter 1930, Romare Bearden left Lincoln, Pennsylvania where he was a freshman at historically Black Lincoln University and traveled north to enroll at Boston University. He majored in science and mathematics, aspiring to be a doctor. Bearden also took art history and instruction classes, those as "a hobby."[44]

Bearden was a student-athlete too. He pitched for the Boston University (BU) varsity baseball team and emerged as a star player. Bearden's pitching caught the attention of recruiters for the MLB Philadelphia Athletics. The owner offered him a position on the team. However, the opportunity came at a human cost: Fair-complexioned Negro Bearden would have to pass as a Caucasian, a White man. Romare Bearden declined.

After two years at BU, in 1932 he returned to his hometown, Harlem, New York, and never played baseball again. He enrolled at New York University and graduated in 1935. In 1940, eight years after tossing his last baseball competitively, Bearden bumped into artist Jacob Lawrence on a Harlem street. Lawrence told him there was a vacancy above his studio on 125th Street. Bearden rented the space for $8 a month and became creative neighbors with Lawrence, poet Claude McKay, and writer William Attaway.[45] Bearden (1911–1988) did not become the medical doctor that he envisioned himself. Moreover, embracing his ethnic heritage rather than hiding it for a chance to sneak past the baseball color barrier was not a hard choice. One of the great artists of the 20th century made the right choice.

***

Negro baseball was revived in the 1930s because of Cum Posey and Gus Greenlee and their Grays and Crawfords teams of Pittsburgh. Ironically, in the early 1940s Negro League baseball had a brief window of profitability and high fan interest (World War II and a labor shortage contributed) at the same time pressure was applied on multiple fronts to desegregate MLB.

Cumberland Willis "Cum" Posey was the sometimes combative, always relentless owner of the Pittsburgh-based Homestead Grays Negro League team. Posey was a member of the Homestead Board of Education from 1931 until his 1946 death, and he was a *Pittsburgh Courier* stockholder. Posey battled like-minded rival Rube Foster of the Chicago team. Sometimes the rivals were friendly, other times not. "[Posey] had a way, even when he became overwrought, of never falling out with you," wrote Young on April 13, 1946.

"He had a way of making his enemies respect him and sometimes win them over as friends. As for his friends, he could rely on their loyalty. He had a forceful way of making you agree with him. That was Cum Posey. And now he is no more."

The existing system of organized Black baseball died in 1932, at that time the peak years of the Great Depression. Greenlee launched the second-generation Negro League in 1933. Greenlee reigned as the Black numbers king of Pittsburgh's North Side. The hub of Greenlee's enterprises – both legitimate and criminal – was his Crawford Grill, the popular Black nightclub when Pittsburgh's Black Hill District was affectionately called "Little Harlem."[46] Greenlee did not have baseball experience but in 1931 he acquired a local semipro team and then branded them as the Crawfords. Greenlee upgraded his club to a professional team and used his money to assemble one of the most dominant baseball teams ever.

Greenlee started by purchasing pitcher Satchel Paige's contract for $250 from the Birmingham Black Barons in 1931. A year later Greenlee raided the crosstown talent from Posey's Homestead Grays: First baseman Oscar Charleston, third baseman Judy Johnson, and catcher Josh Gibson. In 1934, Greenlee acquired centerfielder James "Cool Papa" Bell from the St. Louis Stars and the Crawfords owner had five future Hall of Famers.[47]

The Crawfords dominated Black baseball during the mid- to late-1930s until Greenlee suffered a double come-uppance. First, police vice squads disrupted Greenlee's lucrative gambling operations and he could no longer pay top salaries to his baseball talent.

The second blow occurred in 1937 when pitcher Paige convinced eight Crawford teammates to follow him to the Dominican Republic to play ball at the invitation of dictator Rafael Trujillo.

Despite Greenlee's rise and fall, the second-generation Negro League prospered in the late 1930s through 1940s. A collective revenue producer was the East-West all-star game played in Chicago's Comiskey Park, home of the White Sox of MLB's American League. Attendance at the Negro baseball exhibition often outperformed MLB games, thus giving the Negro League an elevated platform.

Wendell Smith covered Negro League baseball during this period, including the East-West all-star games: "Thirty thousand spectators at the recent East-West game in Chicago proves that Negro baseball has something," he wrote in 1938. "Negro moguls are going to keep fooling around until some White folks' step in and take the game away from them, making thousands of dollars off the same teams that are losing money now."[48] During the 1940s, Negro League owners alleged that by crusading for the racial integration of MLB, Smith, and also Sam Lacy, hastened the demise of Black America's most lucrative business. The critics were partially right, but mostly wrong in their assessment. Right in that in cities where Negro League teams were popular and profitable, they had a multiplier effect in feeding Black businesses that provided, food, drink, lodging, and other services. However wrong because forces much bigger than two Black press sportswriters or MLB led to the demise of the second-generation Negro League. Urban renewal, which often meant the razing of

Black neighborhoods, plus flight to the suburbs, weakened the Black business. Consider that the MLB Dodgers left Brooklyn for California because they could not add parking to accommodate fans who left for Long Island and other New York-area suburbs (as did the Giants, who left Harlem for California).[49] Smith loved the Negro Leagues for what they were but hated the reason the leagues existed.[50]

It became harder for White media figures to caricature and ridicule Black baseball when a large fan base that included White patrons could witness excellence with their own eyes. Frank Young paid close attention to the East vs. West Negro League All-Star games, especially as crowd-attracting revenue producers. That said, he scolded Newark Bears owner Effa Manley for inadequately promoting the 1939 All-Star game at Yankee Stadium, complaining that the better-attended follow-up game in Chicago had 32,000 attendees vs. the 12,000 fans in New York. "Many of Mrs. Manley's objections, as well as some of her arguments," wrote Young, "are, as Shakespeare said in 'The Merchant of Venice,' 'like two grains of wheat lost in two bushels of chaff, you may seek all day ere you find them – and when you have found them, they are not worth their search.'"[51]

**

Even to argue over the efficacy of promoting all-star exhibitions affirmed that Negro League baseball had come a long way as an alternative to White professional baseball that shunned and blocked Black participation during the late 1800s. The New York Cubans – not mixed-race island people but Black resort servers turned sportsmen – formed a team and took on White professional teams, with players like the future Hall of Famer, Minnie Minoso. Black semipro teams populated the Eastern seaboard and Midwest in the early 1900s. Future sportswriter Sam Lacy pitched for teams in Washington and Atlantic City. Rube Foster, a brash Texan, and a better pitcher than Lacy, advanced from the playing field to management and emerged as leader of the NNL. Stars of that 1910s to 1920s era included John Henry "Pop" Lloyd, shortstop, William "Judy" Johnson, third base, and Leroy "Satchel" Paige, pitcher.

Foster's death plus the Great Depression of the early 1930s critically injured Negro League baseball, however, competition was revived elsewhere, led by Pittsburgh teams the Crawfords and Homestead Grays and respective owners Gus Greenlee and Cum Posey. The new challengers and the Monarchs out west in Kansas City, placed MLB owners in hot seats. They rented their ballparks to Black teams and talent that played as well or better than their professional teams were on display. Anecdotally, owners said they wished they had Black players but feared their White customers would storm away. America was very racially segregated, including the north and east. Negro League players and owners were conflicted about whether it was worth the trouble to press for integrated play. But the world war and pre-civil rights era Black agitation would force change in the next decade.

Notes

1. SABC Society for American Baseball Research.
2. Zang, Society for American Baseball Research. Minoso played with the New York Cubans from 1946 to 1948. After joining the Cleveland Indians, Minoso moved on to the Chicago White Sox in 1951.
3. Zang, David W. "Fleet Walker's Divided Heart," University of Nebraska Press, 1995, pp xx.
4. Charles River Editors, "Moses Fleetwood Walker: The Life and Legacy of the Last Black Man to Play Major League Baseball before Jackie Robinson," pps 20–22.
5. Zang, David W., "Fleet Walker's Divided Heart," Lincoln, University of Nebraska Press, 1995, pp 43.
6. Peterson, "Only the Ball was White," pp 29.
7. Ibid.
8. Tsoukas, Liann and Ruck, Rob, "Mal Goode Reporting: The Life and Work of a Black Broadcast Trailblazer," Pittsburgh, University of Pittsburgh Press, 2024, pp 58.
9. Washburn, Patrick S. and Lamb, Chris, "Sports Journalism: A History of Glory, Fame and Technology," Nebraska, 2020, pp 81.
10. Ashe, Arthur, "A Hard Road to Glory: A History of the African American Athlete from 1619–1919," New York, Warner Books, 1988.
11. Parmer, Charles, "For Gold and Glory," New York, Carrick and Evans, 1939. Page 50: No matter how good the ability of a Black jockey, Charles Parma took note of (champion rider Jimmy) Lee's difficulties: "He remained a quiet, courteous fellow ... but some of his compatriots of color became a trifle cocky in the jockey rooms; especially in the east. The White boys retaliated by ganging up against the Black riders on the rails. A Black boy would be pocketed, thrust back into the race; or his mount would be bump out of contention on a White boy's stirrup, and toss him out of the saddle ... those White fellows would slash out and cut the nearest Negro rider ... they literally ran the Black boys of the track." [From 1907–1909 Lee won ten major races, four of those wins on horse Sir Martin].
12. Tsoukas and Ruck, "Mal Goode Reporting," pp 58.
13. Peterson, "Only the Ball was White," pp 35.
14. Peterson "Only the Ball was White," pp 36.
15. Peterson, "Only the Ball was White," pps 59–60.
16. Peterson, "Only the Ball was White," pps 63, 67.
17. The Cuban X Giants was not a member of organized Negro League baseball. The 1903 winners self-identified as the "colored champions." https://www.mlb.com/history/negro-leagues/teams/cuban-x-giants
18. Peterson, "Only the Ball Was White," pps 107–108.
19. Peterson, "Only the Ball Was White," pps 1, III, 64, 103–111.
20. Peterson, "Only the Ball was White," pps 104–105.
21. Ufberg, Ross, "How Much Longer Can Baseball's 100-year Monopoly Last?" Wall Street Journal (WSJ), April 2–3, 2022, pp C-4.
22. Ashe "A Hard Road to Glory," pp 26.

23. Ashe, "A Hard Road to Glory," pp 27.
24. Peterson "Only the Ball was White," pp 108.
25. Ashe, "A Hard Road to Glory" pp 29, MLB attendance (Baseball-Reference.com).
26. 259 US 200 (1922), Ashe, "A Hard Road to Glory," pp 27, Volume II.
27. Paul Finkelman, "Baseball and the Rule of Law Revisited," *Thomas Jefferson Law Review* 25 (2002): 17–52.
28. Ashe, "A Hard Road to Glory," pp 29, Volume II.
29. Ibid.
30. Peterson, "Only the Ball Was White," pps 81, 98.
31. Peterson, "Only the Ball Was White," pp 114; Odzer, Tim, Society for American Baseball Research, https://sabr.org/bioproj/person/andrew-rube-foster/.
32. Paige, Leroy Satchel, "Maybe I'll Pitch Forever," New York, Bison Books, 1993.
33. Peterson, "Only the Ball Was White," pp 77.
34. Holway, John, "Voices from the Great Negro Baseball Leagues," New York, Dodd, Mead, 1975, pp 268. Interview with Sam Lacy, Buck Leonard. Tygiel, "Baseball's Great Experiment," pp 27.
35. "Tygiel, "Baseball's Great Experiment," pp 26, St. Louis (with two teams, the Cardinals and the Browns) and Washington DC with one team (the Senators) were the only Southern cities, where segregation was required by law and where slavery flourished until the Civil War.
36. Tygiel, "Baseball's Great Experiment," pp 29.
37. Chris Lamb "Conspiracy of Silence," pp 49.
38. Lanctot, Neil, "Negro League Baseball: The Rise and Ruin of a Black Institution," Philadelphia, University of Pennsylvania Press, pp 76.
39. Pietrusza, David, "Judge and Jury: The Life and Times of Judge Kenesaw Mountain Landis," South Bend, Indiana, Diamond Communications, 1998.
40. Snyder, Brad, "Beyond the Shadows of the Senators," Chicago, Contemporary Books, 2003, pp xiii. Gates, Henry Louis, Jr., "Black in Latin America," NYU Press, 2012.
41. Spink, J.G. Taylor, "Judge Landis and 25 Years of Baseball," St. Louis, the Sporting News Publishing Company, 1974. Cahan, Richard, "A Court that Shaped America: Chicago's Federal District Court, from Abe Lincoln to Abbie Hoffman," Evanston, Illinois, Northwestern University Press, 2002.
42. Pietrusza, "Judge and Jury: The Life and Times of Kenesaw Mountain Landis," South Bend, Indiana, Diamond Communications, Inc., 1998.
43. $735,000 in 2022 dollars according to CPI Inflation Calculator.
44. Ghent, Henri, "Oral History Interview with Romare Bearden," June 29, 1968, Smithsonian magazine. Archives of American Art, aaa.si.edu
45. Parham, Jason, "The Man Who Spurned a Baseball Career to Become a Renowned Artist," *The Atlantic*, March 14, 2012.
46. Tygiel, "Baseball's Great Experiment," pps 22–23; Borucki, Wesley, "Oxford Encyclopedia of African American History, 1896 to the Present (2009)," pps 42–43.
47. Tygiel, "Baseball's Great Experiment," pps 23–24; https://sabr.org/gamesproj/game/september-22-1935-satchel-paige-takes-the-money-but-not-the-mound-at-yankee-stadium/.
48. Reisler, "Black Writers/Black Baseball," pp 37.
49. A handful of baseball scholars, Black and White, female and male, made the economic analysis in the July 2023 documentary, "The League," a history of the Negro Leagues, directed by Sam Pollard; https://www.rogerebert.com/reviews/the-league-movie-review-2023 and https://www.theleaguedocumentary.com/videos/.
50. Marsh, "The Wendell Smith Reader," pp 179.
51. Reisler, Jim, "Black Writers/Black Baseball," pps 63–64; the Chicago game taught promoters a lesson.

CHAPTER 3

STALLING, THEN JACKIE ROBINSON'S BREAKTHROUGH, 1946

By 1938, Sam Lacy at the *Baltimore Afro-American* and Wendell Smith at the *Pittsburgh Courier* were advocating for Major League Baseball (MLB) to end the color barrier. Eight years later, as World War II was coming to an end, a former Army lieutenant and three-sport University of California at Los Angeles (UCLA) man emerged, in the mind of one major league owner, and the person who could be *the one* to desegregate baseball. Throughout the 1930s, MLB owners said Negroes were capable, but the owners did not act, or they sabotaged any action. By the early 1940s, World War II drained teams of talent because of the military draft, and a surge of Blacks moving north for defense-industry jobs added pressure to fill the baseball vacuum.

Black journalists added more pressure: Lacy, Smith, and Joe Bostic of the *People's Voice* in New York brought Negro League talent to the White ballparks for tryouts. Owners and managers delayed, stalled, and made excuses, but never said the Negro players were not capable. Two unlikely men created a breakthrough, starting with Branch Rickey, who ascended as the Abraham Lincoln of professional baseball, initially seemed the least likely to initiate breaking the color line, especially after blowing up when writer Joe Bostic ambushed him at Bear Mountain, New York. Meanwhile, Albert B. "Happy" Chandler, of Kentucky emerged as the Lyndon B. Johnson of MLB. Like US President LBJ in 1964, Kennesaw Mountain Landis' successor as baseball commissioner was the southerner who appeared to be the unlikely candidate to promote integration. Yet after shaking hands with Black journalists shortly after the announcement that he would succeed Landis (who died), Chandler said, "If a Black boy

DOI: 10.4324/9781003283928-4

can make it on Okinawa and Guadalcanal, hell, he can make it in baseball," then added, "Once I tell you something, brother, I never change. You can count on me. I don't believe in barring Negroes just because they are Negroes."

Chandler meant what he said and played a key role in finally desegregating MLB.[1]

***

At the start of the 1930s Jim Crow oppression of Blacks and pushback by those Black and White northerners was ubiquitous. There was the Scottsboro, Alabama trial of nine Black youths falsely arrested in 1931 for allegedly raping two White women on a freight train. An international campaign that defended the "Scottsboro Boys" applied pressure and saved most of the boys' lives. Some were in jail for many years until their death sentences were overturned. One remained in jail until he escaped in the late 1940s, two others were paroled in 1946.[2]

Black voters who traditionally voted for Republicans – the party of Lincoln – shifted to the Democratic Party and Franklin Delano Roosevelt. That demographic became pronounced in the urban north where several million Blacks had migrated from the south and escaped White segregationist Democrats. And in response to its Black readers, the *New York Times* in March 1930 announced it would begin capitalizing the proper noun, *Negro.*[3]

In 1933, the *Pittsburgh Courier* and *Chicago Defender* – America's two largest and nationally circulated Black newspapers – began pushing harder for the integration of MLB. The writing of Smith and Lacy and other Black sports writers was as influential with their readers as with White press columnists. Black newspapers were far more aware of the historical significance of attempting to break the color line.

Wendell Smith played a major role in shaping coverage. In contrast, White sportswriters largely supported segregation, either intentionally or unintentionally, by barely writing about it.[4]

Black press outlets meanwhile amplified incidents of discrimination. For example, in September 1934, Lacy's *Washington Tribune* reported a Springfield, Massachusetts American Legion Junior Baseball Tournament team withdrew because a Gaston, North Carolina hotel refused entry to Ernest Taliaferro, the team's Black pitcher-outfielder.

During the Depression socialists and communists critiqued American capitalism and also segregation. Leftist media, notably the *Daily Worker*, which was the organ of the Communist Party of the United States (CPUSA) advocated for Black inclusion in professional baseball. For a decade from 1936 to 1946, the *Daily Worker* ran more stories advocating for desegregation of baseball than all of America's predominantly White dailies combined. So stinging was its criticism that baseball management labels its writers "agitators." The *Daily Worker* writers wore the intended rebuke as badges of courage. "We were the conscience of journalism," said Lester Rodney.[5]

So too were the initial crusaders, the Black press journalists led by Sam Lacy. He was wary and feared the communist *Daily Worker* newspaper's involvement could hurt the campaign to end segregation as well as him personally: "It upset me that I might be called a communist," Lacy reminisced in 1999.[6] Showing solidarity with leftists in the 1930s was not as career-killing as it would become after World War II, during the Cold War, America and McCarthyism that dominated the politics of the early 1950s. Yet it was understandable that Lacy was squeamish about the communist stigma.

***

In March 1827, almost four decades after the US Constitution was written, John Russwurm and Samuel Cornish, launched *Freedom's Journal*, the first African-American newspaper in the nation. Published in New York, the newspaper was created in response to printed attacks by White-owned newspapers against Black New Yorkers. Newspaper editor Mordecai Manuel Noah of the *New York Enquirer* was an especially aggressive, menacing proponent of slavery in a state that freed its last slave on July 4, 1787. His newspaper led the chorus of proslavery zealots and condemned of extension of privileges to – and the very privilege of – free Negroes in American society. "Freedom is a great blessing to them. They swell our list of paupers, they are indolent and uncivil; and yet if a Black man commits a crime, we have more interest made for him than for a White," said an *Enquirer* editorial.[7]

Cornish and Russwurm fired back: "Too long have others spoken for us. Too long has the public been deceived by misrepresentations, in things which concern us dearly. We wish to plead our own cause."[8] Blacks, even in free Northern states, had limited rights, however, they could exercise their freedom of speech and press. In 1847, Frederick Douglass, an escaped slave from Maryland who was sponsored by White abolitionists to speak out on slavery's wrongs, started his own anti-slavery newspaper, *The North Star*, in Rochester, New York.

Eight decades after *Freedom's Journal* began, when legal segregation across the South dramatically restricted Black freedom, political rights, and economic opportunity; and private discrimination in the North restricted Black American's opportunities and increasingly ghettoized African Americans, the Black-owned newspapers were instruments used as shields and spears, most evident by three nationally circulated weekly newspapers, the *Baltimore Afro-American*, the *Pittsburgh Courier*, and the *Chicago Defender*.

During the late 1930s and early 1940s, Sam Lacy worked at the *Afro* and briefly for the *Defender*, then returned to the *Afro* and stayed 60 years. Wendell Smith worked for 11 years (1937–1948) at the *Courier*. The *Afro-American* was launched in 1892 by John Henry Murphy Sr., a former slave. He borrowed $200 from his wife and purchased a church publication, the *Afro-American Ledger*, from William N. Alexander, a pastor. The newspaper's mission was to "guide, counsel, educate, help people in trouble and through its columns suggest solutions to problems and means of correcting injustices," explained Elizabeth Murphy Moss, vice president and treasurer in 1969.[9] At its peak during the 1940s through 1960s the newspaper published four editions, twice weekly, in its home base Baltimore, as well as in Washington, DC, Richmond, Virginia, and Newark, New Jersey.

Robert Sengstacke Abbott launched the *Chicago Defender* in 1905. Abbott learned printing at Hampton Institute of Virginia and after graduating earned a law degree in 1898 from Kent Law School (today Chicago-Kent College of Law). Rejected repeatedly for work in the legal field; however, Abbott fell back on his printing knowledge. With 25 cents, a borrowed table, and a break by the landlady from paying rent, Abbott initiated a two-page edition of the *Defender*. At its peak in the 1930s the paper circulated 250,000 copies weekly. Many of the papers were distributed by train to the South, as it became the most important Black paper in the nation. Abbott was largely credited with encouraging the Great Black Migration from the deep south to midwestern cities.[10]

The *Pittsburgh Courier* was launched in 1910 by founder Robert L. Vann, a lawyer who acquired the newspaper from Robert Nathaniel Harleston, a self-published poet and H.J. Heinz security guard. Vann built up his acquisition. He was a crusader, and one of five Black lawyers in town, he vowed to "Abolish every vestige of Jim Crowism in Pittsburgh." Vann's aspirations spread nationally. The *Courier's* memorable World War II crusade was the "Double V," – victory in World War II – slaying anti-Semitism and racism in Nazi Germany and victory by slaying racism in America. His second great crusade was to break the professional baseball color line. That crusade, along with the work of others, would result in Jackie Robinson's breakthrough. The *Courier* printed four editions weekly (local, northern, eastern, and southern) at its peak and circulated 250,000 copies in all 48 states and internationally.[11]

***

In October 1936, 20,000 fans were expected at Chicago Soldier Field for the annual East-West Football Classic. Black gridiron players on two major college football teams were playing, Two Northwestern University running backs were competing against the Ohio State University team. Meanwhile, downstate in Champaign, Illinois, Black stars, Ozzie "Ebony Eel" Simmons, and Homer Harris Jr. of the University of Iowa, were playing against the University of Illinois.[12] Unlike the Jim Crow South, where Blacks were shut out of White major colleges and universities, it was not unusual in the 1930s to see at least one or a few Black football players starring on midwestern college and university teams.[13]

In summer 1937, the National Semipro Baseball Congress considered barring African Americans. Hall of Famer Honus Wagner, the Pittsburgh Pirates shortstop, now turned commissioner of the baseball congress, denied such action was considered.

Meanwhile, a September 25, 1937, Lacy column included a letter by John L. Clark, secretary of the Negro National League, that attacked those Negro League teams that launched a World Series tour not sanctioned by the league. Lacy published the executive's letter on the eve of his September 26, 1937, meeting with Washington Senators owner Clark Griffith to lobby for hiring Black ballplayers. Lacy wrote:

> What with petty jealousies, cut-throat aspirations and willful disregard for rules and agreements on the parts of promoters and club owners, and team-jumping and general wrangling on the parts of players keeping so-called organized Negro baseball in perpetual chaos, it makes one ponder the advisability of entering the breach to submit recommendations.[14]

***

In 1938, there was still resistance to Blacks playing professional baseball with Whites. However, what was different about the status quo rejections were hints that change was in the air. "Colored players will take their places beside those of other races in the major leagues," predicted Washington Senators owner Clark Griffith, who continued to do nothing.

National League President Ford Frick spoke of the "inevitability" of integrated baseball, as did Phillip Wrigley, owner of the Chicago Cubs. Connie Mack of the Philadelphia Athletics in 1935 told Negro League star Webster MacDonald, "I'd give half my ball club for a man like you." MacDonald had just outpitched big-league legend Dizzy Dean during a barnstorming game. And Grace Comiskey, owner of the Chicago White Sox, said to a prospect, "Oh, if you were a White boy, what you'd be worth to my club!"[15] Attitudes appeared to evolve, yet racism persisted, and major league owners refused to sign talented players for many years. Griffith in 1954 – seven years after desegregation – signed Carlos Paula, a Black Cuban player. Paula appeared in a dozen games that year, then played a full 1955 season and gone by the end of 1956.[16]

***

Culture and geography dictated the White owners' indecision and tortured reasoning: One-third of all organized baseball players were southern Whites, accustomed to strict racial segregation and White supremacy in their hometowns. Whites who treated Blacks with dignity, respect, or kindness were usually ostracized or intimidated, sometimes violently. Without hesitation, Hall of Fame players Rogers Hornsby and Tris Speaker plus "Gabby" Street said they were Ku Klux Klan (KKK) members.[17] During the 1930s, the KKK was a mainstream domestic organization that included middle-class professional workers and politicians among its members. So then, why not professional athletes? For many the KKK was a White supremacist social organization or a vehicle for political officeholding, although everywhere in the South its members used violence and intimidation, when necessary, to maintain segregation and to suppress Black rights. Skin color racism was so intuitive in the South that the region's daily newspapers chronicled the humiliation, brutality, and barbarism of Blacks in plain view. White daily's newspaper editors and publishers, notably in Atlanta, Memphis, and Jacksonville, Florida collaborated with industrialists to maintain White domination of Blacks and used their media as weapons.

***

Then in 1938, a jocular and factually dubious comment uttered over the airwaves punched a hole in the stonewalled conspiracy of silence that kept Blacks out of professional baseball. New York Yankee outfielder Jake Powell, who was from Silver Spring, Maryland, said publicly that during his off-seasons, as a police officer, "he derived pleasure from beating up niggers and throwing them in jail."[18]

There was no evidence that in fact, Powell was ever a policeman. But as soon as Powell made the hateful remark, the Chicago radio station recording the words cut off the interview. Nevertheless, hundreds of offended listeners called WGN, the *Chicago Tribune*-owned broadcaster with call letters that proclaimed, "World's Greatest Newspaper."[19] Powell later apologized to Blacks in Harlem. When *The Nation*, a liberal political journal, learned of the trouble, they labeled the incident "*Laffaire* Jake Powell."[20]

In Chicago, where Powell's Yankees were playing, the host White Sox owner and umpires were greeted by an indignant coalition that included representatives from the National Urban League, National Association for the Advancement of Colored People (NAACP), and International Workers Order.[21] Powell was portrayed in some White press as a victim of a "gotcha" radio interview, and the proposed solution was to only allow baseball players in the future to give scripted answers to questions, or just forbid player interviews. But nationally syndicated political columnist Westbrook Pegler, in blunt language, wrote that MLB established and enforced a racist color line and now exposed and embarrassed, Commissioner Landis suspended Powell for ten days because he made a racist statement.[22]

Although Powell claimed he was employed in law enforcement, he did not work as a Dayton, Ohio police officer during the winter off-seasons. Two Black newspapers, the nationally circulated *Chicago Defender* and the local *Dayton Forum*, conducted rigorous reporting and official sources verified that Powell was never a city employee. Granted, he had been offered a chance to work as a police officer but declined the opportunity. The White-controlled daily newspapers meanwhile repeated Powell's false claim. Dayton elected and law enforcement officials were incensed that their city was smeared.[23]

"Say again what you said over the radio," hollered a spectator at a Detroit Tigers game that hosted the Yankees. Instead of his outfield crouch on the field, Powell was sitting in the ballpark behind the heckler. He turned around and saw Black heavyweight champ Joe Louis, "the Brown Bomber," glaring at him. In a rare moment of self-control, Powell kept his mouth shut.[24]

While suspended, Powell was ordered to go to Harlem, across the skinny river separating upper Manhattan from Yankee Stadium in the Bronx to apologize to residents. But while on the apology tour, Powell in a written statement denied he made the racist boast. But this was not true since thousands – perhaps tens of thousands of people – had heard the broadcast.[25] What Powell said over the air left marks. When he visited the Griffith Stadium field on August 16, usually well-behaved Black Washingtonians hurled pop bottles at Powell. A sixth-inning missile barrage caused a 10-minute delay so the grounds crew could clean up the glass.[26] Fay Young of the *Chicago Defender* and dean of Black sports journalists at that time predicted the Negro League East-West all-star game in Chicago would be a turning point for Black baseball because White journalists, baseball executives, and spectators would attend because of the Powell incident.[27]

Jake Powell's playing skill and time deteriorated after his 1938 radio interview. Powell's baseball career had been a reckless life of assaulting players. He habitually slid into bases and injured opponents with his spiked shoes and sometimes jabbed them while running bases. Powell often engaged in ethnic invective on the playing field. Americans of Jewish and Italian descent were among his favorite targets.

Off the field Powell had a record of drunkenness, petty theft, attempted bigamy, and in the end suicide with a gun in November 1940 inside a Washington, D.C. police station after an arrest.[28] A half-century after Powell's death, Sam Lacy remembered the man as "A bigot ... Baseball took care of him."[29] L'Affaire Powell revealed the gaping differences between Black and White America and why the White press routinely ignored protests from the Black community. That community simply was not heard. But this time the Powell incident demonstrated the ability of the Black press to mobilize public opinion and challenge racial injustices.[30] It also illustrates that there were a growing number of White opponents of the color line in baseball, and that even Commissioner Landis, never known for supporting equality, had to take notice of racism.

The campaign to end segregation in baseball became one of the most important stories involving racial equality in the 1930s and 1940s. Black-owned newspaper editors and writers believed that if there could be racial equality in baseball, there could be racial equality elsewhere in society.

To Black sportswriters – *especially* Lacy and Smith, both of whom would be later inducted into the writer's wing of the Baseball Hall of Fame for their contributions to ending the color line in the national pastime – their campaigns were personal ones because they too faced racial discrimination in their profession.

Black sportswriters were barred from press boxes, dugouts, and locker rooms at big league ballparks. Furthermore, they were never hired by mainstream papers, where they would have been paid more and their articles would have been seen by more readers.[31] The papers rarely said that they had a policy against hiring Blacks – they just did not do it. At this time there were virtually laws prohibiting private race discrimination, even in states which had anti-discrimination laws for public accommodations, like restaurants, movie theaters, and hotels.

Black newspapers were far more aware than the White press of the historical significance of the desegregation of baseball, and their stories contained more emotion and more personal insights about Black prospects. At least ten leading Black sportswriters were eloquent, persistent, and occasionally bitter in their advocacy that urged the White baseball establishment to integrate.[32]

***

Between 1940 and 1950, 1.5 million Blacks left the South for cities in the North, Midwest, and West. That was a faster movement than the 1.5 million Blacks who fled the South for the North and the West between 1910 and 1940.[33]

Blacks bound for Midwest cities Chicago, Detroit, Milwaukee, and Cleveland mostly come from Mississippi, Alabama and Louisiana, Tennessee, Arkansas, and Texas. Migration patterns followed train and bus routes. With World War II underway there were jobs at defense industry plants and, in the Brooklyn, and Philadelphia Navy Yards.

In June 1941, President Franklin D. Roosevelt by executive order established the Fair Employment Practices Committee to prevent racial discrimination at government defense plants or other defense-related works. Blacks would work alongside Whites in the factories.

That new reality resulted in rebellions. From June 20 to 22, 1943 in Detroit, as 100,000 Whites and Blacks tried to cool off at a beach at Belle Isle during a heat wave, some jostling followed by rumor-mongering escalated into a fist-throwing melee. Looting of shops followed. By the time federal troops arrived and put down the riot and rampage, 34 people were killed (25 of them Black, 17 killed by police), and 500 additional people were injured.[34]

Even with the steady stream of Blacks escaping the South for freedom and opportunity in the North, three-quarters of Blacks still lived in the South when America entered World War II, the day after the December 7, 1941, Pearl Harbor attack. Regarding baseball, Sam Lacy observed, that despite the growth of northern Black populations, "Black patronage was negligible, so they [White owners] didn't feel that it was worthwhile to appease those Black customers and run the risk of the White customers who were the majority of population." Nevertheless, some Whites who coached or played professional baseball pined for Black talent. In 1942, Brooklyn Dodgers manager Leo Durocher said he would sign Black players if he were allowed to.

Commissioner Kennesaw Mountain Landis, who shut down Black participation with silence and stonewalling, publicly proclaimed, "Negroes have never been barred organized baseball ... and never have been in the 21 years I served."[35] Landis' duplicity was on display.

That year Negro League pitcher Nate Moreland and All-America football star Jackie Robinson requested a tryout with the Chicago White Sox at the team's Pasadena, California spring training camp. Jimmy Dykes, the manager, obliged and said of Robinson, "He's worth $50,000 of anybody's money. He stole everything but my fielder's gloves." Dykes said he was willing to accept Black players but dismissed both athletes. "I can play in Mexico, but I have to fight for America where I can't play," said

Moreland, 42.[36] Moreland did serve in the military during World War II and returned to the United States in 1944 and resumed playing ball.

Flirting, hesitating, and then failing to make a move occurred in Pittsburgh Pirates as well. William Benswanger, the owner of the Pirates, told the *Pittsburgh Courier* that he repeatedly tried to acquire local talent Josh Gibson and Buck Leonard, however, Homestead Grays owner Cum Posey was not willing to let go of his Negro League superstars. Wendell Smith accused Benswanger of "Unmitigated story telling."[37]

Yet the Pirates owner continued talking. In 1940 he surmised, "There's no reason why they [Negro leaguers] should be denied the same chance that Negro fighters and musicians are given." The owner understood Pittsburgh's Hill District, aka Little Harlem, was a destination of Black talent in sports, entertainment, and journalism that were all of national renown.[38] In July 1943, Benswanger made a move. In response to pressure from *Daily Worker* sports editor Nat Low, the owner said yes to tryouts for Baltimore Elite Giants catcher Roy Campanella, plus New York Cubans pitcher Dave Barnhill. August 4 was the Forbes Field tryout date. But the event never happened. Low of the *Daily Worker* received a letter from Benswanger explaining he canceled the audition because of unnamed pressures.[39] Cancelation seemed to be contagious. That same year in Washington, Senators owner Clark Griffith asked Grays stars Buck Leonard and Josh Gibson if they were interested in playing in the major leagues. Both men said yes.

Griffith was familiar with both stars. The Homestead Grays used Griffith Stadium as a second home venue and the Black owners paid substantial rent (and concessions) to use the space. "If we get you boys, were going to get the best ones," said Griffith. "It's going to break up your league." Leonard answered, "Well, if that's gonna be better for the players, then it's all right by me." Did Buck call Griffith's bluff? The owner did not pursue his invitation and Leonard and Gibson remained with the Grays.[40]

Griffith's sincerity seemed doubtful. The Senators would not have a Black player until 1954, Carlos Paula, who was actually from Cuba. The first African American on the team would be Joe Black, a former Dodger, who was signed in 1957, making the Senators one of the last teams to have an American Black on its roster. This was two years after the Yankees placed their first Black player, Elston Howard, and two years before the Boston Red Sox became the last team to have a Black player, in 1959. As the most southern East Coast city with a major league team – and a capital city that was very segregated – it was not surprising that the Griffiths was not really interested in integration.[41]

Nevertheless, another White owner stepped in with an integration scheme. Bill Veeck Jr., the son of Chicago Cubs former president, was the opposite of his reserved, dignified dad. Junior, 29 years old in 1943, was exuberant and iconoclastic. He had purchased Milwaukee's debt-ridden, last place (55–98 won-loss record) minor league team and in two years turned the Brewers into the profitable, pennant-winning enterprise. Veeck Jr. became notorious for his shrewd player deals and wildly imaginative promotions that put fans in seats. His next plan was to buy the floundering Philadelphia Phillies from owner Gerry Nugent, and then stock the team with Black players.[42] Veeck considered the realities of the war that drained the professional ranks: "The only untapped reservoir of players was some of the Blacks who were either older or for one reason or another had not been drafted. I had not the slightest doubt that in 1944, a war year, the Phillies would have leaped from seventh place [next to last] to the pennant."[43]

By containing Blacks to one major league team the act would be akin to the White major leaguers who competed against Negro League teams during the MLB off-season. Veeck's plan had financial backing and he had reached an agreement with Nugent, however, Veeck's transparency killed the transformation. Out of respect he showed the plan to Commissioner Landis, who politely listened and revealed no reaction. When Veeck returned to Philadelphia the following morning he discovered that Nugent turned his club over to the National League and its President Ford Frick sold the Phillies to a wealthy lumber dealer for half the price Veeck had offered. Weeks later Veeck found out that Frick boasted that he stopped him from "contaminating the league."[44] Veeck said, "I had tried to buy the Philadelphia Phillies and stock it with Negro players. ... My Philadelphia adventure was no idle dream. ... The players were going to be assembled for me by Abe Saperstein and Doc Young, the sports editor of the *Chicago Defender*, two of the most knowledgeable men in the country on the subject of Negro baseball. ... I had no doubt that in 1944, a war year, the Phillies would have leaped from seventh place to the pennant."

The silent, nullifying hand of Kennesaw Mountain Landis was evident. But in a year Landis the czar had to cancel William Cox the new owner; Cox was caught betting on his team. And that year in October, Landis, the implacable stone wall opponent of integration, died. Soon, doors would open for transforming professional baseball.

***

MLB owners were intrigued by or caved to relentless nagging by the Black press, the NAACP, the White leftist alternative press, and increasingly liberal politicians in northern and western cities, to consider adding Negro

League stars to their teams. There were openings because many White players were enlisted or drafted during the war. They included such stars as Ted Williams, Hank Greenberg, Bob Feller, Joe DiMaggio, Warren Spahn, and Stan Musial. Many Black stars were too old for military service. For example, Satchel Paige, Buck Leonard, Josh Gibson, and "Cool Papa" Bell were all in their 30s when the war began. From 1942 to 1944 there were a half-dozen tryouts of Black players. Nothing happened. These events were either shams or the owners suffered cold feet and fear of the unknown or were pressured to back off by the baseball commissioner or National and American League presidents.

Yet World War II was changing public opinion. Unlike professional baseball, where Blacks were simply not allowed to play, when the war began Blacks served in the military. A few Blacks had graduated from West Point in the 19th century. In 1936 Benjamin O. Davis Jr. became the first Black graduate in the 20th century. He would later be the first Black general in the US military.

There were other Black officers who had come out of Reserve Officers Training Corps (ROTC) programs at historically Black colleges and universities. But at the same time, for most of the war, Blacks served in separate, segregated units, often with the highest-ranking officer being White. More than a million Black men would serve in the war, as would a significant number of Black women.[45] Red Tails fighter pilots – the Tuskegee Airmen 332nd Fighter Group – protected large bomber planes that pounded German targets.[46] A month before the pivotal Battle of the Bulge at the end of 1944, Gen. George Patton tasked a Black tank battalion, the 761st "Black Panthers" to successfully capture the German-held town Morville-les-Vic in Belgium.[47]

Black government issues (GIs) were patriotic and militant too, as were the Port Chicago, California sailors who mutinied to protest a horrific explosion that killed 320 sailors, the result of overloaded ammunition. Black and White advocates rebelled against pseudo-scientific studies and propaganda that alleged Negroes were cowardly for combat. Most Blacks who were subject to the mandatory draft were assigned to custodial or service tasks. Yet World War II do-or-die urgency chipped away at Jim Crow conventions. During Japan's Pearl Harbor rout, Doris Miller, a Black cook, took over a 50-caliber antiaircraft gun and shot down four Japanese fighter planes while aboard the battleship USS West Virginia. Miller became the first African American to earn a Navy Cross for courage under fire.[48]

GI Joe Louis was not a civil rights crusader; however, the Brown Bomber frequently took principled stands for respect and equality when Louis was in the Army. He was in England on tour and was to give boxing exhibitions at several camps. He arrived at a stadium an hour before the event and watched hundreds of White soldiers enter the gates, but a group of Negro servicemen were standing outside looking forlorn. He asked them if they had tickets.

"We can't go in," one of them said. "This is supposed to be off-limits to Negro soldiers. We were just standing here so we could get a look at you when you arrived." In World War II the US Armed Forces was segregated. Louis entered the stadium in uniform but told the Negro soldiers to stay put. A half-hour passed, and Louis sat in the dressing room. The soldiers inside grew impatient and began clapping and shouting, "We want Louis, we want Louis."

A special services officer rushed in and said, "C'mon Joe. Get dressed, it's time for you to go on." Louis answered he would not perform until the Negroes outside were allowed in. The officer left and returned with the commanding officer, a general. The general pleaded with Louis to box, but the sergeant said no. Then the general issued an order to perform, and Louis stood his ground. Convinced that Louis was resolute, the general allowed the Black soldiers in, and afterward congratulated him for his principled stand, according to Smith.

Black military service would help lead to fundamental changes in American society after the war. Hesitation to change persisted, but not for long. Post-war, the US military would change its racial policies; baseball would change sooner, mere months after World War II ended.

Sam Lacy and Wendell Smith's persistent advocacy for Black player inclusion in professional baseball drove societal change. Both men's opinion columns and well-sourced news reporting had an oversized influence on Black and White readers. Their medium, newspapers, was dominant until 1950 because television for mass audiences was not yet established. TV became available to US masses in 1949; by 1956, 36 million sets were in households and penetration was 72%. Radio was a powerful medium – 28 million units in households – but not as big as newspaper and magazine consumption.[49] Lacy and Smith's footprints would expand during the post-World War II years.

***

Jackie Robinson would be the first of a number of players, including Roy Campanella, Hank Aaron, and Willie Mays, who played Negro League ball briefly, but were elected to the Hall of Fame based on their Major League careers. Robinson played 41 games with the Kansas City Monarchs in 1945. He was not the most talented player on the Monarchs, but his multi-varsity college letters at an integrated, mostly White university, and his service as an Army officer projected him as the best candidate to enter and then survive the hostile atmosphere of MLB.

Jackie Robinson was the first Black baseball player to play major league ball *since 1889*. Some Negro League players were angry or disappointed when he was chosen over them. He was a 28-year-old MLB rookie in 1947 and the year before that Robinson desegregated the top layer of White professional minor league ball with the Dodgers farm team in Montreal, Canada. Branch Rickey, the president, general manager, and co-owner of the Dodgers, believed this experience was vital for breaking the color line in baseball.

The Robinsons – Jackie and Rachel – projected a wholesome image, unlike the boozing, gambling, and skirt-chasing reputation attached – fairly or unfairly – to too many Negro League players and other Black athletes. The couple would have to overcome a racial double standard: No one cared if Babe Ruth were drunk, or Mickey Mantle was a skirt chaser, however, it mattered if Robinson or other Black players did. In addition, Jackie Robinson demonstrated resolute combativeness with the probationary restraint that he would need to survive the majors. Still, some Negro League veterans were upset that a newcomer was given the first chance to break the sports color line.[1]

Jackie Robinson benefitted from the Great Migration: His divorced mother migrated from Cairo, Georgia to Pasadena, California. As a boy, Jackie engaged and competed with Whites in ways that were not imaginable in the Jim Crow South. He and his family still had to face racial animus in California. At the 1936 Olympics in Berlin, Mack Robinson, Jackie's older brother, won the silver medal during Jesse Owens' gold medal-winning heat. That year, after a judge ordered Pasadena pools to allow Blacks to swim, the city government answered by purging Black employees from the payroll, including Olympic medalist Mack.

Still, Jackie Robinson's experiences were unusual for his time, and some Negro League stars, many of whom considered themselves to be better baseball players than Robinson, agreed they did not have the patience or temperament to break the color line. However, Satchel Paige, who was the seventh African American to successfully transition to MLB, albeit at age 42 as a Cleveland Indians rookie in 1948 when most players were long retired, said at the time of the barrier-breaking 1946 Robinson signing: "They didn't make a mistake in signing Robinson. He's a No. 1 professional player. They couldn't have picked a better man."[50]

Paige however was probably masking conflicting emotions. "I'd been the guy who started all that big talk about letting us in the big leagues," Paige wrote later in his autobiography. "I'd been the one the White boys wanted to barnstorm against. I'd been the one everybody said should be in the majors. It was still me that ought to have been first."[51] At Paige's advanced age that was clearly unlikely. It was also unlikely he would be first because of his unpredictable behavior off the field, for example, Paige's contract breaking and team jumping. Rickey could not afford such distractions.

***

Jackie Robinson was the University of California Los Angeles's first athlete to letter in four different sports: Football, baseball, track, and basketball. Robinson's teammates included football letterman Kenny Washington, a running back who was UCLA's first consensus All-American and desegregated the modern National Football League (NFL) in 1946, a year before Robinson integrated MLB. That year, the Los Angeles city council informed the NFL Rams that they had to play Washington because the Memorial Coliseum was a public facility. Washington in turn broke the pro football color barrier: Washington was also an excellent baseball player, perhaps even better than Robinson. While at UCLA Washington was the Pacific Coast League collegiate baseball batting champion.[52] Robinson left the university a semester before graduation to work as an assistant athletic director at a youth camp in California. Robinson then traveled to Hawaii to play semipro football with the Honolulu Bears on weekends, while building houses on the island on weekdays. Robinson left Hawaii 48 hours before Japan bombed Pearl Harbor naval base on December 7, 1941.

By July 6, 1944, Robinson was a US Army lieutenant stationed at Fort Hood, Texas. During World War II the military units were racially segregated. While riding a bus on base and escorting Virginia Jones, the light-complexioned Black wife of a fellow officer, a bus driver who was a local Texan and not in the military, told Robinson to move from the middle to the back of the bus.[53] Looking in the rear-view mirror, the bus driver thought Robinson was sitting with a White woman. Robinson refused to move. He was aware that the Army changed its transportation policy and allowed desegregated travel on base vehicles, and he told the driver this. Still, the driver and dispatcher confronted Robinson when he and the woman stopped to transfer to a connecting bus.

Military police were called, then base officers, because Robinson stood his ground. The lieutenant was charged with insubordination. Robinson now faced a court martial.

Robinson's future could have been altered devastatingly, but he won the day. Robinson argued his case convincingly, unlike the accusing superior officers who were fuzzy on details and appeared vengeful. Robinson dodged a dishonorable discharge and decided to exit the military honorably discharged that November.[54]

Had he been sent to active duty he was to serve with the 761st tank battalion, a Black unit distinguished for the final push against Germany and for liberating concentration camp survivors at Buchenwald.[55] Back to civilian life Robinson at a time of war, signed a contract to play with the Negro League Kansas City Monarchs. His season began in April 1945, just before the war in Europe came to an end. During the 1945 baseball pre-season, Wendell Smith and Sam Lacy agreed that Robinson could succeed as a major league player.[56]

By August Branch Rickey was convinced of Robinson's chances too. The executive dispatched scout Clyde Sukeforth to evaluate the 26-year-old shortstop.

***

On October 23, 1945, in Montreal, Jackie Robinson's signing was announced.[57] He was present and skin color was on the minds of some of the reporters who were present. "This Robinson is definitely dark," wrote Al Parsley of the *Montreal Herald.* "His color is the hue of ebony. By no means can he be called a Brown bomber or chocolate soldier." After Robinson spoke Parsley followed, "He talked with that easy fluency of an educated man. Jack answered a dozen questions fired at him […] with easy confidence, but no cocksureness, nor braggadocio." Dan Daniel of the *Sporting News* framed the momentous event in a column in which he eavesdropped on a discussion in the imaginary "Bijou Tonsorial Parlor," where the debate over baseball integration moved from racial stereotyping to the pros and cons of the Robinson signing.[58]

In March 1945, New York City's three MLB teams had been legally placed on the spot. New York State approved the Quinn-Ives Act that banned discriminatory hiring across a wide range of employment, including professional baseball. The Yankees, Giants, and Dodgers were on the clock to hire Black ballplayers. Irving M. Ives, an upstate Republican who had been in the assembly for 16 years, and state Sen. Elmer F. Quinn, a Manhattan Democrat, were the co-sponsors of the legislation.[59] Gov. Thomas E. Dewey signed the bill and made it law.

Quinn-Ives was a state version of the 1941 federal Fair Employment Practices Commission. The state law's intent was to persuade, not compel employers to hire people of all ethnicities.

A week after Quinn-Ives became state law, Joe Bostic, the Black sports editor of the Harlem-based *People's Voice,* tested the law. On April 6, 1945, he travelled to Brooklyn Dodgers spring training camp at Bear Mountain, New York.

Because of war, Bear Mountain served as an alternative to their traditional Florida training camp. Bostic brought along Negro League stars, New York Cubans first baseman Dave "Showboat" Thomas, and Newark Eagles pitcher Terris McDuffie. Journalists Jim Smith of the *Pittsburgh Courier* and Nat Low of the communist *Daily Worker* came too. General Manager Branch Rickey was not pleased by the announced visit. Initially, Rickey's subordinates told Bostic Thomas and McDuffie could not audition because they had not been vetted by scouts and then invited. But Bostic, who was famously acerbic and tenacious, swatted away the excuses while having lunch that day with Rickey.

"Rickey went berserk, almost with fury," said Bostic. "We went into the dining room at the Bear Mountain Inn, and he told me that he did not appreciate what I had done." Bostic had put the executive on the spot. If Rickey allowed the tryout to proceed, Bostic would get "the sports story of the century," or if he rebuffed the players and writers Rickey would be open to embarrassing criticism. Rickey agreed to and witnessed a 45-minute tryout by Thomas and McDuffie. McDuffie split a home plate with consistent control, throwing pitches ordered up by Rickey. Thomas, a left-handed hitter, faced a lefty thrower and belted numerous long-distance shots in three rounds of hitting.

McDuffie, who told Rickey "I'm a hitting pitcher," showed him by slamming several long shots. Still, Rickey dismissed both men. McDuffie was at least 32, Thomas was at least 37 at the time so advanced age could have been the reason for Rickey's rejections. (McDuffie was a standout pitcher for 14 seasons, since 1931. In 1938 he pitched 27 consecutive complete games for the Newark Eagles and posted a 275 record).[60]

Despite his stony resistance at Bear Mountain, Rickey had been scheming to break the color line on his own terms. On the morning of March 13, Rickey was drinking coffee and reading his newspaper at Bear Mountain. Suddenly he looked up from his paper with an animated expression. "What's wrong, Dear?" Jane Rickey asked her husband. "It was in the paper. Mother, that Governor Dewey has just signed the Ives-Quinn law!" Rickey exclaimed. "They can't stop me now."[61]

Meanwhile Sam Lacy cultivated a relationship with Leslie O'Connor, who because of Landis' death, was named to oversee professional baseball until a new commissioner was appointed. In March Lacy wrote to each of the sixteen team owners and recommended that a committee be created to address the best way to integrate MLB. "This is sort of compromise for me as a colored man, in that it embraces certain elements of appeasement, but if it accomplishes anything I shall feel compensated in some measure for suggesting it. Certainly, it will be a step in the right direction."[62]

On April 24 Lacy presented his proposal to the owners at their meeting in Detroit. Lacy waited for an hour in a hallway of the Cadillac Hotel, then was invited inside a small conference room. He was introduced by O'Connor. Lacy passed out copies of the proposal and made a statement, answered a few questions then left.[63] The owners reacted by establishing a committee on MLB Integration. Lacy was approved as a member. Branch Rickey of the Dodgers was selected to represent the National League and Lee McPhail of the Yankees would represent the American League. During that Detroit owners' meeting the owners chose A.B. "Happy" Chandler as the new baseball commissioner.

Superficially, Branch Rickey appeared to be an unlikely advocate for championing the desegregation of baseball, yet he was a complex and wily character. For example, the committee on baseball integration never met. "[Larry] McPhail always has some excuse," said Lacy," to which Rickey answered, "Well, Sam, maybe we'll forget about Mr. McPhail. Maybe we'll just give up on him and let nature take its course."[64]

If Rickey signaled that he was ready to make a move, Lacy missed the sign. But Rickey was also nicknamed "Mahatma" because like Mohandas Mahatma Gandhi of India, his mood could swing from piety to theatrics. It was a sportswriter who read a portrait of Gandhi that described his persona as a combination of "your father and Tammany Hall."[65] Rickey indeed was a complex man. He was a devout Methodist, so much so that he refused to play Sunday ball games when he was a professional. Rickey said he had empathy for the Black players who were blocked from professional leagues because he recalled Charlie Thomas, an Ohio Wesleyan player he coached who in 1904 was initially refused lodging at a hotel in South Bend, Indiana. Rickey convinced the hotel to place a cot in his room for Thomas to sleep on, as they would a servant.

Thomas, a good-hitting first baseman, wept that night and said to Rickey, "Black skin, Black skin! If I could only, I could make them White."[66] Rickey who played baseball for four years, went on to become a lawyer, then a baseball executive and tactician. While general manager of the St. Louis Cardinals, Rickey created the first minor league farm system that soon became the standard for all teams. The system allowed a team to develop talent until players were ready for "the show," major leagues.

Now that integration was to be discussed in 1945, Rickey deployed several schemes to hide what he ultimately intended. One trial balloon was to create an entire team of Negro professional baseball talent, the "Brown" Dodgers. Another tactic was to front a Negro civic leader to serve on a commission that studied adding Negro players to the three New York teams, Dodgers, Giants, and Yankees.

Working behind the scenes, Rickey would not make a move unless he was comfortable that key stakeholders were on board, whether it meant testing the inevitability of a Black player joining the Dodgers on play-by-play announcer Red Barber, a native Mississippian who was accustomed to his region's racial customs, or Rickey seeking confidential feedback from the business leaders who financed the Dodgers.

Closer to home, Rickey floated his scheme with his wife and adult children. His wife and daughter worried that he would be pummeled by the snarky local media. Branch Rickey Jr., a minor league executive, feared the breakthrough move could be an economic flop.

Before the 1945 MLB season began in April, Sam Lacy and Wendell Smith agreed Jackie Robinson could succeed in the big leagues, even before he played any games with the Negro League Kansas City Monarchs. He was the "ideal man to pace the experiment," Lacy told the periodical *Negro Baseball* because Robinson's west coast college experience acclimated him to interracial competition, "nor would he have the cocky, bulldozing attitude we likewise must avoid." Smith meanwhile rated Robinson his first choice among recruits for a tryout with the Boston Red Sox.[67]

By August, Rickey, who was monitoring Robinson's play with the Monarchs and researched his volatile stint in the military, agreed the prospect could be big-league caliber. The general manager dispatched Clyde Sukeforth to scout the 26-year-old rookie. Sukeforth chatted with Robinson but was unable to witness whether the shortstop had the arm strength to compete in the majors at shortstop. Robinson was resting a shoulder injury. Because of football injuries, Robinson's throws from deep shortstop did not always find its mark accurately. Rickey wanted to meet Robinson anyway and brought him to Brooklyn for an August 28 interview.[68] "It took me a long time to convince myself that Rickey was not just making a gesture," Robinson told Wendell Smith.[69]

For three hours Rickey verbally poked and prodded the prospect, playing dual roles of race-baiting players and spectators or as the team management that counted on the pioneer to keep his cool and not embarrass the team. "Mr. Rickey, I think I can play ball in Montreal. I think I can play ball in Brooklyn," said Robinson. "But you're a better judge of that than I am. If you want to take this gamble, I will promise you there will be no incident."[70]

At the Dodgers' Brooklyn office Robinson signed an agreement to accept a $600 month baseball season salary plus a $3,500 bonus offered by the Montreal Royals.[71] For context, Hank Greenburg in 1947 was paid $100,000 during his final season. Also, the minimum National League salary was \$7,500. The Dodgers front office juggled when to announce Robinson's singing in fall 1945, and how to synchronize with the returning Dodgers who signed their contracts.[72]

Once Robinson was signed, Rickey pivoted to other Black prospects. He did not want Robinson to be the lone Black player in the Dodgers organization. Roy Campanella met on October 17 with the general manager. The Negro League catcher thought Rickey offered a contract with the so-called Brown Dodgers. Campanella initially declined. He was upset after realizing he spurned the chance to break the color line along with Robinson. But Campanella, who at 24 already played nine seasons with the Baltimore Elite Giants, would eventually recover. Then there was pitcher Don Newcombe of the Newark Eagles, whom Sukeforth recommended. Newcombe, was 19, tall and husky, already blessed with a major league fastball, however, he lacked control, discipline, and experience.

"He wasn't by any means the best pitcher in Negro baseball," wrote Wendell Smith, "but Rickey signed him because he's young, big, and has all the natural ability necessary to get him to the big leagues." Robinson, Campanella, and Newcombe had two major things in common: They all grew up either in the Northeast or California and were accustomed to interacting with Whites, and they all played on Negro League teams in 1945.[73] Campanella of Philadelphia was the offspring of an Italian American father and Black mother, and Newcombe was from New Jersey.

Before the Dodgers organization announced Jackie Robinson was signed, the general manager strategically nixed the decision to announce Robinson's signing in October, at the end of baseball regular and postseason. Rickey pushed the announcement into late October\November 1945 when college football was the rage the Robinson news would fly somewhat under the radar. Rickey also wanted to be sure his returning Dodger players signed their contracts for the 1946 season before announcing the Robinson signing.

On October 23 on foreign soil, in Montreal, Canada, the Royals announced that Jackie Robinson signed a professional baseball contract, making Robinson the first Black to break baseball's color line in the 20th century and end the ban on Black professional players that existed since the 1880s.[74]

Sam Lacy meanwhile cast Robinson in the role of greater "national benefactor" than President Harry Truman, quite a comparison considering the commander-in-chief's tough choices – dropping nuclear bombs on Japan, adapting to a Cold War with ally-turned-nemesis the Soviet Union, and coping with a US economy adapting to post-war life. Yes, Robinson now had the main-stage statue of Truman, wrote Wendell Smith because the baseball player "has the hopes and ambitions of thirteen million black

Americans on his broad, sturdy shoulders." Smith worked at the newspaper that was now focused on the second "V" in its double "V" for victories crusade: The first fight was to conquer racism overseas. Now, the latter fight was domestic, to defeat Jim Crow and racism in America.

There was push back against the crack in MLB's glass ceiling. The titans of White professional baseball, from the front office to the playing field, expressed doubt that Robinson, or any Black man for that matter, was qualified to compete with Whites. New York Yankees general manager Larry MacPhail, an ardent and duplicitous opponent of integration, weaponized Sam Lacy's words. Sam Lacy and other Black reporters frequently critiqued the absence of fundamentals among Negro League players. Such tough love was coaching. The advice would have included Robinson, who was playing for the Kansas City Monarchs.

"I am reluctant to say," Lacy wrote in July 1946 "that we haven't a single man in the ranks of colored baseball who could step into the major league uniform and disport himself in the fashion of a big leaguer."

Sam Lacy regretted that piece of writing. As one of the advocates for desegregating professional baseball, he signaled Negro League teams to get their talent ready for imminent big-league play. Be ready. A handful of major league owners for years admitted there was Negro League talent ready to step in and produce but did nothing. Lacy undermined his scouting ability and erred profoundly. But that did not stop MacPhail from using the writer's tough love as a weapon. "Mr. Lacy's opinions are shared by most, Negro or White competent to appraise the qualifications of Negro players," said the Yankees executive.[75]

In addition, and from the field, Cleveland Indians pitcher Bob Feller sprinkled doubts that Robinson could keep up with White major leaguers. Feller, who inspired awe because he could hurl 100-mph fastballs, was criticized by some for his doubts about Robinson. Damning with faint praise, Feller walked back his comments during two November 1945 interviews with Wendell Smith: "I hope he [Robinson] makes good. But I don't think he will."

Robinson rebutted Feller in a three-page handwritten letter to Wendell Smith. In part, it said:

Dear Wendell,

Just read the *Courier*. I must say you write very well (smile). The one article about Bob Feller interested me very much in as much as I was worried more about my fielding than about my hitting. I value what Feller says because I faced him a couple of times and he is a very good pitcher and when I read where he is one of the best, if not the best, pitchers in major league ball I feel confident that if it is left to my hitting, I believe I will do alright ... Just what does Feller mean when he says I have "Football shoulders?"

Robinson reminded Feller that he more than hold his own against the flame thrower during barnstorming games.

***

Like New York, Boston's two MLB teams, the American League Red Sox, and National League Braves, were in the employment crosshairs. City Councilman Isadore Harry Y. Muchnick applied pressure. Boston's municipal laws prohibited businesses from operating on Sundays. Baseball teams needed a special permit to play on that day of rest. Muchnick informed the owners of the Red Sox and Braves that he would vote to deny the license unless they gave Black players a chance to work. Only when the teams agreed in writing to allow African-Americans opportunity would the councilman vote to grant the permits.

Red Sox General Manager Eddie Collins answered with feigned innocence: "I have been connected with the Red Sox for twelve years and during that time we have never had a single request for a tryout by a colored applicant. It is beyond my understanding how anyone can insinuate or believe that all ballplayers, regardless of race, color, or creed, have not been treated in the American way as far as having an equal opportunity to play for the Red Sox."[76]

Boston became the last major league team to integrate, in 1959, 12 years after Robinson became a major leaguer.[77]

Wendell Smith reached out to Muchnick and then offered up Jackie Robinson, who had just reported to the Negro League Kansas City Monarchs, second baseman Marvin Williams of the Philadelphia Stars, and outfielder Sam Jethroe of the Cleveland Buckeyes.

Owners slow walked the aspirants. When the trio reported to Fenway Park on April 14 and 15 management postponed the workouts. Boston sportswriter Dave Egan lambasted Collins in his *Daily Record*: Collins was reminded that he was "living in anno domini 1945 and not the dust-covered year 1865," and "residing in the city of Boston, Massachusetts and not the city of Mobile, Alabama."[78]

***

With news that Robinson had signed to play professional baseball with and against Whites, "Everybody in baseball from the batboy up is expressing an opinion on Robinson's chances of making good," wrote Wendell Smith in the November 10, 1945, *Pittsburgh Courier*.[79] The Baltimore *Afro-American's* Sam Lacy meanwhile cast Robinson in the role of greater "national benefactor" than President Truman, who was trying to return

America to post-war normalcy while grappling with a new reality, Cold War relations with communist adversaries the Soviet Union (Russia and its satellite nations) and China. Furthermore, Robinson, observed Wendell Smith in the December 29, 1945, *Pittsburgh Courier*, "has the hopes, aspirations, and ambitions of thirteen million Black Americans heaped upon his broad, sturdy shoulders."[80]

Among Negro League stars, Satchel Paige, 39 at that time, was publicly supportive but could not hide his angst: "They didn't make a mistake in signing Robinson. He's a No. 1 professional player. They couldn't have picked a better man." Yet, "Signing Jackie like they did still hurt me deep down. I'd been the one everybody said should be in the majors ... It was still me that ought to have been first." Paige was Negro baseball's highest-paid star because of talent and box-office appeal and Paige's initial salary was six times more than the salary Robinson accepted.[81]

The Brooklyn Dodgers organization's signing of Jackie Robinson was the talk of America in the closing weeks of 1945.

NOTES

1. Tygiel, "Baseball's Great Experiment," p 43.
2. Carter, Dan T., "Scottsboro: A Tragedy of the American South," Baton Rouge, LSU Press, 2007.
3. Weiss, Nacy J., "Farewell to the Party of Lincoln: Black Politics in the Age of FDR," Princeton University Press, 1983; Bennett, "Before the Mayflower," pp 563–565; Michaeli, Ethan, "The Defender," pp 83, 122, 197–1198.
4. Washburn, Patrick S., Lamb, Chris, "Sports Journalism: A History of Glory, Fame, and Technology," p 106.
5. Publication began in 1924. At its peak circulation 35,000, however there was a steep decline in CPUSA and readership because the of the 1939 Hitler-Stalin nonaggression pact. Marxists.org.
6. Washburn, Lamb, "Sports Journalism," p 107.
7. Fortenberry, Lawrence, "Freedom's Journal: The First Medium," The Black Scholar, November 1974, Volume 6, Number 3, pp 33–37 (Mordecai Noah); Gilligan, Heather Tirado, "An Entire Man's Village Owned By Black People Was Destroyed to Build Central Park," timelime.com, February 2017.
8. Bennett, Lerone Jr., "Before the Mayflower," p 163.
9. Pride, Armistead, Wilson, Clint C. II, "A History of the Black Press," Washington, DC, 1997, pp 6–7.
10. Michaeli, "The Defender," pps 64–65; Wilkerson, Isabel, "The Warmth of Other Suns," pp 152–153.
11. Wolseley, Roland E., "The Black Press." USA, Ames, Iowa, Iowa University Press, 1990, p 68 Bennett, pp 315; Quill, Khloe, "The Howard Center for Investigative Journalism," February 16, 2022. https://afro.com/robert-vanns-pittsburgh-courier-set-a-pattern-for-what-the-black-press-could-do/; Buni, Andrew, "Robert L. Vann of the Pittsburgh Courier: Politics and Black Journalism," University of Pittsburgh Press, 1974; Pride, Wilson, "A History of the Black Press," p 133. https://www.pbs.org/blackpress/news_bios/afroamerican.html.

12. Schmeling, who was not political or a Nazi, became a Nazi symbol of Aryan superiority, despite Schmeling resisting such labelling. Furthermore, the boxer retained a Jewish manager.

13. Thornton, Jerry, "'Bernie' Jefferson, NU star, school principal," Chicago Tribune, August 19, 1991. Lawrence Bernard "Bernie" Jefferson was one of the two Northwestern student-athletes. He went on to become a decorated World War II Army Air Corps pilot with the Tuskegee Airmen and post war, Lt. Jefferson was a Chicago school system teacher and principal for 35 years.

    Lacy, "Fighting for Fairness," p 34; African-American Registry, Ozie Simmons, Homer E. Harris Jr. https://footballfoundation.org/news/2016/2/1/_55549.aspx (April 29). Coleman, Ken, "U of M celebrates athlete Willis Ward, who was benched for his race in the 1930s: Ward went on to become a prosecutor and judge," Michigan Advance, January 17, 2022 (Ward – 1912–1983 – was a teammate and roommate of future US President Gerald Ford) U of M celebrates athlete Willis Ward, who was benched for his race in the 1930s ★ Michigan Advance.

14. Lacy, "Fighting for Fairness," p 35.

15. Tygiel, "Baseball's Great Experiment," p 32.

16. Negro League Baseball Museum, "Carlos Paula – Barrier Breakers Integration Pioneer," barrierbreakers.nlbm.com.

17. Lieb, Fred, "Baseball as I Have Known It," New York, Coward, McCann & Geoghegan, 1977, pp 57–59.

18. Tygiel, pp 34. Also Lamb, pp 109–110 (Powell also crashed into Hank Greenberg, breaking the Detroit Tiger slugger's wrists. Most people thought the collision was intentional. Powell famously was a bigot who targeted White ethnics, Jews like Greenberg, and Italian Americans). Finkelman, Paul, Dawkins Wayne, "Before the NBA coped with Kyrie Irving's anti-Semitism, baseball faced a similar dilemma," Washington Monthly, November 23, 2022.

19. Lamb, "Conspiracy of Silence," p 113.

20. Lamb, "Conspiracy of Silence," p 110.

21. Lamb, "Conspiracy of Silence," p 115.

22. Lamb, "Conspiracy of Silence," p 109.

23. Lamb, "Conspiracy of Silence," p 114.

24. Lamb, "Conspiracy of Silence," p 120.

25. Lamb, "Conspiracy of Silence," pp 116–117.

26. Snyder, "Beyond the Shadow of the Senators," p 79.

27. Lamb, "Conspiracy of Silence," pp 114–115, 125, 129.

28. Finkelman, Paul, Dawkins, Wayne, "Before the NBA Coped with Kyrie Irving's Anti-Semitism, Baseball Faced a Similar Dilemma," Washington Monthly, November 23, 2022.

29. Lamb, "Conspiracy of Silence," p 119.

30. Lamb, "Conspiracy of Silence," p 120.

31. "From the Great Migration to Charlestown Naval Yard," National Park Service, https://www.nps.gov/articles/great-migration-to-charlestown-navy-yard.htm#:~:text=Great%20Migration%20and%20Boston&text=Between%201910%20and%201940%2C%201.5,these%20migrants%20settled%20in%20Boston.

32. Reisler, "Black Writers/Black Baseball." In addition to Sam Lacy and Wendell Smith, the author spotlighted Frank A. "Fay" Young (Chicago Defender); Joe Bostic (People's Voice, New York); Chester L. Washington (Pittsburgh Courier); W. Rollo Wilson (Philadelphia Tribune); Dan Burley (The Amsterdam News, New York); Ed Harris (Philadelphia Tribune); Romeo Dougherty (The Amsterdam News, New York), and Andrew S. "Doc" Young (Los Angeles Sentinel). Lamb, "Conspiracy of Silence," p 125.

33. "From the Great Migration to Boston's Charlestown Navy Yard," Boston National Historical Park, https://www.nps.gov/articles/great-migration-to-charlestown-navy-yard.htm.

34. Lamb, "Conspiracy of Silence," p 131.
35. Lamb and Glen Beske, "Sports Journalism," pp 110, 213 n96; Boyd, Herb, "Black Detroit: A People's History of Self-Determination," New York, HarperCollins, 2017, pp 150–154.
36. Tygiel, "Baseball's Great Experiment," p 31.
37. Tygiel, "Baseball's Great Experiment," pp 39–40; Nate Moreland integrated baseball in the 1930s: https://www.baseball-reference.com/bullpen/Nate_Moreland ... Tygiel, "Baseball's Great Experiment," p 39.
38. Whitaker, "Smoketown," pp 120–121.
39. Tygiel, "Baseball's Great Experiment," p 40 (Pittsburgh tryout).
40. Tygiel, "Baseball's Great Experiment," p 40. Also include the many "Buts' in Campanella's invitation.
41. Doutrich, Paul E., "September 6, 1954: Carlos Paula integrates the Washington Senators," Society for American Baseball Research, https://sabr.org/gamesproj/game/september-6-1954-carlos-paula-integrates-the-washington-senators/.
42. Tygiel, "Baseball's Great Experiment," p 41, https://www.baseball-reference.com/register/team.cgi?id=3afec9b0 (AA Brewers); https://www.baseball-reference.com/teams/PHI/1943.shtml (Phillies, 64-90-3 won-loss-tied record).
43. Ibid.
44. Veeck, Bill, Linn, Ed, "Veeck as in Wreck," pp 171. Dickson, "Bill Veeck: Baseball's Greatest Maverick," pp 73, 79–80, 93, 357–366. In 1998 in the SABR publication "National Pastime," three authors attempted to debunk Veeck's claim that he tried to buy the Phillies in 1942, but the deal was rebuffed. Authors DM Jordan, LR Gerlach, and JP Rossi claimed Veeck made up his story two decades after the fact for his 1962 autobiography. Instead, SABR members questioned the tone and accuracy of the article. Dickson noted that because the authors could not find confirmation, they assumed the attempted deal did not happen, noting that it was impossible to prove a negative. Tygiel, "Baseball's Great Experiment," pp 41–42
45. Bristol, Douglas Jr., "What We Can Learn About World War II From Black Quartermasters?" August 27, 2021.
46. Ward, Geoffrey C., Burns, Ken, "The War: An Intimate History 1941–1945, pp 111–112, 166–167.
47. Lengel, Ed, "The Black Panthers enter combat: The 761st Tank Battalion," The National WWII Museum-New Orleans, June 18, 2020, https://www.nationalww2museum.org/war/articles/black-panthers-761st-tank-battalion.
48. "Blast death toll now 377, 1,000 injured," San Francisco Chronicle, July 19, 1944. Bennett, "Before the Mayflower," p 572. Miller hunted squirrels with a rifle when he lived in Texas.
49. Journalism.org (2005), After 1950, US newspaper circulation did not keep pace with the population and stagnated, then declined. As for radio, much of its content was appropriated from television when the latter medium became dominant in the late 1950s to 1960s.
   Randle, Quint, "A Historical Overview of the Effects of New Mass Media Influence on Magazine Publishing During the 20th Century," firstmonday.org.
50. Tygiel, "Baseball's Great Experiment," p 78.
51. Ibid.
52. Ashe, "A Hard Road to Glory," pp 36–37, 96–97. Gordon Tokumatsu, nbclosangeles.com, February 10, 2022, https://www.nbclosangeles.com/news/sports/super-bowl-2022/nfl-color-barrier-ucla-kenny-washington-rams/2821840/.
53. Connor, Josesph, "Jackie Robinson refused to move to the back of the bus. Here's how the Army reacted," historynet.com, August 5, 2021. Applewood Books, awb.com. Gordon H. Jones was the husband of Virginia Jones.
54. Tygiel, Jules, "The Court-Marshal of Jackie Robinson," American Heritage, August/September 1984, Volume 35, Issue 5; Ashe, "A Hard Road to Glory II," pp 41–42.

Robinson initially was assigned to Fort Riley, Kansas where his time was also stormy. Robinson was rejected for Officer Candidate School, told off the record that Blacks lacked leadership ability. He confided with a fellow Black soldier on base – boxer Joe Louis – who persuaded a representative of the Secretary of Defense to investigate the case. Robinson's rejection was reversed. Although recognized as a star athlete by White superiors, he was denied a chance to play for the base baseball however Robinson encouraged to play for Fort Riley's football team. He refused to play football. He was transferred to Fort Hood.

Among Black soldiers based in the southwest, Robinson's confrontation with the bus driver made the lieutenant a racial cause celebre. Robinson's hasty transfer between bases led a group of Black officers to believe that the Army was going to try him in secrecy. Those officers wrote letters to the NAACP, and *Chicago Defender* and *Pittsburgh Courier*. The public responded with numerous messages asking about Robinson's whereabouts. A Black underground was able to locate the lieutenant.

The Black press made scant mention of the Robinson case however the Black officers' information campaign was effective: All charges related to the argument on the bus were dropped. Robinson was left to face lesser charges of insubordination related to arguments Robinson had with soldiers and superior officers at the guardhouse. At issue, Robinson refusing to accept being called a "nigger lieutenant" by a private. "I do not consider myself a nigger at all," Robinson later testified. "I am a Negro, but not a nigger."

Robinson was unable to get legal help from the NAACP so instead he was assigned a young Southern lawyer who withdrew from the case. Having been raised in the South, he said, he had not "developed arguments against segregation" that were necessary to defend Robinson adequately. The lawyer arranged for another, Lt. William Cline, a Texan, who was eager to take the case.

55. Potter, Lou, Miles, William, Rosenblum, Nina, "Liberators: Fighting on Two Fronts in World War II," New York, Harcourt, 1992.
56. Tygiel, "Baseball's Great Experiment," pp 47, 64–67. Lacy quote, 64t.
57. Tygiel, "Baseball's Great Experiment," p 69.
58. Tygiel, "Baseball's Great Experiment," p 71.
59. Ives would serve two terms as New York's US Senator from 1947 to 1959: "IRVING IVES DEAD; EX-US SEN., 66; New York Republican was a specialist in civil rights and labor legislation defeated Lehman in '46, Co-authored state's Fair Employment Practices Act – Former Cornell dean, state legislator 16 years was educated at Hamilton, opposed Lehman early, Eisenhower backer bill became campaign issue," New York Times, February 25, 1962.
60. Tygiel, "Baseball's Great Experiment," pp 72–73.
61. Tygiel, "Baseball's Great Experiment," p 45. Age 32 or 34 for McDuffie, 37 or 39 for Thomas.
62. Lowenfish, Lee, "Branch Rickey: Baseball's Ferocious Gentleman," Lincoln, Nebraska, Bison Books, 2009; dodgersblueheaven.com/2010/05/quinn-ives-act.html.
    Lacy, "Fighting for Fairness," p 55.
63. Lacy, "Fighting for Fairness," p 47.
64. Tygiel, "Baseball's Great Experiment," p 42.
65. McCue, Andy, "Branch Rickey," Society for American Baseball Research, https://sabr.org/bioproj/person/branch-rickey/.
66. Tygiel, "Baseball's Great Experiment," p 49.
67. Tygiel, "Baseball's Great Experiment," pp 51–52.
68. Dorinson, Joseph, "The Black Athlete as Hero: American Barrier Breakers from Nine Sports," Jefferson, North Carolina, McFarland & Company, Inc., Publishers, 2022, pp 104, 112.
    Sokol, Jason, "All Eyes Are Upon Us: Race and Politics from Boston to Brooklyn; the Conflicted Soul of the Northeast," New York, Basic Books, 2014, pp 29–30; Tygiel, "Baseball's Great Experiment," pp 43–44.

69. Tygiel, "Baseball's Great Experiment," pp 63–64.
70. Tygiel, "Baseball's Great Experiment," p 65.
71. Tygiel, "Baseball's Great Experiment," pp 66–67, RE baseball salaries, sabr.org; Haupert, Michael, "MLB's salary leaders since 1974," Outside the Lines, Fall 2012 (Baseball Almanac, Year in Review), https://www.baseball-almanac.com/yearly/yr1946a.shtml.
72. Tygiel, "Baseball's Great Experiment," p 67, and Wendell, "Hank Greenberg, First $100,000 Player, Dies," p 66, Los Angeles Times, September 5, 1986.
73. Ashe, "A Hard Road to Glory," pp 41–42.
74. Tygiel, "Baseball's Great Experiment," p 68.
75. Ibid.
76. Athans, Drew, "Red Sox Could Have Signed Willie Mays Before Anyone Else," bosoxinjection.com, May 15, 2020. When Mays was a teenage member of the Birmingham Black Barons, he was scouted by multiple major league teams, including the Boston Red Sox. Sox scout George Digby secured a deal to by Mays' contract from the Barons for $4,500, however the Red Sox front office spurned the offer. Owner Tom Yawkey and General Manager Joe Cronin, according to Digby, "already had made up their minds they weren't going to take any Black players." The missed opportunity came to light because Willie Mays, 89, was promoting his memoir, "24: Life Stories and Lessons from the Say Hey Kid" in 2020.
77. Tygiel, "Baseball's Great Experiment," p 65.
78. Ashe, "A Hard Road to Glory," vol. 3., pp 21, 32. Elijah "Pumpsie" Green of Oakland, California signed with the Red Sox. At that time Blacks were about 14% of MLB players and dominated the record books.
79. Tygiel, "Baseball's Great Experiment," p 71.
80. Ibid.
81. Tygiel, "Baseball's Great Experiment," p 75 (16) Afro-American, May 11, 1946; Spivey, "If You Were Only White," p xvii; Tygiel "Baseball's Great Experiment," p 78. Also, during a June 15, 1945, encounter in the lobby of Harlem's Hotel Teresa, Paige told Sam Lacy, "You fellows (Black press writers) don't understand what we have to go through. You harp on 'give them a chance,' without thinking how tough it's gonna be for a colored player to come out of the clubhouse and have all the White guys calling him nigger and Black so-and-so. It'd be more than a man can stand and nobody can play his best ball unless he's in good spirits, and who the hell could be in good spirits under those conditions.'

"Another thing. You guys cry about fellowship and good will. What I want to know is what the hell's gonna happen to goodwill when one of those colored players, goaded out of his senses by repeated insults, takes a bat and busts fellowship in his damned head?"

Paige and Lacy were both in New York at the time of the Sugar Ray Robinson-Jimmy McDaniels boxing match – Lacy, "Fighting for Fairness," p 59.

FIGURES

Figure 1 Jack Roosevelt "Jackie" Robinson was a four varsity-letter athlete at UCLA and Army lieutenant before joining the Negro League Kansas City Monarchs. Robinson later signed with the Brooklyn Dodgers organization. During a ten-year MLB career, Robinson was Rookie of the Year (1947), a six-time all-star, Most Valuable Player (1949), and played in six World Series, winning in the 1955 championship

Credit: Photograph by Bob Sandberg, Look Magazine. Library of Congress Prints and Photographs division.

DOI: 10.4324/9781003283928-5

Figure 2 Branch Rickey played baseball, was religiously devout, and was a college-educated lawyer. In St. Louis, he built the farm team system that developed baseball players. Rickey moved on to the Brooklyn Dodgers and there vetted then signed Jackie Robinson to play for the minor league Montreal Royals, then the Brooklyn Dodgers

Credit: The Sporting News via Wikimedia Commons.

Figure 3 Kenesaw Mountain Landis, a former federal judge, was recruited to restore integrity to baseball. He also forbids Blacks from playing professional baseball for a quarter century

Credit: Library of Congress Prints and Photographs division.

Figure 4 A.B. "Happy" Chandler, a former US Senator from Kentucky, succeeded Landis as baseball commissioner. Chandler ended the unofficial ban on Blacks playing professional baseball

Credit: Harris & Ewing, photographer, 1940. Library of Congress Prints and Photographs division.

Figure 5 Rachel Robinson, Jackie's wife, sounding board, and confidante
Credit: Official White House photo by Pete Souza.

Figure 6 He was the star quarterback for Syracuse University, but Wilmeth Sidat Singh was benched before a 1938 game against host University of Maryland, a southern school. During World War II Sidat Singh became a Tuskegee Airman, a member of the all-Black Army Air Corps unit. He died during a 1943 training exercise in Michigan

Credit: Charles Henry Alston, 1943, poster from Office for Emergency Management, office of War Information News Bureau. US National Archives and Records Administration.

Figure 7 Monte Irvin was rated as having comparable talent and temperament to be the first Black in professional baseball. But World War II service delayed Irvin's chance. He did join MLB with the New York Giants. Pictured is his June 2010 number retirement

Credit: Chris Shuttlesworth/Flickr.

Figure 8 Jackie Robinson, Roy Campanella, and Junior Gilliam during a barnstorming trip in Japan, 1956.

Credit: Baseball Magazine Co. Ltd, 1956 via Wikimedia Commons.

Figure 9 Althea Gibson broke racial and gender barriers in tennis during the 1950s. Unlike Jackie Robinson, she said publicly that she did not want to be a crusader

Credit: Fred Palumbo, New York World Telegram and Sun, 1956, via Library of Congress Prints and Photographs division.

Figure 10 Sam Lacy, Dan Bankhead, and Wendell Smith before departing for spring training in Santo Domingo (Dominican Republic), 1947

Credit: National Baseball Hall of Fame Library.

CHAPTER 4

ROBINSON AND MONTREAL ROYALS

Dodger Blues

Jackie Robinson signed the papers and agreed to play in the Dodgers organization, yet it was unclear whether the White baseball establishment would accept him. Branch Rickey accepted him, but Major League Baseball's 15 other club owners voted 15-1 – Rickey being the only "no" vote – to block Robinson from playing. The owners initially denied that they rejected Robinson and said there was no written proof of their alleged decision. A draft of the document, owners said, had been destroyed.

However, evidence surfaced. US Rep. Emanuel Celler, D-New York, whose district was in Brooklyn, home of the Dodgers, chaired a committee that was investigating professional baseball. Celler, a monopoly/antitrust stalwart, argued that baseball did not deserve an exemption from operating as a for-profit big business. Among the documents that weighed the merits of baseball's status were meeting minutes that recorded the 15-1 anti-Robinson vote.[1] Exposed, the owners backed away from their earlier denials. Robinson could prepare to play for the Dodgers minor league affiliate in Montreal.

Many White sports writers were also hostile to Robinson's arrival; however, most masked their feelings. On February 3, 1946, the New York chapter of the Baseball Writers Association held their annual meeting at the Waldorf-Astoria Hotel. All of the 1,200 attendees were White. There were speeches, awards, and lampoon-style entertainment. "The burlesque was so broad that the scribes were able to risk bringing into the cast of characters as delicate a subject as Jackie Robinson," wrote *New York Times* columnist Arthur Daley. "But it was all such lampoonery that no one's feelings were really hurt."[2]

DOI: 10.4324/9781003283928-6

Daley's account included dialogue from a skit that opened at a mansion with a butler – a "darky," wrote Daley – in satin breeches and wearing a Montreal uniform. That butler, a sportswriter in blackface, said of Commissioner "Happy" Chandler, "Looks lak de massa will be late dis ebning." Chandler's character entered the stage with four other colonels and then he clapped his hands and called, "Robbie! Robbie!"

The butler returned and said, "Yassuh Massa. Here ah is."

CHANDLER CHARACTER: "Ah, there you are Jackie. Jackie, you ole woolly headed rascal. How long yo' been in the family?"

BUTLER: "Long time, Kunl, marty lone time. Eber since Massa Rickey done bots me from da Kansas City Monarchs."

CHANDLER CHARACTER: "To be sure, Jackie, to be sure. How could ah forget that Colonel Rickey brought you to our house. Rickey, that no good carpetbagger! [an aside] What could he be thinking of?

Wendell Smith, uninvited to the segregated Baseball Writers Association dinner, was not amused. He reprinted the skit dialogue in the February 13 *Pittsburgh Courier* and called the so-called comedy a Nazi Opera: "They were not for equality in sports, and they gave vent to their feelings in this vicious manner. They weren't courageous or brave enough to express their feelings in their respective newspapers, so they put their dastardly act behind closed doors."[3]

As Jackie Robinson prepared for training camp, Smith needed to prepare too. The *Pittsburgh Courier* employee was also hired by Rickey and the Dodgers and became an integral member of the team strategy circle. Rickey paid Smith 50 dollars a week, money comparable to his newspaper salary.[4] Rickey needed someone watching over the Black prospect at the Dodgers' facilities in Sanford and Daytona Beach "Because much harm could come if either of these boys were to do or say something or other out of turn," said the general manager. Accompanied by Black press photographer Billy Rowe, the duo drove south from Pittsburgh to Daytona Beach, Florida. In the 21st century, Smith holding those two jobs would be a conflict of interest, however, in the Jim Crow 1940s, his double duty was a necessary crusade.[5]

The Smith-Rowe trip was fortuitous for Jackie and Rachel Robinson. Jim Crow customs made the couple's travels to spring training camp humiliating, uncomfortable, and slow. The newlyweds boarded an airplane in Los Angeles and flew all night to New Orleans, where they were supposed to change planes.

They were bumped off the scheduled flight and waited for another aircraft. Stranded, the Robinsons learned the airport restaurants would not serve Blacks unless they took their food elsewhere. The dignified couple chose to do without food. They were hungry and had no place to rest inside the airport. The Robinsons checked into a nearby hotel, a dirty, dreadful place, they recalled, and 12 hours passed before they resumed the journey.[6]

They hopped by air from New Orleans to Pensacola, Florida. There, the Robinsons were told by officials to deplane, and two White passengers replaced them. Jackie protested but his words fell on deaf ears. An attempt to stay in a local rooming house was unacceptable; the premises were overrun with children, so the couple chose to catch a bus to Jacksonville, Florida.

They boarded, reclined in the seats, and tried to sleep. Within a few miles, the driver ordered the Robinsons to move to the rear that had straight-back seats that could not recline. For 16 hours they bounced, jogged, and gagged on the exhaust fumes, even as there were empty seats in the buses' White section. At Jacksonville the Robinsons endured another dose of Jim Crow, waiting in a dingy bus station. Food was available if they were willing to take it from a back door, which the Robinsons were not. After a wait, Wendell Smith and Rowe arrived in the car and took the couple to Daytona Beach and training camp.[7] After Rachel went to bed, Robinson spit out anger to Smith and Rowe, recalling the 36-hour odyssey. "Get me out of here!" Smith and Rowe did their best to calm the barrier breaker. Said Rowe, "We tried to tell him what the whole thing meant and that it was something he had to do."[8]

Married for only two and half weeks, Jackie Robinson was fortunate to be partnered with an emotionally strong and resolute confidant as Rachel Isum. "What I liked about him was his smile and the confident air he had about him without being cocky in person," she said. "He also wore his color with such dignity, pride, and confidence. He was never, ever ashamed of his [Black] skin color."[9] Indeed, Rachel was powerfully attracted to Jackie's fierce masculinity, however, she was adept at calming and counseling him when Jackie was near erupting like a volcano.

The Robinsons' arrival called for more adjustments. Rickey believed it was essential that the couple not be isolated from other Blacks during their Southern stay. Thanks to an assist from Wendell Smith, the general manager arranged for the couple to stay at the home of Joe Harris, a local politician. Rickey also searched for a second Black athlete to participate with Robinson.[10] Although Wendell Smith had recommended Robinson's UCLA teammate Kenny Washington, he was unavailable because of committing to play for the NFL Los Angeles Rams. Rickey instead chose John Wright, 27, described by scouts as a willowy right-hand pitcher with good control, a live fastball and a variety of curves, knuckleballs, and sinker pitches. Wright pitched for Negro League teams that included the Newark

Eagles and Homestead Grays, where at the latter he had a 31-5 win-loss season in 1943.

During World War II Wright served in the Navy and pitched well for the all-Black Great Lakes Naval Station team, compiling a 15-4 won-loss record that included a no-hit game. Wright also had the lowest earned run average of any pitcher in the armed services.[11]

"Wright doesn't boast the college background that is Jackie's," wrote Sam Lacy in the *Afro-American* on March 16, "but he possesses something equally valuable – a level head and the knack of seeing things objectively. He is a realist in a role which demands divorce from sentimentality."[12] Unlike Robinson, "I am a Southerner. I have always lived in the South, so I know what is coming," Wright, a New Orleans native, told the March 15 *Montreal Daily Star.* "I have been Black for 27 years and I will remain like that for a long time."

Wright believed he was prepared, but media observers felt uneasy about the future. "Never before in this state, or any other Southern state has a Negro played with Whites in organized ball, nor have Negro teams been pitted against White teams," the *New York Times* opined.

"If Branch Rickey could set up his training camp for his Montreal Royals in a more democratic environment," wrote Sam Lacy in the *Afro* on January 26, "I'd be clamoring for him to abandon Daytona Beach and so would the rest of us."[13] Wendell Smith wrote in the April 6 *Courier,* "this picturesque, tropical city was steeped in the traditions and customs of the Old South."

Strict segregation prevailed in the Atlantic Ocean resort town, but mitigating factors were supposed to be the influence of Mary McLeod Bethune, famed educator, NAACP leader, and founder of Bethune-Cookman College, and local pharmacist and politician Joe Harris, Robinson's host, who managed to give Blacks a modicum of influence.[14] Harris and his wife Dufferin were lauded as a power couple of their time.[15] The wife later became the first Black journalist to work at the daily *Daytona Beach News-Journal.* In the 1970s a park was created and named in honor of Joe Harris, placed near the Bethune-Cookman University campus.

City Manager Jim Titus and Mayor William Perry assured Rickey they would work to reduce racial friction. "No one objects to Jackie Robinson and John Wright training here with the Montreal baseball club," said Perry in a public statement. In an interview with Wendell Smith, Perry described Robinson and Wright not as athletes, but entertainers, and accepted Black participation in the seaside city. "No one gets excited when Cab Calloway comes here," Perry explained.[16] On March 4 ball players began working out on the fields. Robinson and Wright dressed in their Royals uniforms at the home of David Brock, a local Black doctor, before being driven over to the Dodger's other facility in Sanford, 30 miles from Daytona Beach. Two venues were necessary because training camp was unusually crowded with 200 athletes, many of them returning World War II veterans. Jackie Robinson exhaled after his manager Clay Hopper, a Mississippian, greeted him pleasantly: "I was relieved to see him stick out his hand, for even in those days a great number of Southerners would under no circumstances shake hands with a Negro."[17]

Robinson took swings in the batting cage; Wright threw to a few hitters and played "pepper," a game in which players lob the ball to a hitter who gently taps the baseball on the ground to that handful of fielders.

March 4 was also Media Day. Newsmen surrounded Robinson and asked many questions. Few expressed interest in the other Black newcomer Wright. When Wright and Robinson returned to Dr. Brock's home to change clothes, Wendell Smith and Billy Rowe were anxiously waiting. "Pack your bags, we're going to Daytona Beach," said Smith. Once the foursome was in the moving car, Smith explained: A White man visited Smith at the Brock home and said he brought a message from 100 towns-people: "We want you to get the niggers out of town," adding there would be trouble unless Robinson and Wright were "out of town by nightfall." Blacks and Whites would not be allowed on the same field, was the message. Leave immediately.

At this point Wendell Smith overtly wore two hats. He was the journalist corresponding from Florida, and he also engaged in public relations for the Dodgers organization. That meant muting the Black players responses to some of the racial barriers, slights, and even threats that occurred. Telegraphing the incidents in the press might embolden more Whites to strangle the great experiment. Smith was responsible for protecting Robinson and Wright's lives. For Black readers, the setbacks could either agitate or demoralize them. It was not apparent at that moment, but Wendell Smith was drafting the blueprint for the 1950s to 1960s civil rights media strategy.[18] Public protest and civil disobedience was calculated strategy, so too was persuasion even if it meant occasionally turning the other cheek or retreating slightly before pushing ahead or simply getting out of town to avoid violence or a lynching.[19]

At Daytona Beach the Dodgers organization adjusted by having all of the players work out at two venues, the major league contenders on the White side of town, and the minor league prospects at a field in a Black neighborhood. Management waited anxiously for what could happen when the Dodgers and Royals played a scheduled March 17 exhibition game.

That day, 4,000 spectators packed City Island Ballpark. Nearly one out of every four attendees were Black. The local newspapers decades later falsely reported that the city relaxed its segregation laws and let Whites and Blacks sit together. This did not happen. Nevertheless, the game was played without incident, dispelling fears that a race riot would erupt. Robinson played five uneventful innings. Widespread applause drowned out scattered boos when he stepped to the plate to bat.

Sam Lacy noted the *Washington Post* captioned most training camp stories by reporting teams and scores, for example, "Bucs top Chisox" (Pittsburgh vs Chicago), but on the Dodgers-Montreal games, it was "Robinson hitless," or in the *Afro-American,* "Jackie's fielding flawless as Royals best Dodgers," April 6, 1946.[20] Lacy confessed in print on March 16, 1946, that "I felt a lump in my throat each time a ball was hit in his [Robinson's] direction."[21] Lacy also observed in an April 6 dispatch that over time White teammates stopped avoiding the two Black newcomers and had amiable conversations. The *Pittsburgh Courier* meanwhile published front-page accounts of Robinson's activities and promised an "Exclusive picture story of Jackie Robinson and Johnny Wright as they worked out with the Montreal Royals in Florida." Wendell Smith's eyewitness accounts boosted *Courier* circulation by 100,000 during the weeks of March 16 through 30, 1946. Robinson confessed to Wendell Smith on April 20 that fans kept him under tremendous pressure.[22] He developed a sore arm while playing shortstop and was unable to make the long throws required of the position. Robinson was moved to second, but with a throbbing sore arm, he was not effective there either. Rickey ordered Hopper to move Robinson again to first base. After a week Robinson healed enough to return to second base.

His hitting was problematic too. During intrasquad games Robinson failed to hit safely in his first seven at-bats, then he slumped again during a four-game stretch. Sceptics said Robinson was going to wash out. However, Robinson was opportunistic. He was an excellent bunter, and his track-star speed allowed him to manufacture hits.

And nasty opponents helped Robinson improve his slugging. According to his Southern manager Hopper, a fellow Southerner from Kentucky and opposing pitcher signaled he would test Robinson. The former major leaguer threw at Robinson's head and knocked him to the ground. The next pitch came inside and was about to break over the corner of the plate. Robinson held his ground and lashed the ball for a single to left field. Two innings later the 39-year-old pitcher knocked Robinson down again then he lashed the next pitch to left-center field for a triple. "Clay, your colored boy is going to do all right," Paul Derringer, the 223-game winner told Hopper, one White Southerner to another.[23]

Pitcher John Wright struggled too. He pitched well in his first intrasquad game, but in another he walked four batters in four innings. In his final Florida appearance, Wright in one inning walked four batters and hit another. The pitcher's performance was worrisome because pinpoint accuracy was supposed to be his strength. "Wright was wilder than an Egyptian Zebra," wrote Wendell Smith on April 13.[24] Still, Wright accompanied Robinson and the rest of the Montreal Royals north for the regular season.

White New York sports columnists Jimmy Powers of the *Daily News* and Dan Parker of the *Daily Mirror* probably believed they were writing from sympathetic standpoints however they were positioned for stinging rebukes. Parker alleged that Robinson and Wright were "going through the motions," and singled out Robinson as not "living up to his extravagant advance billing." The *Daily Mirror* writer concluded stereotypically "One gets the idea that, although there has been no unpleasantness, on the surface at least, Robinson and Wright are vaguely unhappy about the whole business. They certainly are not having as much fun as they would with their rollicking teammates in Negro baseball." Parker may not have realized that "fun" was not sleeping in uniform on the team bus, or even the playing field, because Negro Leaguers were banned from lodging, or eating canned sardines because restaurants would not serve them. Powers expanded his commentary to general race relations in the South. Powers invited liberal Northerners to cross the Mason-Dixon line and witness racial progress being made in athletic and social arenas:

> "We remember when colored garbage collectors were paid five dollars a week here. Now colored garbage collectors receive $5.50 for a seven-hour day [and] There are more colored colleges with larger enrolments, more colored athletes hitting the headlines." In a scathing rebuttal on March 23, 1946, Smith wrote that Powers "failed to mention that a lot of the fabulously 'rich' colored garbage collectors hold degrees from the 'big' colored colleges but can't get anything better because the South is progressing so rapidly."[25]

Soon it was time for the Dodgers to hop around the Sunshine State and play opponents in other cities. Robinson, a minor league prospect, did not intend to travel with the major leaguers, but that fact did not stop officials in other cities – Miami for starters – to pre-emptively declare they would stop games if the Black man showed up. Paul Waner, the hitting star of the Pittsburgh Pirates during the 1920s to 1930s, who ended his playing career as a Brooklyn Dodger in 1945 and would be voted into the Baseball Hall of Fame in 1952, was manager and part-owner of Miami's minor league team. He pushed back against city officials' segregation edict: "I don't care if I have to build (bleachers) and pay for them myself."[26] Significantly, Waner grew up in Oklahoma, which was the last "southern state" to enter the union and was thoroughly segregated. But he spoke out for racial equality at this time, which suggests that Rickey's experiment was beginning to influence some baseball leaders, who valued talent above race.

On March 23, the Royals were to play the Jersey City Giants in Jacksonville. That city was nearly 50% Black population and many Blacks sat in the segregated seating to watch ballgames. However, in anticipation of "the first time a member of his race had played with the White ball players at the Jacksonville park," reported the city's *Florida Times-Union,* the Jim Crow seating would likely be inadequate. Two days before the game George C. Robinson, executive secretary of the city Playground and Recreation Commission, announced that Jackie Robinson and Wright would not be permitted to play: "It is part of the rules and regulations of the Recreational Department that Negroes and Whites cannot compete against each other on a city-owned playground." Rickey replied that the Dodgers organization "have no intention of attempting to counter to any government's laws and regulations. If we are notified that Robinson cannot play at Jacksonville, of course he can't play." The Giants weighed in and asked the Royals to leave Robinson and Wright in Daytona Beach. Rickey countered with this request: That he be notified on the "official stationery of the city of Jacksonville" so that "neither the Montreal club nor the Brooklyn club would bear the onus." Jacksonville Parks Commission voted unanimously to cancel the game.[27]

"Jacksonville got more bad press banning [them] than any city in Florida has experienced since the Jesse Payne lynching in Madison last October," Wendell Smith wrote in the *Pittsburgh Courier.* Jacksonville officials were condemned by Northerners, including 58 members of a Presbyterian church who sent a letter saying the banning was "a great injury to democracy and brotherhood" in violation of the "Gospel of Jesus Christ."[28]

Despite the advance rejection the Royals returned to Jacksonville hoping to play the scheduled game. A crowd was waiting for the team; however, the ballpark "was as closed and quiet as a funeral parlor at three o'clock in the morning," wrote Wendell Smith in the *Pittsburgh Courier.* City officials had padlocked the gate and city police barred entry. Montreal general manager Mel Jones telephoned city officials for an explanation however the receiver went dead. The Royals returned to Daytona Beach.[29]

The daily *Brooklyn Eagle* reported that "Officials of Southern cities are uniting today in a lockout campaign against the Montreal Royals," on March 26. When the team arrived in Deland for a day game, they were told it was canceled because of a malfunction in the lighting system. On April 7 the Royals traveled to Sanford – the town that menacingly expelled them because of Robinson and Wright – to play the St. Paul Saints. Rickey ignored city officials' request to leave the Black second baseman behind. Robinson took batting practice, nervously, then was penciled into the starting lineup. Batting second, he beat out an infield single. Robinson proceeded to dance off first base and distract the opposing pitcher. Robinson broke for a- second and stole the base easily. He was not done. The next batter singled and Robinson sprinted around third and headed for a close play at home plate. As the crowd roared Robinson slid safely under the tag with the game's first run.[30]

Robinson fielded his position for two innings then "Vicious old man Jim Crow stepped right on the baseball diamond," wrote Wendell Smith on April 13.[31] The chief of police walked onto the field and told manager Hopper that Robinson and Wright had to be removed from the ballpark. Hopper withdrew both players to the dugout.

There was tension because of a shift in Rickey's strategy. Initially, he pledged not to take his Black athletes where they were not welcome, however after the Jacksonville banishment, Dodger spokesmen became more strident. "It will be all or nothing with the Montreal club," said team President Hector Racine. "Jackie Robinson and John Wright go with the team, or there's no game."[32] The Royals transferred road games to Daytona Beach. Soon, the team would break camp to start the season up North in mid-April.

The International League was the professional circuit that banished Black players from competing at the end of the 19th century. White teams had boycotted games or refused to cooperate with Blacks on the field. A half century later Jackie Robinson and John Wright would be tested. Their Montreal Royals opened the season on April 18 on the road, with two weeks of games against Jersey City and Newark, then Syracuse in upstate New York, then Baltimore, the league's southernmost venue. On opening day in Jersey City, Jackie Robinson batted second and was positioned at second base. He faced pitcher Warren Sandell, a six-foot, four-inch hard-throwing left-hander.

Robinson, five-foot, eleven-inches tall with a thick football player torso, did not swing at the first five pitches, resulting in a full count. Something would have to give on the sixth pitch; Robinson would be safe or out. He hit a ground ball to shortstop and was thrown out easily. The ice was broken. Next time at bat, two Royals were on base. Robinson swung at a hard, letter-high Sandel pitch and lined the ball into the left field stands for a three-run homer. He followed up with three more hits and two stolen bases. The Royals won 14-1.[33]

Newspapers all over North America carried news of Robinson's debut. A widely used front-page photo was of teammate George Shuba shaking

Robinson's hand as he crossed home plate. The image was a big deal because of the symbolism, or as one sportswriter claimed, "The most significant sports story of the century."[34]

At the Newark Bears, Leon Treadway, a North Carolinian who previously played for the major league Yankees, refused to play against Robinson. International League officials expressed "considerable consternation" over Treadway's choice, then offered alternative explanations for his defection: Treadway quit in disgust because he did not secure an apartment in Newark, and he opted to play baseball in the Mexican League.[35] Robinson meanwhile opened the season hot. In five games against the New Jersey teams, he hit .417, scored ten runs, and batted in five. The *Baltimore Afro-American* cheered Robinson's performance on the April 23, page 14 sports section: "Robinson on hit spree; hits safely in five straight."

At the next stop Syracuse, some fans were as chilly as the weather. They booed when Robinson stepped to the plate and Chiefs players jeered him from the dugout. As Robinson knelt in the on-deck circle before hitting, an opponent pushed a black cat in his direction and shouted, "Hey Jackie, there's your cousin clowning on the field." Robinson failed to hit safely, but the next night he rebounded with two hits in five at-bats.

One more road stop, Baltimore, America's northernmost Southern city or southernmost Northern city depending on who was asked. What was not in doubt was the city's Jim Crow customs. Shops in the Northwood Center did not serve Black customers, and nearby historically Black Morgan State College's presence so infuriated White homeowners, a brick "spite wall" was built at the intersection of Argonne and Hillen roads to close off the neighborhood from the campus.[36] "For God's sake Branch, don't let that colored boy go to Baltimore," International League President Frank Shaughnessy begged the Dodgers general manager. "There's a lot of trouble brewing down there."[37]

The first of four games on Saturday were frigid. Only 3,415 spectators attended, stoking rumors that there was a boycott. Rachel Robinson sat behind the Royals dugout and heard Whites sitting near her yell, "Here comes that nigger son of a bitch. Let's give it to him now," On Sunday, 25,000 fans – 10,000 of them Blacks – filled Orioles stadium for a doubleheader.

White spectators booed Robinson and continued to hurl insults. The second baseman played poorly, achieving only two hits in ten at-bats and he committed two errors in the field.

Robinson however was better in the Monday finale: "Jackie leads attack as Royals split in Baltimore; 2nd baseman's 3 hits and 4 runs make amends for fatal errors on Sunday," read the April 30, *Afro-American* sports page account. Sam Lacy's newspaper also included a photo spread of four horizontal images of Robinson and Wright to mark their initial, historic appearance in Baltimore.

Calvin Tyler Sr., a Black World War II veteran and Navy cook, attended one of the Royals games in Baltimore. Son Calvin Jr. was at the game too. He drew inspiration from Robinson's barrier-breaking exploits and applied the actions to his career. Calvin Jr. was hired by United Parcel Service. He was promoted to managerial positions in his hometown, then in Texas, Nebraska, and New Jersey. For many years he was the only Black member of the board of directors. As his position and salary grew, so did Calvin Jr.'s shares of stock in the employee-owned company. In addition to the stock he earned, Calvin Jr. bought UPS stock. Eventually he amassed more stock than anyone else in the company, including the CEO. Calvin Jr.'s wealth had increased by 20,000% between 1964 and 1995, the year he retired from the company. Unlike the fiery Jackie Robinson, Calvin Jr. exerted quiet power, working behind the scenes to guide other Black workers into the management pipeline, and he invested strategically. In 2020, Calvin Jr. and his wife Tina Tyler made a $20 million gift to Morgan State University in Baltimore, which at the time was the largest individual contribution made to a Historically Black College or University.[38]

An April 13 *Chicago Defender* editorial read in part, "It is ironical that America, supposedly the cradle of democracy, is forced to send the first two Negroes in baseball to Canada in order for them to be accepted." Robinson and Wright being based in Canada was not a calculated decision; they happened to play for the Dodgers' top Triple-A team. Jackie Robinson and John Wright opened their season on US soil, but indeed they were playing with a Canadian-based team. Now it was time to open before Montreal fans. Canadians were reacting to the news with a mixture of puzzlement, pride, and an air of moral superiority.

Canadians did not lack prejudice. In Montreal, only one hotel regularly accepted Black patrons. The city's Black population was less than 2%, rendering them "forgotten, hidden or overridden," said historian Robin Winks.[39] Still Jackie and Rachel Robinson found their new neighbors welcoming. "The first apartment that I said I wanted, I got," said Rachel. "That alone was very exciting."[40]

Jackie was off to an exciting homestand start. For the May 1 opener, Royals executives anticipated seven thousand fans coming to Delorimier Downs Stadium. It was a weekday and temperatures were chilly. Sam Lacy was there and his May 7, 1946, headline was "Montreal fans acclaim

Jackie – 16,133 rabid Canadians on hand for Royals debut; kids mob star." Robinson silenced hometown sportswriters who predicted his batting average would drop precipitately. Instead, it remained well above .300.

With a banner headline on June 4, the *Afro-American* reported that Robinson was leading the International League in batting with a .356 average. However, the second baseman was benched because of a leg injury.[41] At the season's end, Robinson won the International League batting title. In addition, he stole 40 bases and hit 25 doubles, eight triples, and three home runs. Robinson walked 92 times and struck out only 27 times in 124 games. As a team the Royals coasted to the International League pennant nearly 20 games ahead of the nearest competitor.[42]

Robinson performed so spectacularly that there were murmurs about calling up Robinson to the Brooklyn Dodgers to help the team with the September pennant race battle against the St. Louis Cardinals. Despite key Dodgers in batting slumps, Rickey was unequivocal in not bringing Robinson up. He said if the second baseman played poorly at bat or in the field and the Dodgers lost, Robinson could be blamed for the outcome. The Dodgers were edged out by the Cardinals and Robinson stayed put with the Royals and prepared for the minor league Little World Series.[43]

The Louisville Colonels, champions of the American Association, were the opponents and hosted the first three of best of seven-game series. Sam Lacy was in Louisville to cover the series for the *Afro-American.* "You're smitten with a brazen inconsistency," he wrote. Jim Crow there was a hybrid form: Schools were segregated, streetcars were not. Blacks and Whites went to separate theaters but shopped in the same stores.[44]

Once the games began, Robinson was targeted with harsh verbal treatment from spectators that was edged with loathing and fear. In addition to racial slurs some fans made open threats each time Robinson's name was announced or when he touched the ball in the field.

Although Robinson appeared stoic on the field, the abuse appeared to affect his performance. He hit safely in only one of ten at-bats. Louisville won two of the three games. Numerous letters were sent to the Louisville *Courier-Journal* that expressed dismay at the odious treatment directed at Robinson, and management's decision to turn away Black spectators. A 466-person, segregated section of thirteen thousand-seat Parkway Field was filled to capacity and thousands of Black fans – many of them who traveled for hours – were turned away. Lacy, who called ahead for press credentials was given a spot against the right field wall, "reserved for colored."[45]

The series shifted to Montreal. During game four, when Louisville batters stepped to the plate, Montreal fans booed and snarled unlike the way they normally treated visiting teams. The home fans heard about how Robinson was treated down South, so they expressed their disgust. Robinson came alive. He scored the game-tying run in the ninth inning, then lashed the game-winning hit in the extra-inning tenth. The series was tied 2-2. The next day was game five. Robinson opened with a double to left field and in the seventh inning tripled off the base of a light tower in left-center field. The Royals won 5-3 and was one win away from capturing the series. Montreal won game six 2-0. Robinson smacked two hits and started a double play that killed a Louisville rally.

In the late-day cold exuberant fans carried players and coaches around the field. Fans yelled for "Jackie Robinson!" or "Yakee Rob-een-sen!" and hoisted him on their shoulders and when they put him down, they serenaded, touched, and kissed him. Robinson's face was wet with tears of joy and relief.[46]

Robinson now looked to the future. Rachel, who was pregnant, returned to California before the post-season began. On November 18, Jackie Robinson Jr. was born. His dad was aware that Dodgers training camp in 1947 would be in Cuba, not the American South. However, Robinson had not yet heard from Rickey about his future. Yet the following was certain: Jackie Robinson, a gifted four-sport college athlete, but an inexperienced professional baseball player at start of his rookie season, learned quickly – especially on defense – and emerged as a polished star. He proved many detractors to be wrong. For example, "I don't know what to say about Robinson," said Jim Semler, owner of the New York Black Yankees, just before the start of the Royals season. "I doubt that he will be able to hit the kind of pitching they'll be dishing up to him."[47]

The same fate was not meant for Johnny Wright. Despite his impressive resume as a long-time Negro league pitcher, and reputation for control of his fastball and curve, Wright underperformed. He appeared uncomfortable, even cowed by racial taunts by opponents and spectators, despite his assurances that he was ready for the abuse. Wendell Smith was overly optimistic about Wright's ability. After a handful of bad pitching performances, manager Hopper sat Wright down for two weeks. "Johnny's not ready yet," said the manager. Lacy answered, "Certainly he can't get ready riding the bench."

Wright was demoted to the Three Rivers team in the Canadian-American League. Sam Lacy attributed Wright's demotion to an overabundance of better pitchers on the Royals and was "reasonably satisfied that race had nothing to do with the fact that Montreal Manager Clay Hopper did not use [Wright] as regularly or as often as he might have used him."[48]

With Wright gone, the Dodgers signed Roy Partlow, another Black pitcher, as a replacement. He had pitched for the Homestead Grays and the previous year, 1945, compiled a 9-4 won-loss record with the perennial powerhouse team. Partlow, who also pitched for the Philadelphia Stars, was about 36 years old. He started strong with an effective relief appearance then was rewarded with a starting assignment and won that game. But Partlow's next two games were disastrous. He was shelled by opposing batters in Baltimore and Buffalo. Partlow lasted two months in Triple-A, longer than Wright, but also was dispatched to a lower minor league team. The Dodger organization did not bring in another Black player to keep Robinson company on or off the field.[49]

Jackie Robinson's tumultuous 1946 year had similarities to the shocks, traumas, and breakthroughs ordinary Black Americans were experiencing. Most dramatic was the treatment of 900,000 returning Black World War II veterans, 75% headed South. The sight of Black soldiers in uniforms was an affront to White Southerners. The NAACP reported that 1946 was "one of the grimmest years" and deplored "reports of blowtorch killing, and eye gouging of Negro veterans freshly returned from a war to end torture and racial extermination."[50]

About 1.3 million Black and other warriors of color participated in veteran benefit and education programs at about the same rate (73%) as 14.6 million White Americans. Seismic cultural change was reshaping America. Jackie Robinson, Sam Lacy, and Wendell Smith would experience and witness more of it in 1947.

DODGER BLUES

Jackie Robinson, John Wright, and Roy Partlow were not the only Blacks to play White professional baseball in 1946. Two more players were in the Dodgers organization. Roy Campanella, catcher, and Don Newcombe, pitcher, played that spring and summer for the Class-B team in Nashua, New Hampshire. In fall 1945, when Branch Rickey signed Robinson, the general manager also made an offer to Campanella, but the Negro League star misunderstood the deal. He thought he was offered a chance to play with the Brooklyn Brown Dodgers, Rickey's straw team that was cover for his real strategy. Campanella declined because he was already under contract with the Baltimore Elite Giants.[51]

The missed opportunity to play in Montreal with Robinson tore at Campanella. He had played against Robinson in the 1945 Negro League East-West All-Star game. Months later in October, both men were lodging at Harlem's Woodside Hotel in preparation for travel to Venezuela to play together on a barnstorming Negro League all-star team. While playing gin rummy, Robinson confided that he was "going to be the first Negro in organized ball." Robinson swore Campanella to secrecy.[52]

Campanella wrote a letter to Rickey and asked to be considered again. The G.M. said yes. [53]

The issue next was where to place Campanella. He was already presumed as high-grade minor league talent, but Rickey did not want to place the Philadelphian at one of the Class B level teams in the South. Campanella was placed at the Nashua team that played in the New England League. Newcombe, a New Jerseyan was described as "the most promising hurler," by the *Pittsburgh Courier,* was his teammate in New Jersey. Significantly, both players, along with Robinson, would end up in the Baseball Hall of Fame.

With the news of the signings, Wendell Smith's *Pittsburgh Courier* hyped Campanella as the "best-hitting catcher" in Negro baseball.[54] For more than a decade that crown had belonged to Josh Gibson of the Homestead Grays. However, by 1945 Gibson was drunk, overweight, out of shape, and often AWOL from his team.[55]

Because of unfamiliarity with Campanella, Sam Lacy of the Baltimore *Afro-American* showed less enthusiasm. If the Dodgers organization did in fact obtain the best catcher in Black baseball, it was a "distinction that is definitely on the dubious side," he wrote, alleging the poor quality of catching in the Negro leagues. Lacy assessed Gibson as a great hitter, but poor fielding catcher whose shortcomings were exposed because of overwork.[56]

Once Campanella caught two doubleheaders in one day, first at Cincinnati's Crossley Field, then that night in Middletown, Ohio. "It wasn't so bad," said the catcher. "I grabbed a few sandwiches on the bus after the first doubleheader and I was ready for the next one."[57] Campanella was more supervised and better coached than Lacy realized. He had been playing professional baseball in the Negro leagues since age 15, first with the Bacharach Giants, Lacy's team when the emerging writer played ball. Campanella was permitted to quit high school only by agreeing to have his salary paid to his mother. Also, mentor Tom Dixon counseled Campanella to "Keep your nose clean, a sharp eye out, and keep your tongue in your mouth."[58]

Lacy also said that Campanella's asset was his attitude and love of the game: "He had a dash that was always a pleasure to share," plus a willingness to ignore insults and endure hardships in order to reach the ultimate goal of playing Major League Baseball.[59]

With that assessment Wendell Smith wondered how the catcher and pitcher Newcombe would fit in at Nashua. He described the city, 40 miles north of Boston as "a typical New England town, quite liberal and staid in its ways."[60] Upon arrival, Campanella said, "These people are wonderful. Newcombe and I go anyplace we want to, do anything we please, and are treated like lost sons." Campanella, Newcombe and their wives were the only Blacks in Nashua; however, they said they had no trouble finding housing and experienced no problems at restaurants nor at the ballpark. Said Newcombe, "We were very lucky to play in that area."[61]

The lack of distractions apparently liberated both players at work. Campanella opened the season as a consistent and occasionally spectacular hitter. He walloped a 440-foot home run for a win over the Lynn (Massachusetts) Red Sox. Newcombe started strong too, winning his first four games before a loss at midseason on June 29. And Newcombe, in 21st-century lingo, was a unicorn because of his bat. "They [fans] want to know," wrote Lacy, "Is this guy a pitcher or a hitter?" At that time most pitchers were not great hitters. But some were. An exception from the past was pitcher Babe Ruth, who later became a home-run champion. At this writing there is Shohei Ohtani, the Los Angeles Angel who is equally spectacular as a pitcher and slugger. Newcombe was the team's most reliable pinch hitter.[62] Over a career he hit .270, an acceptable average for a fielder, but a spectacular output for a pitcher.

***

Roy Campanella left the Negro League Baltimore team for the Dodgers organization without incident. However, when Don Newcombe departed the Newark Eagles for the Dodgers, Eagles co-owner Effa Manley balked. Newcombe was still under contract with her team, even though contracts in Negro league baseball were rarely enforced. But with Rickey making moves to racially integrate professional baseball at the expense of the Negro leagues, Manley issued a warning: "I hope you're not going to grab any more of our players. You know Mr. Rickey; we could make trouble for you on the Newcombe transaction if we wanted to."[63] Manley did not follow through on her threat because Rickey in future deals was careful to ask instead of unilaterally snatching Negro talent.

Effa Brooks Manley (1897–1981), co-owner of the Negro League Newark, New Jersey Eagles was a lone woman owner among the Negro league bosses in the 1930s to late 1940s. Furthermore, Manley was not docile or deferential in a male-dominated culture. She was aggressively vocal, a clever self-promoter, and a socially conscious activist.

Manley's male peers often chaffed from her tart critiques, while others grudgingly admired her good sense and instincts. "Mrs. Manley knows a few things about baseball and most of the men club owners could take a few tips from her," wrote *Chicago Defender* sports editor Fay Young in December 1943. "She is a good businesswoman."

Manley complained that fellow owners did not invest enough money in their teams. They would not spend $100,000 ($1.3 million in 2022 dollars), despite Black baseball operating as a multimillion-dollar enterprise during its prime years. The owners competed for Black fans, who attended MLB games despite racial segregation. The same fans attended Negro League games too. Furthermore, as Black sports journalists Sam Lacy, Wendell Smith, and others lobbied in print for the day when the professional baseball color line would be erased, their asks did not mean that Black baseball businesses should be managed on shoestrings.

In 1932 the former Effa Brooks was attending a World Series game when she met her future husband, Abe Manley. The couple took ownership of the Brooklyn Eagles in 1935 and then a year later moved the team across the Hudson River to Newark. Effa's tasks as co-owner included handling contracts, managing travel schedules, and promotion of the team.

Cumberland "Cum" Posey of the Homestead Grays of Pittsburgh said the league could learn from Effa's keen sense of promotion.[64] Noteworthy was Effa's promotion of the East-West Negro League all-star classics that attracted tens of thousands of Black – and White – spectators to Chicago or Greater New York. Effa also cared for players on and off the field, assisting them with off-season jobs and serving as a godparent to some of their children. She also purchased a $15,000 bus for the Eagles' travel. Furthermore, the co-owner worked to get the best available accommodations on the road in Jim Crow America.[65]

When Branch Rickey picked Jackie Robinson from the Negro League Kansas City Monarchs and signed him to crack the White professional color line, Effa Manley put down a marker. She fought for compensation for team owners and recognition of Negro league contracts. Directly, Manley demanded her Eagles receive compensation when the Cleveland Indians picked Larry Doby in 1947 as the second Black to play Major League Baseball and the first to play in the American League. Doby's transaction established a precedent for player compensation.[66] In 1948, Abe and Effa Manley sold the Newark Eagles to a group of investors.

Besides her unique position as a professional sports team owner, Effa Manley was a racial enigma. Her mother Bertha Ford Cole Brooks was German and White. Effa was raised by a stepfather who was either Black or Native American.[67] Effa's biological father was John Marcus Bishop, a White Philadelphia stockbroker who had an affair with Bertha Ford Cole Brooks. "She was a White woman who passed as Black," said author Ted Schwarz. "She could stay in any hotel she desired."[68] Bishop said Effa married "an old Negro man" who bought her a five-carat engagement ring at

Tiffany's that left jewelry store workers gawking. Abe Manley was twelve years older than Effa.

Abraham Lincoln Manley (1885–1952) grew up in rural North Carolina. When Manley migrated to the North he worked as a chauffeur, laborer, and barber. In Camden, New Jersey he became a "numbers banker" and made a fortune in the illegal yet popular African American community pastime. When Manley's Rest-A-While club was bombed in 1932, possibly by a rival, he moved to New York. Two weeks later, Abe met Effa.[69]

Effa Manley channeled her power as an owner to promote numerous social justice causes. Her Newark Eagles invited World War II soldiers to games for free. The club also hosted benefits for causes such as the Harlem Fight for Freedom Committee and the Newark Community Hospital. One benefit game promoted a "Stop Lynching" theme where sash-wearing ticket takers collected donations.

The Newark Eagles won the 1946 Negro League World Series, the same year Jackie Robinson played for Montreal in the International League. The Eagles' rosters included future Hall of Famers Larry Doby, Monte Irvin, Ray Dandridge, Leon Day, Biz Mackey, Mule Suttles, and Willie Wells. In 2006, Effa Manley was inducted into the Hall of Fall in Cooperstown.

***

In 1946 there were 16 Major League Baseball teams, eight each in the American and National leagues. The two westernmost teams were based in St. Louis (National League Cardinals and American League Browns. St. Louis, at the mouth of the Mississippi River and in a state that shared a border with Arkansas, was also the southern-most Major League Baseball city.) Along with Washington, DC, it was the only major league where local and state law required strict segregation of schools, hotels, restaurants, and almost all other facilities. Along with Washington, DC, it was the only major league city where slavery was legal when the Civil War began. Seven of the 16 teams were concentrated in the Northeast: Boston (AL Red Sox and NL Braves), New York (NL Dodgers, Giants, and AL Yankees) and Philadelphia (NL Phillies and AL Athletics), and Pittsburgh (Pirates).

Washington, DC, wedged between Virginia and Maryland, was also southern city. St. Louis, Baltimore, and Washington in the 1950s remained legally segregated until the 1964 Civil Rights Act. The remaining teams were in the Midwest [American League White Sox and National League Cubs in Chicago, and then Detroit, Cleveland, and Cincinnati].[70]

At the December 1946 Major League Baseball owners meeting in Los Angeles, it appeared none of the executives were interested in following

Rickey's lead and desegregating their teams.[71] Some of the peers expressed interest in Jackie Robinson's progress. Bill Veeck, the new owner of the American League Cleveland Indians, was mentioned as a possible candidate to hire Blacks. Connie Mack of the Philadelphia Athletics, who lambasted Rickey the previous spring for bringing Robinson to Florida training camp, hailed a "new day" for professional baseball.[72]

Still there was no real interest in integration. Wendell Smith feared a counterrevolution was underway and owners in both the Major Leagues and Negro Leagues were working behind the scenes to prevent player defections from one organization to the other.[73]

That month it was still not clear if Robinson would get a shot at joining the Dodgers. Yet a strong hint was Rickey's decision to hold 1947 training camp away from the US mainland in Cuba with some of the Caribbean sojourn spent in Panama. There was no legal segregation on the island or isthmus, and both places had substantial Black citizens.

Robinson remained on the Montreal Royals roster and a few more Blacks were expected to join him. The new venues were expected to shield the team from the stubbornly segregated American South. The moves were also intended to acclimate the returning Dodgers veterans, many of them Southerners, to having Black teammates. A tryout was arranged for Roberto Avila, a Cuban League second baseman. Lacy and Smith speculated that the Brown-skinned player was being used to measure reaction by the White Dodgers. Although Lacy assessed Avila as ordinary, and Smith dismissed the player as "definitely not big-league material," both writers metaphorically swung and missed. Alvia joined the Cleveland Indians in 1949; in 1954 he was the American League batting champion.[74]

In Cuba and Panama there would be frequent intrasquad games between the Dodgers and Royals thus many chances for Robinson to show off his talents. Observers estimated that Rickey and the Dodger organization would lose $50,000 ($697,650 in 2022 dollars) for the additional cost of importing rival major league teams to play exhibition, plus other expenses. Host Havana had 35,000-seat El Gran Stadium. Sam Lacy wrote, "I had heard that Cubans are a deeply religious people. In two days here I have learned that baseball is their religion."[75]

***

In July 1946, Sam Lacy stepped away from covering Jackie Robinson's historic professional baseball debut and traveled across the southern US border to cover baseball in Mexico. That summer numerous Negro league stars left their teams, lured by promises of better pay. They included Satchel Paige, John Wilson, Sam Bankhead (older brother of pitcher Dan

Bankhead, Robinson's future teammate), Jim Crutchfield, and Willie Wells.

At least a dozen major league players jumped to the Mexican League too, chasing higher pay. Unlike the United States, Blacks and Whites were competing professionally on baseball diamonds on foreign soil. Lacy was intrigued. Jorge Pasquel, president of the Mexican Baseball Leagues, brazenly raided major league baseball for many stars. He owned the Vera Cruz Blues team and stacked it with White players, notably pitcher Max Lanier of the St. Louis Cardinals, outfielder Danny Gardella of the New York Giants, and catcher Mickey Owen of the Brooklyn Dodgers. Pasquel lured these players by promising to pay about two times what they were offered by their major league employers. For example, the Giants offered Gardella $4,500 after hitting 18 home runs, driving in 71 RBI, and batting .272 in 1945. Gardella balked at the amount and preferred Pasquel's $10,000 offer.[76]

Pasquel also held a controlling interest in a second team, the Mexico City Red Devils. The Monterrey Monties had no White major league talent and was stocked with Black and Latino players: Art Pennington of the Chicago American Giants, Ed Stone of the Philadelphia Stars, Claro Danny and Ramon Heredia of the New York Cubans, and Johnny Taylor of the Pittsburgh Crawfords. The Monties were managed by Larazo Salazar of the New York Cubans.

The Tampico Lightermen (Alijadoeres de Tampico) was an all-Black and Latino team too, co-managed by Willie Wells and Santos Amaro.[77] In head-to-head competition the predominantly White Blues failed to win a series against any of the teams stocked with Negro League and Latino players. The Blues won only three of ten games against Mexico City, which had Negro Leaguers Ray Dandridge of the Newark Eagles, Bill Wright of the Baltimore Elites, Carlos Colas of the New York Cubans, and Theo Smith of the Cleveland Buckeyes.

Some of the White players blamed Mexico's high-altitude thin air for their failure to win often. Danny Gardella however dissented, telling Lacy the altitude was not a hindrance.[78] The *Afro-American* placed Lacy's correspondence on the front page, or with banner headlines across the inside sports page. The July 9 edition carried a front-page locater map tracking Lacy's sojourn and depicting a sombrero that hopped from Mexico City to Vera Cruz, Tampico, and Neuva Larado. Lacy also reported from US border city San Antonio during his three-week stay.[79] Lacy resumed the Jackie Robinson Montreal Royals watch July 30 with reporting from Baltimore.[80]

***

On January 20, 1947, about a month before the players arrived at training camp, Josh Gibson, the greatest Negro League player other than Leroy "Satchel" Paige, collapsed and died near his Pittsburgh home. He was 37. The "Black Babe Ruth" was revered for the tape-measure home runs he hit. Gibson played for the Homestead (Pittsburgh-area) Grays and he played winter ball in the Caribbean and Latin America. Almost everyone agreed he would have been a major league superstar had he been White.

***

In Cuba, Jackie Robinson, and his Black Royals teammates Roy Campanella and Don Newcombe, both promoted from Class A, attracted more media attention and fan interest than the Dodger players.[81] Wendell Smith wrote the Black athletes were accorded better treatment from spectators (Panama). Actually the situation was familiar, not ironic. The Royals and Dodgers were training in the African diaspora. Culturally Cubans acknowledged that their heritage was partially or mostly African. When US armed forces arrived in 1898 to fight the Spanish-American War, they were stunned to find Black and White Cubans fighting side by side against the Spanish colonizers, with Black generals, notably Antonio Maceo, leading the charge. About 60% of the revolutionary army was Black. After the war, and through US influence, Cuban elites who identified as White and Spanish pressed de facto racism on their Black and Brown countrymen.[82]

As for Panama, the Central American isthmus was populated not only by indigenous and Spanish people, but also by Black Caribbean people who came there to build the Panama Canal. Panama declared its independence from Colombia in 1903 with help from the United States. Laborers from Barbados, then Jamaica came to Panama to work, and in large numbers intermarried with the natives. Furthermore, Africans, enslaved and free, had deep roots in the 16th to 17th-century Spanish New Kingdom of Granada, an Americas region that included present-day Colombia, Panama, and Venezuela.[83] It was not a racial utopia. There was a social and economic caste system, tied to race. But legalized segregation – Jim Crow laws – did not exist there.

Still there were exceptions and contradictions despite, Cuba's tolerance. In Havana, Robinson and Black teammates stayed in segregated, uncomfortable quarters and greasy-spoon dinning, while their White teammates lodged in a comfortable hotel run by a White, American company.

Sparse crowds, about 2,000 fans, came out to see the Dodgers play against General Electric, champions of the Panama Professional League; however, those crowds tripled when Robinson, Campanella, Newcombe, and the other Royals played in the same tiny wooden stadium.

Robinson hit well during spring training. He also received guidance about the fine points of fielding second base from Eddie Stanky, the Dodgers' regular second baseman. On April 10, Robinson was informed that he would be a Brooklyn Dodger.[84] Rickey meanwhile squashed a player rebellion in Panama. A handful of Dodgers circulated a petition stating that they would refuse to play with a Black teammate. Manager Leo Durocher, who was a Robinson ally, gathered the rebellious players late one night. Dressed in a bathrobe Durocher read the riot act:

> I'm the manager of this ballclub, and I'm interested in one thing, winning. This fellow is a real great ballplayer. He's going to win pennants for us. He's going to put money in your pockets and money in mine. And here's something else to think about when you put your head back on the pillow. From everything I hear, he's only the first. *Only the first boys!* There's many more coming right behind him and they have the talent and they're going to come to play. Unless you fellows look out and wake up, they're going to run you right out of the ballpark.[85]

Unrelated to quashing the White player rebellion, Durocher was relieved of his duties. Baseball Commissioner Chandler suspended the manager for one year for "conduct detrimental to baseball." just before Jackie began playing.[86] Durocher's friends included actor George Raft, alleged to have worked at gambling clubs, and mobster Bugsy Siegel too. Furthermore, Durocher was denounced by Brooklyn's Catholic Youth Organization for having an affair with actress Laraine Day, who was married. Weeks before spring training began, Durocher and Day married in El Paso, Texas, one day after Day obtained a divorce across the border in Juarez, Mexico.[87]

News of Robinson's promotion to the big leagues excited Black fans. However, Rickey moved to tamp down the enthusiasm. How would White spectators and opposing players receive Robinson in such unchartered territory? Also, how would the New York press behave? Some outlets underplayed the Robinson story. The *Brooklyn Eagle*, a daily, made no mention of Robinson, who started on opening day. Metropolitan New York at that time had eight daily newspapers (television would not become a widely accessible and used medium until the 1950s) yet there was indifference or little-to-no coverage of the unique rookie.

For completeness, plus cheerleading, opinion, or cornball, readers were left to consume Black or left-wing weeklies. Sam Lacy of the Baltimore *Afro-American* on April 12 wrote, "The Dodgers to a man, feel that Jackie will be one of them before the club completes its exhibition series here [in Brooklyn against the Yankees]. And they're prepared to take it – or else." Lacy opined days before the Dodgers bought Robinson's contract from Montreal. The *Pittsburgh Courier* in a front-page April 19 account attributed robust exhibition game attendance to Robinson: Jackie Robinson might easily dislodge [Dodger star] Dixie Walker as "the Peepul's choice in Brooklyn."

The previous week the *Courier* reacted ominously to Rickey's announcement that Robinson was promoted to Brooklyn: "If Robinson fails to make the grade, it will be years before a Negro makes the grade."

"Robinson on Dodgers!" exclaimed the *Daily Worker,* the communist newspaper on April 11, that had steadfastly lobbied for racial integration of the national pastime.[88] Robinson would start the 1947 season as the lone Black player in Major League Baseball. Wendell Smith roomed with Jackie because of a prohibition on interracial roommates lodging together while on the road. Smith was also ghost writer of Robinson's column that appeared in the *New York Post.* Furthermore, the *Pittsburgh Courier* journalist gathered content for Robinson's autobiography, scheduled for 1948 publication.[89]

A banner headline in the daily *Boston Chronicle* read, "Triumph of Whole Race Seen in Jackie's Debut in Major League Ball."[90] Robinson answered skeptics, well-wishers, and race mongers this way: In his rookie season he batted .297, three percentage points shy of A-grade .300, smashed 12 home runs, and batted in 48 runs. He also led the National League in stolen bases with 29. Robinson's closest competitor swiped 14. Robinson endured name-calling racial epithets from opposing players, coaches, and spectators.[91] In Philadelphia, Robinson was baited incessantly from the opposing dugout by Phillies Manager Ben Chapman. A conflicted Sam Lacy saw value in exposing Chapman's stance.[92] White players of Jewish and Italian ancestry were often heckled therefore Robinson the rookie would have to put up with abuse in order to prove he was mentally tough enough to stick. Words shouldn't hurt according to the trite saying but sticks and stones do. Robinson endured brushback pitches that forced him to crash-land to the dirt and Robinson was hit often with pitches, 72 times in 11 seasons.[93] As a defense, Robinson inserted a metal plate into his wool ballcap to provide minimal protection. Batting helmets were not used yet.[94]

His wife Rachel attended many games to support her husband and witnessed the physical and verbal pounding. Jackie effusively praised her moral support. Then there were Brooklyn fans, attuned to the historic moment, who showed their admiration and appreciation. Wendell Smith painted word pictures in his April 19 dispatch from Brooklyn, New York:

"'Grab Jackie Robinson,' cried a hysterical woman standing on top of the Dodger dugout. "Don't let him get away before I get his autograph." The Dodgers had just beaten the crosstown, opposing league Yankees 14-5 in an exhibition, days before the regular season would begin. "When he [Robinson] finally reached the street, he was mobbed again. There seem to be 1,000 people standing directly outside that door. When he stepped out they gave him a deafening roar and surged upon him. Despite the efforts of another squadron of police, he was absorbed in a sea of slapping hands and was literally carried away. Flashbulbs were exploded with machine-gun-like rapidity and the whole world seemed to be screaming in unison: 'Jackie Robinson!'"

White fans, like Black ones, stormed baseball stadiums to see Robinson. The St. Louis edition of the *Pittsburgh Courier* warned readers that tickets for the Dodgers' visit were "going like hot cakes and it isn't just the Sepia fans that are buying the bulk of them." Sam Lacy observed Brooklyn fans waiting more than an hour after games for Robinson to emerge from the runway to get autographs or simply to touch him: "It was just as though he had suddenly been transformed into some kind of matinee idol."[95]

***

Three months later in July, Larry Doby joined the Cleveland Indians of the American League, thus becoming the second Black Major League player. Maverick owner Bill Veeck wanted to bring Black players into the majors since 1944 but was thwarted by fellow owners. Like Robinson, Doby was college-educated, starting at integrated Long Island University in Brooklyn, then finishing his degree at Virginia Union College, a historically Black school in Richmond.

Otherwise, Doby was the opposite of Robinson. He was shy and soft-spoken. Born in South Carolina, he lived there for the first 15 years of his life before the family moved north to New Jersey. During World War II Doby served in the Navy and was shocked by its segregated customs, but he kept silent. Also, unlike Robinson, he had a lengthy career in Black baseball, beginning in semi-pro as teenager, then polishing his skills for years with the Negro league Newark Eagles as an adult. Veeck bought Doby's contract for $15,000 from Eagles owner Effa Manley.[96]

During his first time in the Indians clubhouse, numerous players refused to shake his hand or acknowledge his presence until Joe "Flash" Gordon broke the ice and played catch with the newcomer. Manager Lou Boudreau also warmed up the rookie. Doby's debut was dubious. He struck out in his first at-bat, and the recently converted outfielder misjudged a fly ball – it hit him in the head – that resulted in three runs for the opposing team and an Indians loss. Yet, strong, silent Doby recovered from that colossal opening failure. The next day he hit a game-winning home run. During a full 1948 season, Doby smacked 14 home runs and batted in 66 runs, affirming he would remain in the majors.

***

By May, Robinson, whose debut was muted in New York press, blossomed into a national phenom. Robinson's presence on the team shattered the common belief that White consumers would reject coming and paying to see Blacks compete in major league ball. Yet on May 11, a Dodgers-Phillies doubleheader drew the largest crowd in Philadelphia baseball history. Two days later in Cincinnati, one of the most southern cities in the North, just across the Ohio River from segregated Kentucky, 27,000-plus fans turned out despite all-day rain to "size up Robinson."[97] Games in Pittsburgh and Chicago respectively attracted 34,800 and 46,600 fans. In print Wendell Smith crowed: "Jackie's nimble/Jackie's quick/Jackie's making the turnstiles click."[98] By the season's end, five National League teams, including the Dodgers, set new attendance records. The Dodgers attracted more than 1.8 million fans for the first and last time in the club's Brooklyn history.[99]

***

Among the fans eager to see Jackie Robinson were the Caldwells, a Black family that lived in a Clearfield, Pennsylvania small town in the mountains about 120 miles east of Pittsburgh. The father ordered *Ebony* and *Jet* magazines, the *Pittsburgh Courier, Grit,* the Sunday *Philadelphia Inquirer*, or Pittsburgh *Post-Gazette*. Of all the periodicals arriving and devoured by the reading family, said son Earl Caldwell, "the Pittsburgh Courier was most impressive." He followed Wendell Smith's sports columns and dispatches from far-away places. In the summer of 1947 Caldwell was 12 years old and obsessed with the life and career of Jackie Robinson.

Although the *Courier* was published in Pittsburgh, copies of the newspaper reached the Caldwell family every week in Clearfield. The family intended to travel to Pittsburgh and Forbes Field when the Pirates were hosting the Brooklyn Dodgers. Mr. Caldwell, who never attended sports events, told his children that to show support for Jackie Robinson, he would go with them to a game in Pittsburgh. And he did.

As that spring turned to summer, the threats against Jackie and hints of riots at stadiums where he played began to subside. Crowds attending games began to grow. Some attitudes toward Robinson were starting to change too. The Detroit Tigers of the American League traded star slugger Hank Greenberg to Pittsburgh. Greenberg, who was Jewish, had hit 58 home runs in one season but as his production began to fall, he was traded and as the Pirate first baseman, he reached out to Robinson during a game against the Brooklyn Dodgers. Wendell Smith, the *Courier* sportswriter had the story. He wrote that Greenberg told Jackie that he too had been subjected to racist slurs on the ball field and he urged Jackie to stay strong. The two eventually developed a friendship that lasted the rest of Jackie's life.

Late that July, on a beautiful Sunday afternoon, the Caldwells attended a Major League baseball game for the first time. The oldest brother drove from Clearfield to Pittsburgh. The father sat in the front passenger's seat. In the back, Earl was seated alongside another sibling. Earl Caldwell had no memories of the game, only the bigness of the stadium.

Once Earl reached his seat, he began to scan the players on the field. Every one of them had arms that were white coming out from their uniform shirts. Then, suddenly, there were these dark, very dark arms that seemed so large and that was his introduction to Jackie Robinson. Earl followed his every move on the field, but those pictures along with those from the game, have not faded away.

What stuck in his mind was what happened next. The game was over, and the family were in the parking lot directly across the street from the stadium. Most of the cars were gone from the lot but the Caldwells were enjoying the lunch the mother had packed. As they ate and told stories from the day, Earl saw a sight to behold. Coming out of the stadium by himself was Jackie Robinson and he was crossing into the parking lot where the Caldwells were gathered. He was moving right toward them. With Robinson approaching, Earl was thinking autograph, or offer him a sandwich. Suddenly, Robinson was only a few feet away. Earl, his siblings, and father we're just staring and saying nothing.

Robinson smiled, waved a greeting and the Caldwells waved back. Jackie Robinson kept moving; in a blink, he was gone. The family was frozen with their thoughts. They began to criticize each other for not offering a sandwich, a piece of pie, not even a proper greeting. they were left dumbfounded. Why was Robinson alone? Where was he headed?

Wendell Smith, the sportswriter from the *Courier* newspaper solved the mystery. "Beyond the outfield wall from the Pirates stadium," he said, "was Schenley Park and a giant building, a part of the University of Pittsburgh and alongside that, a swanky hotel that was for-Whites-only. All of the Brooklyn entourage stayed there. The players, coaches, managers, and team executives – everybody except Jackie Robinson. After the game, Jackie was left alone to make his way to the Hill District, which was the colored neighborhood that had a colored hotel. I've never been able to shake that from my mind or to excuse the Brooklyn baseball club for not fighting for Jackie. I knew that some cities, especially in St Louis, had segregated hotels and Black players were not allowed. But Pittsburgh? In Pennsylvania?"

Four years later in 1951 Earl Caldwell was the high school battling champion. The coaches wanted him to go to Valdosta, Georgia, and play minor league baseball. He said "no" to leaving his small, Black colony and venture into the Jim Crow south. Locally, Caldwell joined the staff of the daily Lancaster *Democrat & Chronicle* as a sportswriter. In 1960 he was sent to cover the first two games of the Yankees-Pirates World Series in Pittsburgh. Jackie Fennell, the Yankees public relations guy, introduced Caldwell to Shirley Povich of the *Washington Post* and Bob Considine, a gregarious writer with the Hearst-affiliated *New York Mirror* and New York *Journal American.*[100]

While in the press box, Caldwell complimented Povich on his story about Yankees pitcher Don Larsen. Caldwell said he memorized it. Povich and Considign couldn't believe him. So, he recited the piece word for word. Povich answered, "Thanks! He's gonna sit and drink with us."

Then a New York *Daily News* writer came over and snatched Caldwell's drink then said, "He can't drink with us. He's too young." Caldwell at the time was about 25 years old.

Earl Caldwell had an iconic newspaper career. He became a reporter with the Rochester *Democrat & Chronicle* in upstate New York then he joined the staff of the *New York Times.* As a national correspondent, he was the only journalist present during the 1968 assassination of the Rev. Martin Luther King Jr. in Memphis. Two years later as a Times' West Coast correspondent, he covered the dramatic trial and acquittal of activist professor Angela Davis.[101]

***

The 1947 Brooklyn Dodgers won the National League pennant, seven games ahead of the nearest competitor, and in large part because of Robinson. Tom Spink, a Robinson skeptic and publisher of the *Sporting News*, bestowed the Rookie of the Year Award on Robinson.

Spink flew to Brooklyn to personally give Robinson the award. Spink wrote that the judges had "sifted only stark baseball values. The sociological experiment that Robinson represented, the trailblazing that he did, the barriers he broke down, did not enter into the decision."

Dixie Walker, a native Georgian and an unrelenting opponent of integration, nevertheless conceded, no other ballplayer on this club, with the possible exception of (catcher) Bruce Edwards, "had done more to put the Dodgers up in the race as Robinson has."[102] Previously, Walker was so opposed to Robinson joining the Dodgers, he demanded to be traded, and Brooklyn gave Walker his wish, sending him to the Pittsburgh Pirates.

Next was a subway series: Brooklynites would travel an hour north to the Bronx and the American League champion Yankees. The championship required four wins out of seven games. This led to every game in this series being ranked among the most thrilling in baseball history. The Dodgers had only made it to the world series three times, losing in 1916, 1920, and 1941, when Brooklyn won only one game in a five-game series. The 1947 series was different. The series went to seven games. There was a near no-hitter in game four. Robinson played well hitting solidly, fielding flawlessly, and rattling Yankee pitchers while on the basepaths.

In the end the Yankees won the pivotal seventh game. Wendell Smith concluded, "If we must get racial conscious about it in determining the wreath of heroism, we'll have to pass the laurels to the players of Italian extraction." Smith referred to Yankees stars Joe "Yankee Clipper" DiMaggio, Yogi Berra, and Phil Rizzuto, and Robinson's Dodger teammates Ralph Branca and Al Gionfriddo, who made a leaping catch of a DiMaggio line drive. Added Smith, "It's been a great series no matter who your parents were."[103]

Jackie Robinson's 1947 was so triumphant in addition to successfully breaking the color line he was a *Time* magazine cover story on September 22. "He and his boss took a chance" (Sport) read the cover caption. Yet Robinson's breakthrough was in no way spontaneous. Branch Rickey sensed that post-World War II America was poised and probably ready for racial integration in professional baseball and other modes of American life, yet the wily owner knew he had to plan carefully and advance cautiously.[104] Robinson, instinctively proud, indignant to insults, and confrontational, suppressed those urges for the hatched experiment to work. Robinson coped with attacks – verbal, psychological, and physical – for the first three months of the season, then another Black man, Larry Doby, broke the color barrier in the rival American League.

That year civil rights was a lead story. The Congress of Racial Equality and the Fellowship of Reconciliation sent 23 Black and White Freedom Riders through the South to test compliance with court decisions. The archbishop of St. Louis said he would excommunicate Catholics who continued to protest integration of parochial schools. President Truman's Committee on Civil Rights condemned racial injustices in America in a formal report, *To Secure These Rights.*[105]

A few more Black players joined Robinson in the National League that season. Pitcher Don Bankhead, Robinson's Montreal teammate, reunited on Dodgers in August 1947, but was not on their World Series roster, and the American League St. Louis Browns acquired outfielder Willard Brown and infielder Henry Thompson, but released both players that same year.[106]

Of the 16 Major League teams only three – Brooklyn, Cleveland, and the St. Louis Browns – signed any Black players. The three had signed just four Black players, St. Louis signed two, evidence of grudging, grinding progress.

Yet post-World War II America was steadily transforming ethnically. Americans of Jewish and Italian descent were visibly successful – with caveats – in New York, America's most populous city that also had three MLB teams. By 1937, a decade before Robinson's Dodger season, Jews were 25% of New York's population but 65% of the city's lawyers, 64% of its dentists, and 55% of its physicians. Jewish New Yorkers had great success in the professions because of a paradox: Their cultural emphasis on education and near-total exclusion from high-level jobs in large corporations. One out of four Jewish immigrants moved into self-employment in small businesses, or professional services like law, medicine, or dentistry, as soon as possible.

Furthermore, once the subway system extended into the outer boroughs in the early 1900s many Jewish immigrants left the overcrowded, stifling lower Manhattan ghetto for Flatbush and Brownsville in Brooklyn or Grand Concourse in the Bronx.[107]

Italians were a concentrated New York interest group too. Ninety-seven percent of those immigrants landed in New York harbor and as late as the 1990s nearly half of them lived within one hundred miles of Manhattan. Extended family-oriented Italians – also shunned or scorned by the WASP establishment – created small businesses. A few of them made it big: Amedeo Obici, founder of Planters Peanuts in Virginia, and A.P. Giannini, founder of the Bank of America.[108]

As for Black/Negro/colored people, many of those men – and some women – returned from the war in uniform, visuals that enraged and moved some White Southerners to assault and maim. The attackers insisted that the proud returning veterans go back to surf-like, subservient lives.

However, progress could not be reversed. The Great Migration from the South to Northeast, Midwest, and California cities accelerated. There was a boom in Black students attending college. Now and then mainstream America would read or hear about Black professional experts such as the medical doctor Charles Drew invented a way to store blood for blood banks, scientist Percy Julian, who synthesized soybeans into medicines and other products, William Hastie, the first federal court judge, or scholar John Hope Franklin, who in 1947 published the seminal Black history *From Slavery to Freedom*, and in the 1950s became the first Black history department chairman at a predominantly White college.[109]

With all the fast-moving change, baseball, so interwoven in American culture and folklore, could not be separated from the momentum. Sam Lacy and Wendell Smith chronicled Jackie Robinson's breakthrough, and the addition of Larry Doby and a few more compatriots in 1947. More stars would shine in the galaxy the next year. Wendell Smith's pre-civil rights crusade strategy, a mix of deadline reporting and public persuasion, shaped the monumental change.

NOTES

1. "Report of the Major League Steering Committee" is in the Chandler Papers plus the US Congress. Also see Lowenfish, Lee, "The Imperfect Diamond," pp 147–152,* 174–181, and US Congress, "Organized Baseball," pp 504–507. Tygiel, "Baseball's Great Experiment," pp 82, 85–86.
2. Tygiel, "Baseball's Great Experiment," p 92.
3. Lamb, "Conspiracy of Silence," pp 309–311; Tygiel, "Baseball's Great Experiment," pp 92–93.
4. Tygiel, "Baseball's Great Experiment," p 107; Lamb, "Conspiracy of Silence," p 309.
5. In 1938, Sam Lacy tried to manage a semipro basketball team while serving as sports editor of the Washington Afro-American. Lacy's publisher said he could not do both. Lacy agreed to be transferred to the Afro's Baltimore base to cover the news. Wendell Smith however operated with the blessing of Pittsburgh Courier management.
6. Tygiel, "Baseball's Great Experiment," p 100.
7. Ibid.
8. Lamb, "Conspiracy of Silence," p 313.
9. Kashatus, "Jackie & Campy," p 61.
10. Tygiel, "Baseball's Great Experiment," p 102.
11. Tygiel, "Baseball's Great Experiment," p 103, Lamb, "Conspiracy of Silence," pp 309–310.
12. Tygiel, "Baseball's Great Experiment," p 103.
13. Tygiel, "Baseball's Great Experiment," p 101.
14. Tygiel, "Baseball's Great Experiment," p 104.
15. In 1952, Harris successfully sued to force the integration of Daytona Beach's municipal concert hall, Peabody Auditorium. Harris et al v. City of Daytona Beach et al, US District Court, Southern District, Jacksonville Division, June 5, 1952. Declaration of judgment and final decree, June 23, 1952.
16. Tygiel, "Baseball's Great Experiment," p 105.
17. Tygiel, "Baseball's Great Experiment," p 106.

Sam Lacy said that Hopper did want Robinson on the team and furthermore questioned whether Blacks were human. When the Royals were in Baltimore and Robinson muffed a play, Lacy felt compelled to write an open letter editorial to Hopper:

> You, like Jackie, are on the spot, if for no other reason than that you come from a section of the country that is generally hostile to Robinson's people.
> The Afro-American appreciates your position the same as it understands Jackie's … Jackie muffed an easy putout at second base in that second game … another player would have been bawled out by you immediately after the game was over. If you didn't give him hell, you should have.
> Jackie's people don't want him treated any different from the rest.

Lacy, "Fighting for Fairness," p 61. May 4, 1946, Afro-American. Tygiel, "Baseball's Great Experiment," p 131.

After initially meeting Robinson and surveying the prospect on the field, Hopper told Red Barber, "Well, when Mr. Rickey picked one, he sure picked a Black one," noting Robinson's complexion. On another day as a Black child scampered near a spring training field, Robinson overheard his manager Hopper suggesting that the child would "make a nice mouthful for an alligator." Yet in a short time, Hopper's behavior evolved and he became a Robinson ally. Hopper complimented the rookie without prompting from peers and opposing players. From the dugout, he called out encouragement to Robinson as he would teammates. Whatever the motivations of Hopper's alliance, it did not take him or any member of the Royals to see what Robinson could do for the team. Kennedy, "True," pp 16–17.

18. Schall, Andrew, "Wendell Smith: The Pittsburgh Journalist Who Made Jackie Robinson Mainstream. The Story of the Writer Whose Careful Coverage of Jackie Robinson Created the Media Strategy for the Civil Rights Movement. Wendell Smith's Secret Weapon? Exerting Soft Power Over Public Opinion," Pittsburgh Post-Gazette, June 5, 2011, p B7.

19. Tygiel, "Baseball's Great Experiment," pp 106–107, Lamb, "Conspiracy of Silence," pp 314–315.

20. Tygiel, "Baseball's Great Experiment," pp 112–113.

21. Tygiel, "Baseball's Great Experiment," pp 114–115.

22. Tygiel, "Baseball's Great Experiment," p 112.

23. Tygiel, "Baseball's Great Experiment," pp 116.

24. "Baseball's Great Experiment," pp 118.

25. Tygiel, "Baseball's Great Experiment," p 113.

26. Lamb, "Conspiracy of Silence," pp 317.

27. Tygiel, "Baseball's Great Experiment," p 108.

28. Smith, Pittsburgh Courier, March 30, 1946. Bradley Hobbs, Tameka, "Democracy Abroad, Lynching at Home: Racial Violence in Florida," New York, Oxford University Press, 2015, pp 156–188: On October 11, 1945, in Madison, Florida, Jesse James Payne argued with his landlord. Because of the disagreement, Payne was hunted, kidnapped, and shot. The national reaction to Payne's death signaled that many Whites were no longer looking the other way as Blacks were denied due process and full protection of the law. Tygiel, "Baseball's Great Experiment," pp 108.

29. Smith, Pittsburgh Courier, April 6, 1946.

30. Tygiel, "Baseball's Great Experiment," p 109.

31. Smith, Pittsburgh Courier, April 13, 1946.

32. Tygiel, "Baseball's Great Experiment," p 110.

33. Kennedy, Kostya, "True: The Four Seasons of Jackie Robinson," New York, St. Martin's Press, 2022, pp 6, 32–33.

34. Kosta, "True," p 34.

35. Tygiel, "Baseball's Great Experiment," pp 120–121.

36. A section of the "spite wall" was still standing until April 2023 when it was demolished. Lucas, Tramon, "Morgan State U. demolishes historic 'spite wall' built to segregate campus from the city," Baltimore Banner, April 12, 2023, https://www.thebaltimorebanner.com/morgan-state-spite-wallbarrier-QVLQFFBEGVEGHPLRXKIDKRYRUU/.

   Cassie, Ron, "The Great Migration: How Black Families Came 'Up South,' Faced Down Jim Crow, and Built a Ground-Breaking Civil Rights Movement," Baltimore Magazine, (February 2020) https://www.baltimoremagazine.com/section/historypolitics/the-great-migration/

37. Tygiel, "Baseball's Great Experiment," p 121.

38. Wickham, DeWayne, "The Calvin Tyler Story," Maryland Public Television, September 5, 2022. https://www.morgan.edu/news/calvin-tyler-documentary

   Calvin Tyler Jr. earned a reputation as a reliable, self-starting employee at a local printing company however he was passed over when he applied for a managerial opportunity. When he asked why, Calvin Jr.'s boss told him he believed the White co-worker "had a better knack for the job." Rather than see over the suspected racism, Calvin Tyler Jr. pursued a new opportunity. United Parcel Service arrived in Baltimore during the early 1960s and advertised that it was hiring drivers. Calvin Jr. visited the package delivery service and then took and aced the written test.

   Yet there was one more thing, a potential barrier. He had to take the driving test. The bulky brown trucks were operated by manual transmission which was unfamiliar to Calvin Jr. With one week to prepare for the road test, he was undeterred. Calvin Jr. borrowed a stick-shift car and practiced driving on the upper floors of downtown parking garage. He passed the test. (From the MPT documentary).

39. Tygiel, "Baseball's Great Experiment," p 123.
40. Tygiel, "Baseball's Great Experiment," p 124.
41. Afro, Kennedy, "True," pp 13–15. June 4, 1946, pp 17: (banner) Robinson leads International League batting – Montreal 2nd baseman on top with .356 average; benched since May 29 on account of injury, star also sparkled afield (Syracuse dateline, no byline).
42. Kennedy, "True," p 4.
43. Kennedy, "True," pp 52–53.
44. Tygiel, "Baseball's Great Experiment," p 140.
45. Tygiel, "Baseball's Great Experiment," p 141.
46. Kennedy, "True," pp 55–56, 58–59.
47. Kennedy, "True," p 30.
48. Tygiel, "Baseball's Great Experiment," pp 126–128, Kennedy, "True," p 44.
49. Ibid.
50. Butler, Kirstin, "The Blinding of Isaac Woodard," American Experience, March 25, 2021, https://www.pbs.org/wgbh/americanexperience/features/blinding-isaac-woodard-seeing/. Dawkins, Wayne, "City Son: Andrew W. Cooper's Impact on Modern-Day Brooklyn," Jackson, University Press of Mississippi, 2012, pp 18–19.
51. Tygiel, "Baseball's Great Experiment," p 145.
52. Campanella, "It's Good to be Alive," pp 109–112.
53. Kashatus, "Jackie & Campy," p 73.
54. Pittsburgh Courier, April 13, 1946.
55. Snyder, "In the Shadow of the Senators," pp 226–228.
56. Snyder, "In the Shadow of the Senators," p 229.
57. Kashatus, "Jackie & Campy," p 75.
58. Kashatus, "Jackie & Campy," p 70.
59. Tygiel, "Baseball's Great Experiment," p 147.
60. Tygiel, "Baseball's Great Experiment," pp 148–149.
61. Ibid.
62. Tygiel, "Baseball's Great Experiment," p 149.
63. Tygiel, "Baseball's Great Experiment," p 147.
64. Whitaker, "Smoketown," pp 113, 119.
65. Effa Manley | Hall of Fame biography.
66. Effa Manley | Baseball Hall of Fame profile.
67. Grigsby, Darryl Russell, "Celebrating Ourselves: African Americans and the Promise of Baseball," Indianapolis, Dog Ear Publishing 2012.
68. Schwarz, Ted, "Cleveland Curiosities: Eliot Ness and his Blundering Raid, a Busker's Promise," 2010. Effa Manley's oral history at the Louis B. Nunn Center at the University of Kentucky.
69. Essington, Amy, "Abe Manley," Society for American Baseball Research, https://sabr.org/bioproj/person/abe-manley/.
70. Ashe, "A Hard Road to Glory," Vol. 3, p 11.
71. Nechal, Jerry, "1946 Winter Meetings: Tranquility and Turbulence," Baseball's Business: The Winter Meetings, 1901–1957. Sabr.org.
72. Tygiel, "Baseball's Great Experiment," p 161.
73. Pittsburgh Courier, December 14, 1946, Tygiel, "Baseball's Great Experiment," p 161.
74. Smith, Wendell, Pittsburgh Courier, March 15, 1947.
75. Lacy, Sam, Baltimore Afro-American, March 8, 1947.
76. Lacy, "Fighting for Fairness," pp 62–63.
77. Lacy, "Tan players backbone of baseball in Mexico," Baltimore Afro-American, July 16, 1946, pp 1, 16.

78. Lacy, "Major leaguer denies Mexican air is hindrance – Danny Gardella, ex-Giant, say altitude is helpful; star's assertion breaks down alibi of former big leaguers who haven't clicked," Baltimore Afro-American, July 23, 1946, p 17. "Major leaguers outclassed in Mexican baseball – high-priced Vera Cruz nine can't win games. Two top teams in loop have none of the White celebrities. Big shots flounder in 7th place," Baltimore Afro-American, July 16th, 1946, p 16.

Max Lanier, Danny Gardella, Mickey Owen, and other White defectors returned to the United States and asked to return to their former teams. Commissioner "Happy" Chandler barred them by issuing a five-year suspension. Several players sued MLB in federal court. Their cases were dismissed, however the Second Circuit Court of Appeals voted 21 to allow a trial. Chandler ended the suspensions and players were reinstated in June 1949.

79. Lacy, "Weather hot, food bad; pay less than Whites in Mexico, player tells Afro," July 9, 1946. From San Antonio, Lacy covered a track meet ("Tan athletes take 11 of 16 events at Texas meet – Harrison Dillard annexes 200-meter hurdles in 23.2 seconds"). The following week, Lacy covered a gubernatorial election ("Texas liberal expected to face fight for election").

80. Lacy, "Montreal star answers boos with stellar play – Treated better after he hits homer, steals home in opening game of series," Baltimore Afro-American, July 30, 1946.

81. Baltimore Afro-American, March 8, 1947, Baltimore Afro-American, March 15, 1947, Pittsburgh Courier, March 15, 1947. "Roy Campanella's 1947 Season in Montreal was a Career Turning Point," cooperstownersincanada.com.

82. Tygiel, "Baseball's Great Experiment," p 164.

83. Gates, Henry Louis, "Black in Latin America," pp 185–186; French, Howard W., "Born in Blackness," pp 243–245. Tygiel, "Baseball's Great Experiment," p 173; Buffalo Soldiers: https://www.nps.gov/prsf/learn/historyculture/buffalo-soldiers-and-the-spanish-american-war.htm.

84. Lacy, "Fighting for Fairness," pp 65–66.

85. Marlett, Jeffrey, "1947 Dodgers: The suspension of Leo Durocher," Society for American Baseball Research https://sabr.org/journal/article/1947-dodgers-the-suspension-of-leo-durocher/.

86. Lamb, "Conspiracy of Silence," p 153, Tygiel, "Baseball's Great Experiment," pp 176–177.

87. "Some of the most infamous baseball scandals," CBS News, May 2, 1012, https://www.cnn.com/videos/business/2023/01/26/navaroli-twitter-whistleblower-speaks-out-donie-pkg-lead-vpx.cnn.

88. Sandomir, Richard, "In Print, Cheerleading and Indifference," New York Times, April 13, 1997 (April 12, 1947, Ashe, "A Hard Road to Glory," Volume III).

89. Tygiel, "Baseball's Great Experiment," p 201.

90. Baltimore Afro-American, May 17, 1947. Sporting News, May 21, 1947.

91. Ashe, "A Hard Road to Glory," p 10.

92. Reisler, Jim, "Black Writers/Black Baseball," pp 57–60, also Tygiel, "Baseball's Great Experiment," pp 183, 192, 195.

93. Baseball-reference.com. Among early Black major league stars, Frank Robinson was hit by pitches 198 times in 21 seasons, and Minnie Minoso was hit 197 times in 20 seasons.

94. Anderson, Stefan, "Jackie Robinson's Special Cap to 'Protect His Head From Beanballs' Up for Auction By Lelands," New York Daily News, September 27, 2017.

95. Pittsburgh Courier, April 26, 1947, Baltimore Afro-American, April 19, 1947

96. Dorinson, Joseph, "The Black Athlete as Hero: American Barrier Breakers from Nine Sports," McFarland, 2022, pp 131–134.

Branson, Douglas M., "Greatness in the Shadows: Larry Doby and the Integration of the American League," Lincoln, Nebraska, University of Nebraska Press, 2016.

97. Sporting News, May 21, 1947.

98. Smith, Wendell, Pittsburgh Courier, May 31, 1947, p 189.

99. Tygiel, "Baseball's Great Experiment," p 205.
100. Bob Considine, 68, Dies After Stroke, Newsman, Hearst Columnist Also, New York Times, September 26, 1975.
101. Caldwell interview with author, April 20, 2023.
102. Smith, Wendell, *Pittsburgh Courier*, October 11, 1947. Araton, Harvey, "The Dixie Walker She Knew," New York Times, April 10, 2010.
103. Tygiel, "Baseball's Great Experiment," p 207.
104. Tygiel, "Baseball's Great Experiment," p 206, Bennett, "Before the Mayflower," pp 579–580.
105. Tygiel, "Baseball's Great Experiment," p 261, Ashe, "A Hard Road to Glory," pp 14–15, Bennett, "Before the Mayflower," p 580.
106. Bennett, "Before the Mayflower," p 580.
107. Barone, Michael, "The New Americans: How the Melting Pot Can Work Again," Regenery Publishing, Inc., 2001, pp 218–220
108. Barone, "The New Americans," pp 128, 132.
109. "John Hope Franklin Dies at 94; Scholar Wrote Pivotal Text on Blacks in US History," Los Angeles Times/AP, March 26, 2009. Rutland, Robert Allen, editor, "Clio's Favorites: Leading Historians of the United States 1945–2000," University of Missouri Press, 2000, Finkelman, Paul, pp 49–67. Futterman, Allison, "5 Interesting Facts About Chemist Percy Julian: Julian Isn't a Household Name, but He Should Be," Discover Magazine, February 1, 2023.

CHAPTER 5

JACKIE FIGHTS BACK; WENDELL'S BOXING BEAT

In 1949 Americans were fearful of communism. There was the Soviet Union and 15 European and Asian countries it conquered (or occupied after the USSR liberated Poland from the Germans, but then would not leave) and imposed a communist ideology. The Chinese mainland was communist too. A minority of capitalist-minded citizens fled to the island of Taiwan off the Chinese coast. Like-minded communist allies were in Korea and Indochina (later renamed Vietnam).

In Europe after World War II, Germany was partitioned, with the eastern portion in the communist Soviet sphere. The western portion, two-thirds of the German land mass, was democratic and aligned with America and Western Europe. Bonn became the latter's capital city. Soviet leader Stalin initiated a blockade and attempted to starve and eventually conquer former capital city Berlin. The United States and Western allies successfully countered with an airlift of food and supplies. The American and the Western allies, and Soviets were locked in Cold War political tension, and military rivalry. The United States was armed with nuclear bombs. The Soviets successfully tested a nuclear bomb in 1949, raising fear of annihilation.

American communism was muted during the post-World War II years. The change explained a conflict that erupted regarding baseball that involved Wendell Smith and the *Daily Worker* newspaper. Allan B. Tine, a contributing writer, wrote that his paper advocated for Satchel Paige and other Negro league stars inclusion in the major leagues. Smith hotly disagreed: "He sounds like a Russian diplomat trying to sell communistic propaganda to someone Stalin just kicked in the seat of the pants. The

DOI: 10.4324/9781003283928-7

Daily Worker did not personally interview those big-league players and managers. The *Pittsburgh Courier* made those interviews and ran a series of articles on their views and reactions."

True, indeed, because Smith was the writer of those enterprise pieces. But Smith, considering the tense political climate, overstated his point: "So, for a matter of record and so that our kids won't come up with ideas that the 'great' communist party is responsible for Negroes playing in our national pastime, let me assure you that the Reds had nothing to with it at all. The most they did was bungle the campaign up at times when it appeared some headway was being made."

"Like a bad penny, they always turned up when least wanted."[1]

Daily Worker writer Lester Rodney took offense to Smith's dismissal because in the 1930s and early 1940s he wrote numerous articles promoting Black participation in professional baseball.

Rodney confronted Smith by reminding him of the 1939 letter he wrote to Rodney praising his advocacy of Negro inclusion. Rodney threatened to republish the letter and embarrass Smith. Smith cooled his rhetoric.

In an April 26, 1997 letter to Wendell Smith biographer Michael Scott Pifer, Rodney said: "I was quite hot about it at the time, not about [Smith's] anti-communistic views, to which I had no right to object, but to his allegation that we falsely took credit for his interviews, and that it was obscene for us to say that we went to bat for Satchel Paige. I responded with a letter to Smith telling him that our attorney said the column was libelous, that I decided not to pursue it because of our past cooperation and good relations, but that if he [Smith] ever repeated those falsehoods, all bets were off. He never responded to my letter, and to my knowledge never repeated the charges, at least not in print." Rodney speculated that because Smith was still working for Branch Rickey, a staunch anti-communist, at the time he wrote the column, it was the reason for the harsh tone.

***

In July 1949 Jackie Robinson was summoned before the House Un-American Activities Committee (HUAC). The previous fall HUAC investigator Alvin Stokes, a Black man, contacted the Dodgers organization and persuaded executives to have Robinson, their celebrity athlete, appear as a friendly witness. At that time the congressional committee was investigating suspected red or pink influences in Hollywood. HUAC wanted to be sure the national pastime, remained ideologically pure, Stokes implied.

When Brooklyn opened its 1949 season in April against the crosstown New York Giants, HUAC had trained its sights on another Black icon, Paul Robeson, the intellectual, performing artist, athlete, outspoken social activist, and outspoken supporter of the USSR and a communist fellow traveler. Robeson was in Paris, and he was invited to address the World Congress of Partisans for Peace. He sang solidarity songs to an adoring audience. Before speaking, an Associated Press correspondent filed a dispatch to the United States with this quote attributed to Robeson: "It is unthinkable that American Negroes would go to war on behalf of those who have oppressed us for generations against the Soviet Union, which in one generation has lifted our people to full human dignity."[2]

Those words were never uttered by Robeson; historians would debunk many years later. But Robeson did say that Black America's true fight lay at home, in the land of Jim Crow.[3]

However, in 1949 Robeson was scorned as an enemy of the American people. National Association for the Advancement of Colored People (NAACP) leadership immediately condemned Robeson. HUAC members saw Robinson as a human club to use and bash the upstart. Robinson was put on the spot. "I didn't want to fall prey to the White man's game and allow myself to be pitted against another Black man," Robinson wrote in his second autobiography.[4] "I knew that Robeson was striking out against racial inequality in the way that seemed best to him. However, in those days I had much more faith in the ultimate justice of the American White man than I have today."

On July 18 Robinson was dressed in a tan suit and seated at the committee table. If, in fact, Robeson uttered that inflammatory statement overseas, said the Brooklyn Dodger, it was silly. Then Robinson said:

> White people must realize that the more a Negro hates communism because it opposes democracy, the more he is going to hate any other influence that kills off democracy in this country – and that goes for racial discrimination in the army, and segregation on trains and buses, and job discrimination because of religious beliefs or color or place of birth.

Robinson's 1949 testimony did not sack Robeson, his communist ties did. Robeson was erased from mainstream public life: he was blacklisted from theaters, his records were banned from stores, and blocked from concert venues, notably that August in Peekskill, New York. The civil rights benefit concert was canceled because of a menacing swarm of anti-Robeson demonstrators. That evening the roving bands attacked concertgoers trapped on the show ground. As the Robeson supporters tried to leave, they were stoned and beaten as police stood by, some hoisting their bill clubs and then joining in the ambush.[5] Unwelcome domestically, Robeson's passport was confiscated, preventing the 51-year-old from touring overseas.

Robinson's testimony the previous month indirectly criticized Robeson. Robinson bluntly critiqued American race relations. The investigators, however, conveniently ignored the latter message. "I have grown wiser and closer to the painful truths about America's destructiveness," said Robinson near the end of his life. "And I do have an increased respect for Paul Robeson who over the span of 20 years, sacrificed himself, his career, and the wealth and comfort he once enjoyed because, I believe, he was sincerely trying to help his people." Robeson indeed sacrificed and suffered immensely. Within three years of the 1949 conflict, his annual income plummeted from $104,000 to $6,000.[6]

In March 1949 Wendell Smith's cordial relationship with Robinson changed. The Brooklyn Dodger complained that some sports reporters were treating him unfairly after he had a confrontation with a teammate during spring training. Robinson's complaining was contrary to the praise he showered on 33 sports reporters in "My Own Story," his autobiography told to Smith.[7]

Smith slammed Robinson in the March 19 *Pittsburgh Courier.* The writer who roomed with Robinson, transported him, and was his confidant was particularly annoyed with the Brooklyn Dodger. Call it a case of familiarity breeds contempt, or Smith the reporter wrestled with objectivity and concluded Robinson protested too much. The heat was evident in three cadences of the column. Smith wrote in part:

> This it seems, is time for someone to remind Mr. Robinson that the press has been especially fair to him throughout his career. Not only since he made his debut in organized baseball but all the time he was in college. If it had not been for the press, Mr. Robinson would have been just another athlete insofar as the public is concerned. If it had not been for the press, Mr. Robinson would not have been in the majors today. If it had not been for the press – the sympathetic press – Mr. Robinson would have probably still been tamping around the country with Negro teams, living under what he has called "intolerable conditions." We do not know whether he was right or wrong in the conflict with [spring training rookie] Chris Van Cuyk. We hope he was justified in saying the things he is reported to have said. We do know however, that Mr. Robinson's memory, it seems is getting shorter and shorter. That is especially true in the case of the many newspapermen who have befriended him throughout his career.[8]

Robinson, added Smith, "isn't as popular in the press box as he once was." The writer's claim may have been exaggerated. At the time of Robinson's 1949 clash with pitcher Chris Van Cuyk in Vero Beach, the barrier breaker announced that his boss' turn-the-other cheek moratorium was over. "I'm not keeping myself under wraps anymore," Robinson told Branch Rickey. The player was 30 years old and had been uncharacteristically polite for three seasons, two in the majors and one in the minors. "They'd better be rough on me this year," Robinson told a reporter that March, "because I'm going to be rough on them." Robinson kept his promise. He taunted pitchers verbally from the basepaths, bristled at umpires when there were close plays, and shouted expletives toward the mound when hit with pitches.[9]

In Smith's April 23 column, published a month after he criticized Robinson, the writer revealed more details about the Van Cuyk incident after talking to MLB Commissioner "Happy" Chandler. Chandler noted that Robinson and Van Cuyk, a pitcher, nearly tangled in a physical fight. Van Cuyk admitted to throwing at Robinson. Chandler reminded the pitcher his act was against baseball rules. Van Cuyk said he was angry at the time and sorry for his behavior. As for Robinson, Chandler received reports that Robinson promised to confront players who physically or verbally abused him. When both men met, Robinson said he had been misquoted. "I accepted that without further ado," said the commissioner.[10]

Unchained, Robinson hit .342 that season, drove in a career-high 124 runs, scored 122 runs, stole a career-high 37 bases, and hit 16 home runs and 56 total extra-base hits. He was the National League Most Valuable Player (MVP), besting Stan Musial by 38 points. Van Cuyk, who the Dodgers signed in 1946 as a free agent, made his major league debut with Brooklyn a year later in July 1950. The 6-foot, 6-inch-tall lefthander compiled a 7-11 won-loss record in three seasons.[11]

After falling out, Smith and Robinson did not speak to each other for ten years, according to a *Chicago Tribune* writer's 1993 article.[12] That did not mean that Smith stopped writing about Robinson; the player was the unavoidable standard that incoming Black baseball professionals were measured against. Smith's widow Wyonella insisted that both men remained friends despite their disagreement, which was akin to adult siblings not speaking to each other because of a spat that occurred decades ago. Rachel Robinson offered a concurring perspective.

Smith, 58, and Robinson, 53, died one month apart in 1972, Robinson in October, Smith in November. One of Smith's last articles was an appreciation of Robinson, written when he was dying from cancer. "He had a feud with manager Leo Durocher and never hesitated to shower an opposing pitcher he thought was throwing at him with a volley of obscenities," Smith wrote. "He slid into Roy Smalley of the Cubs here at Wrigley Field and they almost came to blows."

"But through all this Jackie Robinson was always himself. He never backed down from a fight, never quit agitating for equality. He demanded respect too. Those who tangled with him always admitted afterward that he was a man's man, a person who would not compromise his convictions."[13]

Smith biographer Michael Marsh said the journalist and Robinson, "eventually reconciled their differences. It was easy to respect Jackie Robinson. It was not always easy to like him. … Wendell just knew that

Jackie was going to say what he thought, not necessarily what people wanted to hear. That was the Jackie Wendell sometimes liked and always respected."[14]

Respect for Robinson was evident that year when the Brooklyn Dodgers daringly took a spring 1949 preseason exhibition road trip to the Jim Crow South. The team was in Macon, Georgia beginning April 8 to play the Atlanta Crackers. Since January, Dr. Samuel Green, Grand Dragon of the Ku Klux Klan, tried to prevent the game. Green had the unconditional support of Governor Herman Talmadge, however, Eugene Cook, the attorney general, sided with Rickey. Inside the clubhouse before the first game, Robinson was handed a stack of death threat letters. Manager Burt Shotton read one of the letters out loud to the entire team: "Take the field and you're going to be shot!" The Dodgers sat, frozen in silence, until outfielder Gene Hermanski said, "Why don't we all wear No. 42?" Robinson's number) "Then the nut won't know who to shoot at!" The players laughed then prepared for the game.

"White fans came out early to see them," wrote Sam Lacy of Robinson, Roy Campanella, and Don Newcombe, "booed while watching them, but stayed after the game to get their autographs."[15]

More than 6,500 spectators overwhelmed 4,000-seat Ponce de Leon Park. Black attendees packed the bleachers and overflow sections of the outfield and roared in support of the Black Dodgers. Robinson smacked three hits and drove home two runs.

The pre-season had truly dangerous moments elsewhere. In one of them, Sam Lacy intervened. Previously at Vero Beach, Newcombe got into an altercation with Fermin Guerra, the Philadelphia Athletics catcher. An American Hispanic, Guerra's fair complexion made him indistinguishable from other Whites. An observer to the dispute handed Guerra a wooden post and told him to "kill the Black [expletive] with it." Lacy grabbed Newcombe and hustled him off the field.

"There was talk that I was going to be lynched," said Newcombe. "Nobody took it lightly. At five in the morning, Jackie convened a meeting at Branch Rickey's house. Jackie, Mr. Rickey, [Dodgers organization executive] Buzzie Bavasi, the mayor of Vero Beach, the sheriff and the chief of police were all there. They were prepared to get me out of town if they had to. The whole time they were talking they had an airplane waiting for me at the local airport. It was finally decided that I could stay, but I wouldn't be able to leave camp until the end of spring training."[16]

Branch Rickey was among four 25%-owners of the Brooklyn Dodgers. In 1950, one of the owners departed and sold his share to Walter O'Malley, which made him the 50% majority owner. The power shift signaled the beginning of the end for Rickey. He cashed out and left the Dodgers for the Pittsburgh Pirates front office.

Rickey's departure was bad news too for Jackie Robinson. O'Malley did not care for Robinson's combativeness and favored Roy Campanella, the team's other Black star, because he was productive and not controversial.

O'Malley scorned Robinson as Rickey's prima donna and the relationship would be tense and testy through the early to mid-1950s. Robinson was distraught over Rickey's exit. He wrote a letter – on Dominican Republic hotel stationary left over from the 1948 spring training stay – expressing gratitude and continued friendship.

Robinson's relationship with new boss O'Malley would also be uncomfortable and awkward because the player emerged as the leader of the Dodgers. Many White teammates did not like Robinson's antics, with teammates, opponents, and umpires. They respected him but kept their distance. Robinson, however, was very close with Pee Wee Reese, Carl Furillo, and Gil Hodges – certainly the three best White players on the team, two of whom would end up in the Baseball Hall of Fame (as would Robinson, Newcombe, and Campanella). The trio defined Robinson as fearless, a defender and motivator of teammates, and deserved respect for enduring unimaginable abuse during his first three years in the majors.

The Robinson and Campanella tensions were complex and multilayered. Biographer William Kashatus called Robinson the clubhouse's WEB DuBois, taking the stance that Black men had to demand respect and not shrink from insults or inequality. Campanella meanwhile was the clubhouse's Booker T. Washington: Look at what I do. I produce and excel without rancor, and that should affirm that I belong. Robinson and Campanella were at odds over each other's approaches. Nevertheless, during their productive 1950s seasons, both suppressed their mutual loathing so the behavior would not poison the Brooklyn Dodgers clubhouse.[17]

Robinson, Campanella, and their teammates had to stay focused on rivals. When the 1950s opened, New York was the "Capital of Baseball," according to filmmaker Ken Burns. Of the 16 major league teams the Yankees, Dodgers, and Giants dominated the postseason with pennants and World Series appearances. It was an era of "Subway Series" because road games were 40-minute train rides.

There was a crosstown National League rivalry between the Dodgers and Giants. While more than half of all major league teams had not desegregated, the Dodgers and Giants both were stocked with Black talent, Robinson, Campanella, and Newcombe with the Dodgers, and Willie Mays, Monte Irvin, and Hank Thompson with the Harlem-based Giants.

Leo Durocher, Robinson's former manager and advocate in Brooklyn, was now the Giants' skipper. Trash-talking during Dodgers and Giants games at times was spectacularly mean and personal. During a game, Durocher called Robinson swell-headed. He fired back that the manager was a "traitor" for leaving the Dodgers for uptown.

During another game, Robinson, fielding second base, began needling Durocher about his wife, Hollywood actress Lorraine Day. Durocher who was standing in the third base coaching box charged Robinson and screamed a stream of racial epithets. Pee Wee Reese stepped between both men and cooled the conflict.[18] When Durocher regained his composure, he looked at his Black players, Irvin, and Thompson, standing on bases. Embarrassed, "Leo the Lip" hung his head realizing the invective he spewed.

"We didn't like them [the Dodgers] off the field and we hated them on the field," said Irvin.[19]

On the field in 1951 was an epic Dodgers-Giants battle. In mid-August the Dodgers were cruising along in first place, 13 games ahead of the struggling Giants. Earlier in May, Durocher and general manager Horace Stoneham called up rookie Willie Mays from the minor leagues. Mays struggled initially however Durocher assured Mays he would be all right. Monte Irvin was tasked to mentor Mays. Irvin, an experienced Newark Eagles Negro League star, was projected as a better prospect than Jackie Robinson to break the baseball color line.

Irvin matched or exceeded Robinson's pedigree: College, World War II veteran, star Negro League stats. But when Irvin returned from the war, he said he was not yet in baseball shape and declined inquiries from Rickey to make history.[20]

Center fielder Mays indeed caught on and caught fire; in fact, he was named National League Rookie of the Year. The Giants caught up to Dodgers and tied them on the last day of the season. That forced a three-game playoff to decide which team would face the Yankees.

In the tiebreaker third game, Giant Bobby Thomson hit the game-ending home run off Dodger hurler Ralph Branca that gave the NL Pennant to New York. The Yankees beat the Giants four games to two in the World Series. For the first time, the championship fielded an all-Black outfield, Giants Hank Thompson, Willie Mays, and Monte Irvin.[21]

***

Just across the Harlem River in the Bronx was the New York Yankees, who beat Brooklyn in the 1947, 1949, 1952, and 1953 World Series, infuriating and demoralizing the Brooklyn faithful. The Yankees also beat the

Philadelphia Phillies in 1950, and the New York Giants in 1951. In 1954, the Yankees missed the championship because Cleveland won the AL pennant, then lost the World Series to the New York Giants.

The Yankees stridently remained an all-White team. A Black prospect, Elston Howard was signed in 1950 and was working his way through the farm system, becoming a Yankee in April 1955. Jackie Robinson publicly denounced the Bronx Bombers as bigoted, annoying his boss O'Malley and angering Yankees General Manager Larry MacPhail, who before Branch Rickey arrived built the Dodgers' winning foundation before departing. MacPhail and fellow executive George Weiss insisted they would not be pressured to place Blacks on the team.

McPhail and Weiss vehemently denied that they and Yankees organization were not anti-Black; however, many observers were suspicious and skeptical. Multiple people alleged that they overheard Weiss at 1952 cocktail party say, "I will never allow a Black man to wear a Yankee uniform. Boxholders from Westchester don't want them. They would be offended to have to sit with niggers."[22]

The Yankees did have two probable stars in their system, pitcher Ruben Gomez, an Afro-Puerto Rican, and Vic Power, also Afro-Puerto Rican, a power hitter acquired in 1951 who looked like a can't-miss talent. Yankee executives hedged, claiming Power (born Victor Felipe Pellot) "wasn't the Yankee type" and worried that the player liked to date light-complexioned women. In 1953 he was traded to the Philadelphia Athletics. Elston Howard, who was Power's teammate in Kansas City, endured as a Yankee, and in 1963 would be the first Black American League MVP.[23]

Power played 12 major league seasons and batted .284 and socked 169 home runs. The Yankees were already well-stocked with White talent.[24] During 1953 spring training, Sam Lacy published allegations that the Yankee management engaged in anti-Black tactics. With Vic Power traded and Gomez released from the Kansas City farm team, Lacy alleged there was a scheme to undermine another Black prospect, Elston Howard.

The New York baseball writing fraternity, Lacy alleged, were co-conspirators with Yankees management in resisting integration. Dan Daniel, a *World-Telegram* writer, called Power "a bad actor" with a "poor attitude." Lacy called that writer a "Yankee yes-man." Joe Williams, a fellow *World-Telegram* writer, called the departed Gomez a boy "with poor attitude." Lacy wrote that the anti-Power drumbeat built up Howard as a better prospect who would stick with the team. So why was manager Casey Stengel recommending that Howard the outfielder be converted to catcher?

The optics at that time appeared fishy. The Yankees catcher was Lawrence "Yogi" Berra, 29, a five-time all-star and 1951 league MVP (Berra would win MVP again in 1954 and 1955). Berra was going to own the catcher's spot for a long time. Stengel did not help matters by uttering a crude joke: "They finally get me a nigger [Howard] and he can't run."

Stengel assessed that Howard was too slow to make it as a major league outfielder; however, his cannon-like arm made Howard ideal to play catcher. New York baseball beat writers and Stengel recoiled from Lacy's fiery allegations. Lacy reached his conclusions in part from interviewing Howard. Howard said he thought their conversation was off the record. Howard held a press conference with the writers Lacy called Yankee "house men" and insisted that Casey treated him fairly and he looked forward to learning how to convert to catcher.

Chicago Defender sports editor Fay Young chastised Howard, 24, for denouncing Lacy: "Facing Boss Stengel's white New York reporters, Howard backtracked from what he told Sam Lacy, who is a sagacious sports reporter and editor. But all his [Howard's] bootlicking did was get him a train ride to Toronto [a Triple-A team, one step from the majors]. And the New York Yankees remain lily white. A piece of advice to Howard. Never call a newspaperman a liar. It isn't a nice thing to do."[25] Indeed, Howard was sent to minors for more seasoning, and he returned and broke the Yankees color line in 1955.

In May 1952, Wendell Smith did a head count of Black prospects in the minor league pipeline for the entire major leagues. In all, 104 were in the farm team system, 54 of them in the American League, and 50 in the National League. Three teams – Detroit Tigers, Boston Red Sox, and St. Louis Cardinals – had no Black players in their systems.

The leaders included the St. Louis Browns (22), the Boston Braves (14), the Pittsburgh Pirates (12), and the Washington Senators and Chicago Cubs, both tied with nine.[26]

Smith's outlook was sunnier compared to December 1949 when he warned that after two full seasons of Black inclusion in the major leagues, plenty of jobs were available, evidenced by Brooklyn and Cleveland diving in quickly and aggressively to sign talent, and that in 1948, "there were 36 Negro players in organized baseball, the majority of whom were stretched across the country in the minor leagues. ... If ten of them come up within the next three years we will be surprised."

Smith's concern was that the major league-capable talent was already extracted from the Negro Leagues, which were collapsing foundationally, so where would other Black prospects come from? He recommended that colleges and lodges and fraternities sponsor baseball leagues for youth who want to play ball.[27]

"The teams that sign Negro players now to increase attendance are in the minority," reported Smith. "The majority sign them more out of necessity than anything else. If a good Negro player is available, for instance, he is signed because he might help that particular club win a pennant or championship. It is a case of self-preservation." The attitude of most owners now is: "If we don't sign him, some other club will, and that very club may then beat us out for the pennant."

The year 1954 was history for civil rights and Black excellence in baseball. In May, a unanimous US Supreme Court asserted in *Brown vs. Board of Education* that "separate but equal" public school education was unconstitutional. The Brown decision did not overrule *Plessy vs. Ferguson* in 1896, but that change would come later. Legally the decision undermined the entire public-school systems in 17 states, and as well as local segregation in a few other states. The Brown decision was a social earthquake.

In major league ballparks, Willie Mays returned to the New York Giants. After the team's 1951 pennant-winning season, the rookie sensation was drafted into the US Army. He served a one-and-half-year stint in Virginia and returned to the Giants in spring 1954. Fortuitous because for two seasons New York fell out of contention. The Giants rallied and won the NL pennant. They faced the AL Cleveland Indians, led by Black stars Larry Doby and Al Smith. The Giants won the World Series in a four-game sweep.[28]

In 1954, Henry Aaron and Ernie Banks debuted as rookie National League stars. Aaron was a Boston Braves outfielder; Banks was a Chicago Cubs shortstop. That year Dodger veteran Roy Campanella was National League MVP. Furthermore, the American League St. Louis Browns moved to Baltimore, changing their name to the Orioles, after an earlier International League team. A decade later another Robinson (Frank) would help lead the team to World Series glory.

The year 1955 was another year of excitement. Brooklyn Dodger Jackie Robinson was prematurely gray, overweight, and statistically a shell of great player he once was. Many of his teammates were declining too because of aging, and this crew failed multiple times to beat the Yankees and win a World Series. Robinson, hitting a mediocre .256, was moved from second base to third to make room for a new Black star, Jim "Junior" Gilliam, who was 1953 Rookie of the Year.[29]

But what Robinson lacked in physical ability he made it up with ferocious determination. He challenged his teammates to win it all. Brooklyn won the NL pennant again. So, did the Yankees in the American League.

The October championship was full of drama. During game one at Yankee Stadium, Robinson acted recklessly, but succeeded. After reaching base safely, he made it to third base, 90 feet from scoring. Robinson walked off the bag, then sprinted for home plate, alarming pitcher Whitey

Ford and his catcher Yogi Berra. Ford's throw home reached Berra as Robinson was into his slide.

"Safe!" waved the umpire. Berra leaped and screamed in protest. Robinson emerged from the dust cloud and walked to his dugout with a satisfied grin. He and his Dodgers would not be beaten. Yet the Yankees did win the first two games of the best-of-seven series, in part on a home run by Elston Howard, the first Black on the Yankees. After the first two games the Dodgers appeared doomed to fail once more. Brooklyn rallied and won games three and four at home and tied the series 2-2. Then the Dodgers won game five at Yankee Stadium. But Yankees ace Ford won game six in Brooklyn, setting up a climatic game seven in the Bronx.

Robinson injured his Achilles tendon and had to watch from the dugout. On October 4, Brooklyn won 2-0 thanks to Johnny Podres' pitching, Gil Hodges' hitting, and Sandy Amoros' late-inning catch of a deep drive hit by Berra. The Dodgers and their long-suffering Brooklyn fans finally earned a championship.

Their win also signaled the end of Robinson's ten-year run in Brooklyn. Robinson was despised by G.M. O'Malley, and the icon had a toxic relationship with Campanella, who was generally liked by the front office and teammates. After playing the 1956 season, O'Malley that fall arranged to trade Robinson to the rival New York Giants. Robinson decided in early 1957 to trade his baseball uniform for a suit and tie, take a corporate job, and continue to press for civil rights.

At the end of the 1940s, it was evident that baseball's great experiment succeeded. Jackie Robinson quickly became a Dodgers star. By 1949, he stopped suppressing attacks – verbal and physical – and responded in kind. Black teammates joined him, and a subway ride away, the New York Giants desegregated in 1949 and quickly added additional Black talent.

In the Midwest, the Cleveland Indians added Black players, and won a World Series with them. The rival St. Louis Browns acquired Black talent with mixed results. These four teams were the exceptions compared to the remaining twelve big league teams that still resisted integration.

Before the 1950s began, Wendell Smith worried in print that after about a dozen of the best Negro League players were extracted from that circuit, there would not be enough credible talent in the pipeline to populate the remaining teams. Sam Lacy meanwhile accused the Yankees and reputed sportswriter enablers of inventing schemes to discredit or reject Black talent.

But by 1954 change was blowing in the wind. The New York Giants powered by Willie Mays and Monte Irvin won the National League pennant and then World Series.

The next year the Dodgers, with Robinson, Roy Campanella, Don Newcombe, and others won the pennant and the World Series. Rookies Henry Aaron and Ernie Banks arrived in 1954 and quickly proved they would become steady superstars. In 1957 the Braves, led by National League MVP Henry Aaron, would win the World Series. By the latter part of the decades every team eventually desegregated.

At the end of the 1956 season, Jackie Robinson was traded to the crosstown New York Giants. Robinson chose to retire from baseball as a Brooklyn Dodger, and he transitioned to other work as an executive at Chock Full of Nuts, a coffee company and restaurant chain. The Dodgers transitioned too, moving from Brooklyn to Los Angeles in 1958.

Baseball was connected to what was going on generally in American society. In August 1955 Emmett Till, a Black schoolboy from Chicago was murdered in Mississippi by White men for allegedly whistling in the direction of a White woman. The killers denied that a slaying occurred, but the 14-year-old's body was recovered. Emmett's mother Mamie insisted that her son's grotesquely disfigured corpse be displayed for America and the world to see. That December, seamstress Rosa Parks was arrested in Montgomery, Alabama for refusing to give up her seat to a White man. A year-long bus boycott ensued, led by a young pastor, Martin Luther King Jr.

Other changes were not as tumultuous, but still significant. Late in 1954, the US Defense Department announced the elimination of all segregated regiments in the armed forces.[30]

More Blacks were joining the White-collar job ranks. The Great Migration of Blacks from the south to the north, Midwest and West Coast continued and such movement dramatically changed the nation's culture and attitudes. Lacy and Smith would continue to chronicle these events, often when sports and society intersected.

BOXING SUMMONS SMITH, LACY

Wendell Smith and Sam Lacy devoted most of their careers to covering baseball, however, because of the pressing needs of the Black-owned newspapers they worked for, both men were pressed into other duties. Wendell and Sam both covered multiple sports, notably boxing, plus track and field, basketball, football, tennis, and golf.

Sam Lacy and Wendell Smith were journalists, period. Smith served as city editor of the *Courier* in the 1940s during World War II. Lacy covered "straight" news briefly for the White-owned daily *Chicago Sun* (now known as the *Sun-Times*). He also covered news for the *Chicago Defender* because he was blocked from sports by "Doc" Young, the *Defender's* territorial sports editor. When he returned to Baltimore, Lacy's boxing reporting was elevated to front-page placement:

LOUIS METHODICAL, CONN APPEARS OVERTRAINED

DURING AFRO VISIT TO CAMPS OF THE TWO RIVALS FOR JUNE 19 BOUT

The four-column headline was Sam Lacy's May 28, 1946, sports page 17 preview of the upcoming championship fight between Joe Louis and Billy "the Pittsburgh Kid" Conn.

On June 18, 1946, Lacy's reporting from New York was elevated to the front page:

"LOUIS, CONN AWAIT GONG:

Afro Sees Champ KO'ing Challenger by 9th Round;

Joe's 40-percent Cut of the Gate Will Net Him Over One Million for Fistic Job."

At the top of the front page was a skyline promo: "All-Star AFRO Coverage for Louis-Conn Title Bout Wednesday Night." There were five mug photographs that included Lacy.

Previously on June 18, 1941, Joe Louis' fight against Conn was his 18th title defense, his seventh in seven months. Louis knocked out Conn in the 13th round of a 15-round fight in New York. At that time Conn was leading on two of the three scorecards. The Louis team counseled the champion to knock out the challenger or risk losing. Conn's team urged their man to "stick and run" and not trade blows with Louis, who had a 25-pound advantage. Conn did not heed the advice, got too close, and took a monster right Louis blow that dropped him to the canvas. Had the challenger stood up, Conn had a chance to win; however, he was unable to beat the referee's ten-second count before the bell. *Sports Illustrated* called the Louis-Conn match one of the greatest ever. In defeat, Conn made fun of his tactical error, "What's the sense of being Irish if you can't be dumb."[31]

Joe Louis earned champion status in another sport, golf. He won the Professional Golfers Association of America (PGA)-sanctioned Eastern Golf Association Amateur Championship, reported Wendell Smith in his Sports Beat column. Louis beat Jacques "Bearded Wonder" Isler, in the final round.[32]

"The king of the heavyweights got a great wallop out of winning," wrote Smith. "He has been trying for a number of years to win a tournament and when he finally struck paydirt on the fifteenth hole of the tricky South Park [Pittsburgh] course he was all smiles." Smith wrote that

Louis gained the upper hand over Isler by hitting tee shots that averaged 250 yards that Isler could not match. "Isler found himself in a position where he had to win the last four holes to gain a tie. Louis got a par three and when Isler tried for a birdie and missed, after landing on the green about fifteen feet from the cup, Louis emerged victorious. The gallery swarmed around him and shook his hand, pounded him on his broad back and begged for the ball he was using. The heavyweight champion was his usual gracious self and went stalking off with the championship [trophy] in the bag and a broad smile on his deeply tanned face."[33]

What went unsaid was Louis' Black History pioneering. The boxer broke through in a sport that was perceived as for Whites only and for the country club elite. At the time of Louis' win, Jackie Robinson was finishing his season as the first Black to play major league baseball.

Smith's column also referenced Negro golfer Ted Rhodes, who Louis had hired as his personal golf tutor. "Today," wrote Smith, "he [Rhodes] is probably the No. 1 Negro golfer in the country ... Here in Pittsburgh, he shot a sizzling 283, five under par ... Rhodes is a stylist on the links. He plays par golf – or close to it – consistently. He hits a long ball and plays his irons like a champion. ... In another year he should be able to compete in the big tournaments against the best White golfers and hold his own."[34]

***

Walker Smith Jr., better known as boxer "Sugar Ray" Robinson, was an outstanding fighter with an odious reputation away from the ring. His career scoresheet was 175 wins out of 202 matches. Of those wins, 109 were by knockout. Robinson lost 19 times and fought to a draw or tie six times. He won welterweight and middleweight titles. Away from the ring, Robinson had sexual liaisons with multiple women, and when his second wife Edna Mae complained about the infidelities, Robinson beat her. Son Ray Robinson Jr. suggested that his father's spousal abuse resulted in Edna Mae having multiple miscarriages.

Lacy did not hide his contempt for Robinson's outside-the-lines behavior: "I have said many times that Sugar Ray Robinson was the greatest athlete in any given field I have had the pleasure of covering. I have also said that he can be one of the most disgusting figures one is compelled to meet in this business."[35] In the June 25 edition, Lacy analyzed Louis' win:

LOUIS DEBATES NEW TITLE BOUT: Considers meeting Marciano in September; Changes Mind; Believed Persuaded by Promoter Jacobs.[36]

Lacy also criticized Sugar Ray Robinson because when in Baltimore, the boxer complained about the lack of a working elevator. At the downtown building where Robinson was staying the elevator was not working. Sugar Ray threatened to get in a car and go back to New York. Had it not been for trainer George Gainford's intervention, Robinson would have made good on the threat. Lacy wrote that the champ should have shown more courtesy to his hosts because he knew the inconvenience was out of the building management's control. Dan Parker of the New York *Daily Mirror* quoted Lacy. Parker accepted Lacy as one of the boxing beat writers, but was distant. He did not hesitate to quote Lacy when the latter wrote critically of Black athletes.[37]

One of Lacy's March 1951 "A to Z" columns, dateline Miami, reported this Sugar Ray incident: At Gulfstream Racetrack. The world middleweight champion became the first colored enthusiast to "graduate" from the Jim Crow bleachers for the Florida racing circuit. ... Robinson showed up in tow of Walter Winchell. Gulfstream officials made their resentment quite clear. The next day, Sugar Ray was back again, this time again accompanied by Winchell plus E.L. Hopkins, owner of a powerful racing stable headed by the handicap champion, Three Rings. Mrs. E.L. Hopkins explained that Robinson was her guest and was to have access to her clubhouse box as long as she was racing her string in Florida. "Track people don't like to cross folks like the Hopkins, the Whitneys, the Vanderbilts, and Calumets," wrote Lacy, "people who run 'big money' horses, so Robbie had another 'kayo' [knockout] to his credit."[38]

When Joe Louis retired as heavyweight champion, Wendell Smith assumed a sarcastic tone in his Sports Beat column. He did not take digs at the champ in "Fight Mob Member Talks to Himself ..." Smith saved his jabs for the indignant entourage hanger-ons who now had to exit the Joe Louis gravy train.[39] Smith wrote in the voice of character "Hotnose":

> Believe me, when I tell you, I am irritated no little. I am around with this Louis for fourteen years. In all that time I served him faithfully. I travel with him. Eat with him. Sleep with him. I even go to Europe with him, and to South America. I am even considerate enough to take his money from him. Sometimes he doesn't know it. But I always say it is better to have your friends take your money than a stranger. After all, you may never see a stranger again. But this Louis could always depend on seeing me again. In fact, the only time I ever leave him is when he goes off to war.

When Louis hung up his gloves and walked away intact, he could have commanded a half million dollars per fight according to Hotnose, millions in 21st-century money. But now, poor Hotnose would have to get a job, so he could eat and not become skinny.[40]

On June 11, 1949, dateline Chicago, Sam Lacy wrote about Joe Louis' optimism about the chances of spectacular attendance and anticipated gate revenue, $400,000, for the June 22 Jersey Joe Walcott vs. Ezzard Charles heavyweight championship at Comiskey Park.

Louis at the time was boxing director of the International Boxing Club (IBC) of New York.[41] Lacy in his A-to-Z column suggested Louis and Harry Mendel, his White publicity chief, curb their enthusiasm. Mendel, Lacy wrote, "scurries about like a kangaroo with racehorse battery tied to his tail, only louder." Lacy preferred the less blustery, yet confident tone of Truman K. Gibson Jr., ticket sales supervisor, who the sportswriter identified as the brains behind the IBC.[42]

Wendell Smith's August 22, 1949, Sports Beat column spotlighted boxing promoter Fred Irvin, whose prestige as a promoter soared, according to the writer, because Irvin signed six boxing champions of varied weight classes to battle on the same card September 2 in Chicago, Smith's new home base. Smith was far from kind, calling Irvin "fat and forty" and a "fast talker." The writer also recalled an incident six years previous in St. Louis: Irvin promoted a title bout between light heavyweights John Henry Lewis and Bob Olin. Lewis, managed by Gus Greenlee, won. Afterward, "it seems some very crude-looking gentlemen, referred to by the police and other respectable people as mobsters," wrote Smith, called on Greenlee to get a cut of the prize money. Irvin promised the money to the gang, unbeknownst to Greenlee, the Negro league baseball team owner.[43]

"But instead of cutting them in," wrote Smith, "Mr. Irvin got his loot and cut out for the nearest railroad station. Foiled by Irvin's ingenuity, the mobsters decided to declare themselves in on Mr. Greenlee's part of the purse." Despite implied threats of bodily harm, Greenlee managed to escape, excusing himself to find the messenger with the money, but instead slipping away on train, like Irvin.

Joe Louis was not a civil rights crusader; however, the Brown Bomber frequently took principled stands for respect and equality, wrote Wendell Smith.[44] What happened was White daily newspaper journalists were surprised that Louis took a public stand in alleging racism at a PGA event in San Diego. Smith informed readers and "the writers from the other side of the tracks" that Louis did not shy away from racial conflicts. His style was to operate behind the scenes, but up close and personal.

On August 25, 1956, Wendell Smith wrote about heavyweight Hurricane Jackson, "the weird man with the amazing amount of stamina," who was scheduled to fight big Bob Baker in Pittsburgh on September 26 and possibly have a title fight against champion Archie Moore two months later. Smith's analysis: Strange things happen in the business of punching. If Jackson won, he would be "the darndest of champions," wrote Smith, like Jersey Joe Walcott, who would resent the comparison. Smith explained: "It was a twist of fate, actually, that he [Walcott] ever won the crown and had the chance to strut around in his pompous manner with it perched on his balding head. He lost it to the first good, young fighter who came along – [Rocky] Marciano." Smith did not hide his scorn that Walcott reached the top very late and did not have the champion longevity of Jack Dempsey or Joe Louis.[45]

New light heavyweight champion Dick Tiger, an African whose given name was Richard Ihetu, had been fighting professionally for 14 years and looked ancient, like 100 years old, wrote Wendell Smith. However, during a Madison Square Garden bout against Jose Torrez, the Tiger "fought like an inspired teenager," wrote Smith in his Sports Beat column. Smith's analysis was Torrez foolishly followed the advice of his former manager, Cus D'Amato, to cover his face with his fist and allow the opponent to pound away unmercifully at his midsection.[46]

Smith called the strategy amateurish. It was the same advice D'Amato gave Floyd Patterson, which worked until that former champ faced legitimate challengers.

Wendell Smith did not hide his disgust in a January 1957, Sports Beat column. He loathed mediocrity and style over substance. Both sins occurred when Smith watched the once-great Sugar Ray Robinson fight Gene Fullmer:

> Robinson was nothing more than a gaudy, cheesecake champion when he climbed into the ring before those 18,000 fans in Madison Square Garden. His primary mission was to collect $138,000. That's what the 'Pretender' to the throne taxed his subjects and the public for the privilege of watching him flounder and stumble … and fall and fumble … for 15 inglorious rounds.

Smith landed a verbal left hook on another target: "'His Majesty' is all through as a super fighter and any boxing commission anywhere that permits him to milk the public at top price again is guilty of collaboration." As for Fullmer, Smith called the winner "a butcher without a cleaver. He chops away and chops away but couldn't dent [Robinson's] chin with an axe." Yet Smith wasn't faulting Fullmer for who he was but condemning Sugar Ray for sinking so low. Four months later Robinson beat Fullmer in a rematch and regained his middleweight crown. Yet Smith was correct, Robinson's skills were seriously degraded. He lost the title again in 1957 then regained it the next year. Robinson retired for good in 1965.[47]

In the late 1950s the nation's boxing writers rated Jack Dempsey "The fighter of the century." Wendell Smith cast a dissenting vote in his January 3, 1959, Sports Beat column. "There are a few of us, however," Smith wrote, "who will always frown upon that selection because the Manassa

Mauler never did match punches with the outstanding challenger of his time – Wills."

That was Harry Wills, a heavyweight who was victimized because of the time in which he lived. Wills, who had died the previous week, was the Black boxer who followed Jack Johnson, the fighter who inflamed White America for knocking out contenders and violating social mores by consorting sexually with White women. Wills was denied any chance to challenge Dempsey because of the Jack Johnson legacy. "Throughout the last half of his career," wrote Smith, "Wills stalked Dempsey, trying vainly to lure the heavyweight champion into the ring and a title fight.

He once collected $50,000 after signing a contract for a title fight with Dempsey when the latter found it 'inconvenient' to live up to the obligations of the pact."

Smith also quoted Dempsey's manager who explained, "Wills was a dangerous opponent, the easier contenders could be picked for Dempsey, and they gave 'racial prejudice' as their excuse for keeping Wills from fighting for the crown." In contrast, Smith concluded, "Joe Louis fought everyone and anybody when he was champion. He ducked no one, offered no excuses."

"Louis, not Dempsey is the greatest in this book."

"Wills may have been … but he never got the chance."[48]

Danny "Bang Bang" Womber, 30, was an energetic middleweight class boxer who appeared on preliminary fight cards in front of headliner stars such as Sugar Ray Leonard. Moreover, Womber was good enough to be Leonard's sparring partner. But what apparently motivated Wendell Smith to spotlight Womber in a Sports Beat column was the man's steady job as a skilled barber in champ Leonard's barber shop.[49] As for Womber, Smith did not wonder, why was it that so many fighters, especially those on top, end up destitute or broke? Thousands of ordinary, undistinguished pugilists, Smith mused, knew when to say when. If they weren't winning often, most of these ordinary men acted like other regular men: get a job, get a lunchbox, a car, and home. As for stars who crash and do not recover, why can't they get up and become public wards? Is it foolish pride? A destroyed ego?

"I knew I had to learn a trade of some kind," Womber told Smith, "Because eventually I'd have to get out and look for a job. So, I went to barber school. I also had a few side jobs. I'd work during the day and train at night."

He continued, "I'm not ashamed to walk out and face the people who once paid money to see me fight. And I get the impression that those people like me just as much now as they did then, maybe more. I think people respect me."[50]

"Was it appropriate to cheer for heavyweight champion Floyd Patterson, or root for the challenger?" wondered Sam Lacy in his A-to-Z column.[51] The dilemma: Cus D'Amato, Patterson's manager, committed numerous "promotional sins," aka conflicts of interest, wrote Lacy such as handpicking opponents, paying both fighters, setting ticket prices, and naming the referee. In 1956 when Patterson won the heavyweight crown after taking it from old, poorly conditioned Archie Moore, Lacy said Patterson was "champion of what?" In 1959 a judge ordered the IBC dissolved because of the shenanigans.[52]

***

Wendell Smith criticized Patterson's boxing harshly too, but not in a January 28, 1961, column. Patterson ascended as a hero. The heavyweight was about to battle Ingemar Johansson for a third time in March and in Miami Beach, Florida. When Patterson signed the contract for the bout, he demanded that the promoter, Feature Sports, Inc., post a $10,000 bond that guaranteed there would be no segregated seating of Negroes and Whites at the fight. Patterson would be the sole judge of the seating arrangement, reported Smith, basing it on if there were any complaints. "Always when I get in the ring, I look over the crowd," said Patterson, "and I can tell then if there is any segregation."

Patterson's demand and guarantee was unequivocal and bold. He was telling a city in a Jim Crow state what it must do if he were to perform. Patterson's demand occurred days after John F. Kennedy was sworn in as the 35th US president. At that moment Black press journalist Simeon Booker questioned why no Black cadet was in the color guard of the US Coast Guard Academy. JFK ordered a recruitment effort as a remedy. In April, Booker of *Ebony/Jet* magazines asked the president if he believed the White House News Photographers Association should continue to bar Blacks. "No, I don't," answered Kennedy. Therefore, the barrier fell.[53]

Patterson's act furthermore spurred Smith to initiate a crusade and goad Black major league players to demand acceptable lodging and an end to segregation in Florida when they reported for spring training a month later in February. "Why should a Negro baseball star making a salary of $50,000 per year submit to conditions which a White rookie making $7,000 would not stand for?" Smith wrote. He did not name names but called Black stars "fat cats" and "Uncle Toms," language he used sparingly.

This time he was prodding players because the 1954 Brown vs. Board of Education victory placed Florida's segregated customs on the wrong side of the law. Fifteen years ago, Jackie Robinson and a Black teammate ran through figurative rings of fire in navigating where to sleep, eat, and train in Florida. Smith concluded it was time for action. He did his part in writing a multipart series of articles that spurred positive change.[54]

***

Heavyweight champion Sonny Liston was scorned and feared by much of the public, but did he deserve to be harassed, asked Wendell Smith in his October 20, 1962, Sports Beat column. While driving in along sprawling Fairmount Park, Liston was stopped by Philadelphia Police and charged with driving too slowly. Liston's explanation: he didn't realize he wasn't permitted to drive with care and safety. "Fearless shakedown experts," wrote Smith, "notified the newspapers that they had nabbed the nation's No. 1 criminal."

Meanwhile in New York, the joint legislative committee on boxing demanded that Liston appear and testify "on claims by ex-sparring partner Cortez Stewart," reported Smith, who called the probe phony because the State Athletic Commission expressed no interest in taking action against the fighter.[55]

***

June 22, 1937, should be an unforgettable Black advancement date, asserted Wendell Smith in his September 21, 1963, Sports Beat column. Joe Louis knocked out James J. Braddock in the eighth round 26 years ago, to win the heavyweight title. Louis, 23 at the time, did not win easily in Chicago. Braddock, the aging and clever veteran, knocked Louis to the canvas. Much of the Comiskey Park crowd gasped.

Louis was stunned too, but he got up, dusted resin off his trunks, and hammered Braddock with repeated left jabs for at least five rounds until the opponent succumbed. "He'll be a great champion," Braddock predicted. "He'll be good for boxing in and out of the ring."

Smith called the gracious loser's words prophetic. Louis went on to defend his title 25 times Despite performing in what was the "red light district of sports," wrote Smith, quoting fellow sports scribe Jimmy Cannon. Louis' behavior and image were above reproach. Smith wrote that before a fight in New York, mobsters approached Louis' managers and proposed that Louis take a dive: "Let [Primo] Carnera win this one," they advised, "and then, when he wins the title again, we'll give you a shot at it." The managers John Roxborough and Julian Black answered that there would be no deals.

That choice set Louis' dramatic journey. After knocking out Carnera, Louis famously was knocked out by Max Schmeling in a spectacular upset. Louis recovered by beating Braddock then getting a rematch with

Schmeling, whom he knocked out in one round. Louis, Smith wrote, "did as much for Negro advancement – particularly in sports – as the Rev. Martin Luther King and the late Medgar Evers of Mississippi accomplished in the field of civil rights."

This was not hyperbole. Louis was the strong, silent type, but when he spoke up the words were powerful like his fists. When Lt. Jackie Robinson was under attack for allegedly being "uppity" or insubordinate, Louis behind the scenes spoke on Robinson's behalf.

And on more than one occasion, Louis shamed major league baseball owners, asking "How come you don't have any Negro players on your team?" rendering bosses sheepishly silent. Robinson survived his tumultuous military stint and made it to big league baseball. Once the Brooklyn Dodger opened the door, Black players who immediately followed made the grade and excelled based on ability.

"It was Louis," wrote Smith, "who set the stage for baseball's racial revolution by virtue of his conduct and impact on the American public."[56]

***

When Wendell Smith filed his August 3, 1963, Sports Beat column, brutish heavyweight champion Sonny Liston disposed of Floyd Patterson, who Smith described as "the strange, introvert and frail-hearted ex-titleholder." Liston's next challenger was Cassius Clay, a precocious 21-year-old. For a writer like Smith, Clay was great material. He was colorful, unlike the sanctimonious Patterson, and a long line of dull, undistinguished fighters. Clay declared that Liston "is a disgrace as a fighter," and "uglier than a bear drinking hot vinegar," reported Smith.

But quotability and championship-caliber boxing were different things, Smith discerned. He had doubts that the "Louisville Lip" and "Filibuster Fighter" could beat Liston. By trash-talking, Smith believed Clay made the same mistake as Tony "Two Ton" Galento, who bragged that he would "knock Joe Louis flatter than a two-day-old glass of beer." Louis listened, and when it was time to fight, bopped Galento with a left hook, then destroyed him. The challenger faded from memory. Was such a fate awaiting Clay?

Liston was universally disliked. For shock value *Esquire* magazine dressed the boxer in a Santa Claus suit for a holiday photo shoot and convinced him to balance a six-year-old White girl on his knee. "The scariest man coming down your chimney this Christmas" was the cover story title. Outraged readers canceled their subscriptions.[57]

"Even if people don't like me," said Liston after whipping Patterson, "they may as well get used to me as heavyweight champion. They're going to have to tolerate me for a long time."

Smith wrote that many fans wanted to wish Clay onto the heavyweight throne, but fight veteran sources said lean, young, Clay wasn't ready. "Clay doesn't know how to fight," a trainer told Smith. "He can't punch to the body; he stands up too straight and he had no defense. He refuses to keep his hands up, and as far as I can determine, he hasn't learned a thing since he fought in the Olympics." Soon, fight enthusiasts would learn the verdict of the Clay-Liston collision.[58]

Cassius Clay proved Wendell Smith and other experts wrong. The challenger dethroned champion Sonny Liston in Miami on February 25, 1964. Liston, a menacing seven-to-one favorite who was guaranteed 40% of all net revenues, quit at the start of the seventh round.

Although Liston was widely despised and would not be missed as an ex-champion, the World Boxing Association was not happy with Clay. The WBA recognized every US state except two as bona fide members and shunned Clay as champion, plus Liston as No. 1 contender. The outlier states were New York and Massachusetts. Instead, the fight for the heavyweight champion was scheduled on March 5 between Ernest Terrell and Eddie Machen.

It was Wendell Smith's turn to ridicule the WBA's hollow and opaque logic. The WBA wanted to eliminate Clay because he supposedly violated a no-return bout clause, Smith reported.[59] Clay was stricken with a hernia complication on the eve of a rematch with Liston in Boston. The WBA then fell back to a second excuse to block Clay: He failed to conduct himself with the dignity expected of a heavyweight champion.

Smith demolished such nonsense in print. Yes, young Clay immodestly rants and raves in public, however, that annoyance could be solved: "you should find a fighter who belts him in the mouth hard enough, and often enough, to take the title. Championships are won in the ring ... not outside of it."

Smith also said what WBA officials would not: They were uncomfortable that Clay associated with the Nation of Islam, Black Muslim separatists who at that time made most Americans uncomfortable, including Smith. Still, that was not just cause to sideline a legitimate champion and attempt to manufacture a "synthetic" one.

On May 25, 1965, in Lewiston, Maine, the former Cassius Clay, self-identifying as Muhammad Ali, defeated Liston in a first-round knockout rematch.[60]

Ten months after insisting that Cassius Clay was heavyweight champion until beaten in ring, Wendell Smith in his December 11, 1965, Sports Beat column wrote that skeptics were taking Clay, aka Muhammad Ali seriously. Smith used most of his column to quote Ali's description of how he defeated former champion Floyd Patterson. Some writers called Ali's punishment of Patterson sadistic and added he could have knocked the man out in the early rounds.

Ali told Smith, "Patterson had no business in the ring with me. All he had was a big heart. I tried to knock him out in the fifth round and again in the sixth. He took a terrible beating but stayed on his feet. I admired him for that and let up on him."

To the critics, Ali answered, "I can't do anything right for them. They don't like me because I talk too much and am right so often. If I had knocked Patterson out in the first or second round, they would have rapped me for taking advantage of him. So, I let him go. I was nice to him in that I didn't put him in the deep freeze early." Wendell Smith well aware that the boxer self-identified as Muhammadcenveo

Ali, chose to ID to man by his birth and new name.[61,62,63,64,65,66,67,68,69]

THE ANTI-JACKIE

During the 1950s, race made the female athletic phenom Althea Gibson a political paradox, a godsend, and kryptonite all at once. Sam Lacy and Wendell Smith experienced the challenges of covering the tennis champion. Except for sports competition, Gibson was the anti-Jackie Robinson. She said she was not pining to serve as a representative of racial progress; Gibson just wanted to win.

Furthermore, Gibson was wary – often justifiably – of the press. Writers pried into her family upbringing, which the tennis star guarded, and more over there was obsession about Gibson's tomboyish appearance, her romantic encounters, and whether she was lesbian or queer. Also, Gibson had to cope with instances of patriarchy and sexism, especially from the Black Press. The whirlwind spinning around Gibson made her appear at times arrogant, haughty, and unfriendly. Or it was very likely Gibson created a perimeter so she could block out the noise in order focus on playing championship tennis at the highest level.

While Jackie Robinson broke racial barriers in America's national pastime, the game of the masses, Gibson, a Negro daughter of the deep South and later Harlem streets, was groomed for a social game of the White elites. She was largely unwelcome, despite Gibson's frequent denials and dissembling to the contrary. Understandably, she was willing to go along to get along until she could achieve her athletic goals. Gibson was spotted on Smith and Lacy's respective radar while a student-athlete at Florida A&M College (now university) in 1950. For years she was mentored by the Black-owned American Tennis Association, whose members where the Black elite professionals (lawyers, doctors, politicians) who were shut out of mainstream tennis clubs. ATA sponsored their own tournaments, many of them at historic Black campuses in the south that included Hampton institute in Virginia, Tuskegee Institute in Alabama, and Florida A&M in Tallahassee. By 1950, ATA leaders believed Gibson's talent made her eligible to compete in the US Open tournament at Forest Hills, New York. To qualify, Gibson began playing in pre-qualifying matches against White competition.

Gibson was under scrutiny. Tennis was a sport where there was social mixing at dances and banquets that could lead to relationships and marriage. Gibson's ATA chaperones counseled her not to fraternize. She complied.

While in Chicago, Gibson ate dinner at a private residence when Smith of the *Chicago American* appeared, unannounced. Gibson did not rush to finish dinner. Smith waited. When Gibson appeared, he was pleased with her appearance and painted word pictures for his readers. Smith found Gibson's summer smock attractive because it was "short and sleeveless and dangled from her trim body in a casual sort of way." At 5-feet, 10 ½ inches, Smith reported she was a "well-proportioned 130 pounds" with "marvelously efficient arms" of a "smooth bronze color" that was only "slightly muscular," while her legs were "like two columns of polished mahogany."

Combined, Smith assessed Gibson, 23, as "a handsome woman with an abundance of personal charm." Smith asked Gibson if she was dating anyone. "I haven't had time to think of boys or marriage," she answered. "All my time has been devoted to tennis. I eat and sleep the game and when I go to bed, I dream of playing at Forest Hills. The game of tennis absorbs my very life."

Smith's objectification of Gibson, sexist and cringeworthy by 21st-century standards, was purposeful in the last year of the 1940s. The lesbian athlete stereotype was alive then in the public consciousness. Smith portraying Gibson as feminine, attractive, and physically appealing signaled that she was heterosexual, an acceptable female athlete, and a normal woman.

Three weeks later in August, the USLTA announced that Gibson qualified to be among the 52 invited to play in the US Open at Forest Hills. White daily newspapers signaled shock in its headlines: "Title Tennis Admits First Negro, a Girl," from the *New York Times*, and in the *New York Herald Tribune*, "New York Negro Girl Will Enter National Tennis Championship." Jackie Robinson's 1947 major league debut was muted in the New York daily press; however, Gibson's arrival was loud like blaring trumpets.

In the Black press, Gibson was a conflicted source of pride and patriarchal resentment. Unabashed Gibson fan Sam Lacy of the *Baltimore*

Afro-American wrote a celebratory profile saying her debut would mark, "the first time in history that a colored girl has been given a shot for a world championship in tennis." At the *Philadelphia Tribune*, the editors churlishly concluded that "the door will be open from now on to other qualified women players of color." Gibson's success and historic first were of little use or meaning to Black men and boys, concluded *Tribune* leaders.

Whatever people thought of Gibson, an amateur competitor, what mattered was her performance on the courts. Gibson won her opening match against Barbara Knapp of Birmingham, England. Gibson's next round opponent was Louise Brough, 1947 Forest Hills champion, and 1950s Wimbledon champ. Gibson, leading 7-6 in the third set of the match, was one game short of winning, then a dramatic thunderstorm forced postponement. When play resumed the next day, Gibson's calm and concentration abandoned her and in eleven minutes she lost to Brough 7-9. Nevertheless, when Gibson returned to Florida A&M for her sophomore year her effort at one of the four leading global tennis championships was praised. She "pioneered for her race in the stodgy atmosphere that belongs to the prim West Side Tennis Club," wrote Lacy. Meanwhile the *Chicago Defender's* editors credited Gibson with "[striking] a blow for democracy ... that is still echoing in the snooty precincts of country clubs and exclusive sports associations throughout the land."

As Gibson pierced the rarefied tennis establishment, she chafed from the obligations expected of her. Gibson had become a symbol and commodity to be used for civil rights advancement, or as Cold War soft power, an instrument to counter Soviet Union criticism that America oppressed its Black people. When Gibson complained to Black elders that she would rather play tennis and not serve as a civil rights torch bearer, she was reminded that her comfortable travel, lodging, and wardrobes were underwritten by the civil rights community, so don't be an ingrate was the message. Still, instinctively rebellious Gibson considered quitting college so she could turn pro and probably make money and have independence. Jack Gaither, Florida A&M's athletic director and renowned football coach, insisted Gibson, a physical education major, finish college. Gibson would storm out of such exchanges with the coach, then return and heed her trusted mentor.

During the early 1950s, Gibson made incremental gains on the White pro-am tennis circuit. She ventured out of the United States and competed in the Caribbean championship in Jamaica. Stateside, Gibson made an impression in Jim Crow-Miami at the Good Neighbor Tournament. She was the first Black player to enter a competition organized by Whites in the South. Gibson was allowed to stay at the Admiral Hotel, which previously was off-limits to crossover Black entertainers Ella Fitzgerald, Harry

Belafonte, Louis Armstrong, Sammy Davis Jr., and Nat "King" Cole. Gibson however became lonely during her stay and switched to the Black-owned Mary Elizabeth Hotel.

In summer 1957, Gibson made history: She became the first Black to win the women's single title at Wimbledon in England. Weeks after Wimbledon, Wendell Smith criticized Gibson for her alleged rude behavior toward reporters after completing at a tournament in Chicago. "Her curt manner and insulting responses to friendly writers of all papers in Chicago justifiably won her the dubious title of 'Tennis Queen and Bum of the Court,'" Smith wrote. "It might be wise for Althea to take stock of this time and realize that while she wields a mighty racket, she is still only a tennis player and nothing more."

The *Pittsburgh Courier* ran an editor's note with the column that said Gibson told reporter Evelyn Cunningham that she feared the friends she gained after she became famous would keep her from the friends who had helped her achieve success. Smith complained about the note attached to his column to the editor Percival Prattis. Prattis told Smith he did it because he had to contend with falling circulation that could cause the paper's eventual purchase by Sengstacke of the *Chicago Defender* chain. Prattis explained in a letter to Smith:

> Althea is on top. She won at Wimbledon. She won at Chicago. She won in the Wightman Cup matches. She won the Essex tournament. She's riding the crest of victory, so what are you gonna do? She's an IDOL. When your article came in, I had to say to myself, "Well, Wendell is smattering one of our idols. Our readers won't like that, no matter how true what he writes is." So I dutifully turn to my typewriter and peck out an editor's note, designed to soften [just a wee bit] the blow you were delivering. Please believe me when I write you that the next week, we were bombarded with letters – against your article. We used the one from New York to symbolize the avalanche.
>
> As a personality, I think the gal is lousy. I went to a dinner and cocktail party where she was. I introduced myself and tried to start a conversation. I got exactly nowhere.

For the rest of Althea Gibson's life, she was an enigma, a champion multi-sport athlete, a pop singer, New Jersey's athletic commissioner, and a Black woman who alternately complained that she did not quite receive the recognition she deserved, but also said she should not be obligated to serve a civil rights hero. Smith meanwhile felt the sting of accessing a particular sports star critically.

The end of the 1940s, the entire 1950s decade, and the early 1960s were a transitional period for sportswriters Wendell Smith and Sam Lacy. The era began with a near-exclusive focus on baseball, then shifted dramatically to boxing because multiple Black fighters were successful and popular with Black and White fans.

Althea Gibson's emergence as tennis champion brought Black women into national and global sports conversations and was a transformative phenomenon, chronicled by Smith and Lac

Notes

1. Wendell Smith, *Pittsburgh Courier*, August 23, 1947.
2. "The story behind Jackie Robinson's moving testimony before the House Un-American activities committee," Eric Nussbaum, *Time magazine*, March 24, 2000 https://time.com/5808543/jackie-robinson-huac/
3. Rickford, Russell, "1944–1949: The Black Left," from "Four Hundred Souls: A Community History of African America, 1619–2019," New York, One World, 2021, p 313.
4. Robinson, Jackie, Duckett, Al, "I Never Had It Made: An Autobiography," New York, G.P. Putnam's Sons, 1972.
5. Rickford, "The Black Left," p 315. Wintz, Cary, ed., "Harlem Speaks: A Living History of the Harlem Renaissance," Naperville, Illinois, Sourcebooks, 2007, pp 361–383.
6. Faulkner, "Great Time Coming," p 202.
7. Robinson, "My Own Story," p 171.
8. baseballhall.org.
9. Kennedy, Kosta, "True," pp 76–77.
10. Wendell Smith's Sports Beat, "The Commissioner Talks Shop," *Pittsburgh Courier*, April 23, 1949; Kashatus, "Jackie & Campy," pp 118–119.
11. "Jackie and Campy," p 132; baseball-reference.com https://www.baseball-reference.com/bullpen/Chris_Van_Cuyk
12. Wendell Smith's Sports Beat, *Pittsburgh Courier*, March 19, 1949, p 10.
    Holtzman, Jerome, "Jackie Robinson and the Great American pastime: And the man behind him," *Chicago Tribune*, April 11, 1993, pp B4, 5, 15.
13. Smith, Wendell, "The Jackie Robinson I Knew," *Pittsburgh Courier*, via *Chicago Sun-Times*, November 4, 1972, p 9.
14. Pifer. Michael Scott, Marsh, Michael, "The Wendell Smith Reader," p 121.
15. Lacy, Sam, Baltimore Afro-American, April 14, 1949; "Jackie & Campy," pp 123–125.
16. Kashatus, "Jackie & Campy, p 130.
17. Kashatus, "Jackie & Campy," pp 136–160.
18. Durocher and Linn, "Nice Guys Finish Last," pp 208–210; Irvin and Riley, "Nice Guys Finish First," pp 146–147.
19. Kashatus interview with Irvin, "Jackie & Campy," p 150.
20. Kashatus, "Jackie & Campy," pp 35, 41–42.
21. Swaine, Rick, "The Integration of the New York Giants," 1951 New York Giants Essays, https://sabr.org/journal/article/the-integration-of-the-new-york-giants/
22. Madden, "1954," p 100.
23. Tan, Cecilia, "Elston Howard," Society for American Baseball Research.
24. Wolinsky, Russell, 2004, "Vic Power: 'Power to the People,'".
25. Madden, "1954," pp 99–101.
26. Smith, "Plenty of Jobs for Negro Ball Players …" Pittsburgh Courier, December 29, 1949.
27. Smith, "Teams Now Find It Necessary to Sign Negroes …" Pittsburgh Courier, May 23, 1952.
28. Madden, "1954," pp 232–250.

29. Gilliam previously played for the Negro League Baltimore Elite Giants https://thisdayinbaseball.com/jim-gilliam-page/
30. Bennett, "Before the Mayflower," p 589.
31. Deford, Frank, "The Boxer and the Blonde: Billy Conn Won the Girl But Lost the Fight," Sports Illustrated, February 13, 2015.
32. Smith, "Louis Amateur king; Rhodes tops pros in Courier meet," Pittsburgh Courier, August 16, 1947, p 14.
33. Ibid.
34. Ibid.
35. Hauser, Thomas, "Sugar Ray Robinson Revisited," Muhammad Ali: His Life and Times, New York, Touchstone, 1991.
36. Dorinson, "The Black Athlete as Hero," p 22; Lacy, "Fighting for Fairness," p 59.
37. Lacy, "Fighting for Fairness," p 100. Dan Parker.
38. Lacy, "Fighting for Fairness," p 107.
39. Smith, "Fight Mob Member Talks to Himself," Pittsburgh Courier, March 12, 1949.
40. Ibid.
41. The IBC, formed by James D. Norris and Arthur M. Wirth in 1949, promoted bouts at Madison Square Garden, the Polo Grounds, Yankee Stadium, St. Nicholas Arena, Chicago Stadium, and Detroit Olympia. Boxrec.com.
42. Lacy, Baltimore Afro-American, "From A to Z," June 11, 1949.
43. Smith, "Mr. Irvin, fight promoter," Pittsburgh Courier, August 22, 1949.
44. Smith, Pittsburgh Courier, January 26, 1952.
45. Smith, Pittsburgh Courier, August 25, 1956, "Baker or Jackson to fight Archie."
46. Smith, Pittsburgh Courier, December 31, 1956.
47. Smith, Pittsburgh Courier, January 12, 1957; Pifer, Wendell Smith Reader, pp 194–195.
48. Smith, Pittsburgh Courier, January 3, 1959.
49. Smith, Pittsburgh Courier, July 18, 1959.
50. Smith, Sports Beat, Pittsburgh Courier, Why Do Boxing Champs Go Broke? Courier, January 18, 1959.
51. Sam Lacy, "For Floyd or against him?" From A to Z, Baltimore Afro-American, May 9, 1959.
52. Ibid.
53. Booker, "Shocking the Conscience," p 174.
54. Smith, "Time for diamond stars to follow in footsteps of Patterson's fight against bigotry," Pittsburgh Courier, January 28, 1961.
55. Smith, "Cops Stooges vs. Liston," Pittsburgh Courier, October 20, 1962.
56. Smith, Pittsburgh Courier, June 22, 1963.
57. Cosgrove, Stuart, "Sonny Liston – The Santa That Scared America," bigissue.com, December 19, 2019.
58. Smith, "Clay is Next in Line to Feel Wrath of Sonny Liston," Pittsburgh Courier, August 3, 1963.
59. Smith, "Clay is Still Champion Until Someone Beats Him," Pittsburgh Courier, January 16, 1965.
60. Ashe, "A Hard Road to Glory," Volume Three, pp 93–97.
61. Smith, "Muhammad No Longer a Laughing Matter," Pittsburgh Courier, December 11, 1965.
62. Brown, Ashley, "Serving Herself: The Life and Times of Althea Gibson," New York, Oxford, 2023, p 198.
63. Smith, "There's Gold in Them Thar Forest Hills," Pittsburgh Courier, July 29, 1950, p 11. Brown, "Serving Herself," pp 102–103, n73, n74
64. Brown, "Serving Herself," p 103.

65. Brown, "Serving Herself," pp 112–113, n108–109. Lacy, "Althea Gibson, A Profile," editorial, "Tennis Comes of Age," *Philadelphia Tribune*, August 16, 1950, p 4.
66. Brown, "Serving Herself," pp 117, n8, 9.
67. Lacy, "From A to Z," Afro, April 7, 1951, p 16; Lacy, "Vanquished Rival Lauds Althea Gibson," Afro, April 7, 1951, p 16. Brown, "Serving Herself," pp 124–125, n42, 43.
68. Smith, "Has Net Queen Althea Gibson Gone High Hat?" *Pittsburgh Courier*, July 27, 1957, p 24.
69. P. L. Prattis letter to Wendell Smith, August 20, 1957. The letter is part of the Wendell Smith file, courtesy of the National Baseball Hall of Fame and Museum.

CHAPTER 6

WENDELL SMITH AND CHICAGO TV
Sam Lacy's Long-Distance Run to the 21st Century

In early 1961, nearly 15 years after Jackie Robinson arrived in Florida for spring training and endured segregation and racism, Major League Baseball's racial climate changed dramatically. Black and Brown players on the playing field had become accustomed to being treated as first-class citizens. However, about a month before spring training at Florida training sites, Negro players anticipated humiliating, Southern-style segregation, and told reporter Wendell Smith they no longer wanted to be treated as second-class citizens at lodging and at restaurants. That led to a major story on January 23 in the *Chicago American.*

"The Negro player resents the fact that he is not permitted to stay in the same hotels with his teammates during spring training," Smith wrote, "and is protesting the fact that he cannot eat in the same restaurants, nor enjoy other privileges. At the moment he is not belligerent. He is merely seeking help and sympathy, and understanding, and a solution."[1]

Southern cities such as St. Louis, Baltimore, and Washington were initially required by local laws to be segregated, but local custom led to segregated hotels in Philadelphia, Chicago, and other northern cities. By 1961 this had stopped in most Major League cities. Segregation in Florida meant inconveniences for Blacks. Often, they were housed at least a mile from their White teammates, which required extra arrangements to get to the practice fields. Furthermore, if the Black players had wives and children, the players had to make additional segregated accommodations for their families. But segregation in the South during spring training was more than inconvenient, it was humiliating, degrading, frightening, and hateful. Smith reported that approximately 100 Negro players were

DOI: 10.4324/9781003283928-8

expected to train at camps in Florida, Arizona, and California. In most cases the western venues allowed entire teams to lodge under the same roof regardless of race; however, in 1961 Florida locations became stridently against integration.[2] The Chicago White Sox trained in Sarasota, Florida. Its Black players had to lodge in a separate motel. Meanwhile, the Chicago Cubs, based in Mesa, Arizona, were kept together; however, if there were exhibition games across the border in Texas, the Black players had to scout for places to stay overnight.

Milwaukee Brave Hank Aaron's face appeared in Smith's front-page article. The son of the Deep South was an all-star, MVP, and World Series champion. The article quoted star Black players, but not by name. Said one, "We think we should enjoy equality the year around and intend to get it. We are tired of staying in flophouses and eating in second-rate restaurants during spring training. If we are good enough to play with a team, then we should be good enough to share the same facilities and accommodations as the other players both in spring and summer."

The Black players who spoke anonymously wanted help from their employers, the team owners. Smith wrote that baseball owners were sympathetic but acting with caution because the South was rebelling against the enforcement of mass integration. Smith did not urge all MLB teams to move to Arizona and California for spring training; however, a Negro player told the writer, "Major league clubs not only spend thousands of dollars in the cities where they train, but they are responsible for luring millions of dollars to those towns in tourist trade. Very few towns would be willing to lose that revenue if the owners threatened to move their clubs to California or other places where there aren't as many racialized situations. This situation can be worked out. It must be worked out."[3]

In February 1960 four North Carolina A&T college students launched the lunch counter sit-in movement. By March there had been sit-ins at lunch counters in other North Carolina cities, as well as in South Carolina, Tennessee, Maryland, Alabama Virginia, Florida, Texas, Louisiana, Arkansas, and Georgia.[4] The previous fall, during the 1960 presidential campaign, Martin Luther King Jr. was arrested at an Atlanta sit-in and then sent to the Georgia State Prison to serve a four-month sentence. Democratic presidential candidate John F. Kennedy called Coretta Scott King to express his concern. After eight days King was released from prison on bond. Political observers said Kennedy's call increased the number of Black voters, who helped JFK's 1960 win over Republican candidate Richard M. Nixon. And on January 11, 1961, a riot occurred at the University of Georgia because of the enrollment of two Black students, Charlayne Hunter and Hamilton Holmes. Both students were suspended, but a federal judge ordered Hunter and Holmes reinstatement. They returned to class on January 16.

On February 6, 1961, Smith's *Chicago's American* column carried a photo of Cincinnati Reds outfielder Vada Pinson drinking from a segregated water fountain labeled "Colored" in Tampa, Florida. Yet Smith wrote he was happy to report "as a result of that [January 23] story, many constructive steps have been taken to remedy what everybody agrees was an intolerable situation." They included:

- White Sox owner Bill Veeck secured lodging for the entire team at Miami's Biscayne Terrace Hotel when the team visited to play two exhibition games. Veeck also began negotiations with the Sarasota Terrace Hotel, the team's headquarters, to accept Black players Minnie Minoso, Al Smith, and four others;
- Florida Governor Farris Bryant supported the integration campaign and said he did not know of any state laws that would be violated if Negro players are integrated. Bryant also said he believed "in the freedom of association";
- At least three other baseball executives said they supported integrated lodging for teams.[5]

Meanwhile a hotel owner rejected the propositions. "When either the Yankees or the Cardinals, or both, feel the situation has developed so they must insist on housing all of their personnel in the same hotel, then the Yankees and the Cardinals should look for other hotels," said C.H. Alberding, president of the firm that operated the two St. Peterburg hotels. Kansas City Athletics general manager Frank Lane said, "if it has been accepted in the past that Negroes use different hotels, then we have to subscribe to what has been done in the past." However, Lane added, "We won't play in cities where Negroes can't play, and we won't have any working arrangements with teams that do not accept Negro players."[6]

Milwaukee Braves Executive Vice President Birdie Tebbetts endorsed a statement by National League President Warren Giles that he had: "never heard one word of complaint on the subject from any ballplayer, White or Colored." Hank Aaron, who had emerged as one of the two best players on the team, publicly disagreed with Tebbetts. Describing the accommodations for Black Braves in Bradenton, Florida, Aaron said, "There is really only room for four men, and last year, there were eight or ten living there. Beds have to be put in the hall and if players don't hustle to the bathroom in the morning, the last man up doesn't get any hot water."[7] Unlike the conspiracy of silence in the early 1900s, there were signs of incremental progress for Blacks or at least debate about conditions.

In early April, Smith launched a series of stories about the conditions Black baseball players endured during spring training. "To the average White player, the six weeks spent here training is merely a blink of a pleasant time in a ballplayer's life," wrote Smith, "but to his Negro team-mate it is an eternity of humiliations and frustrations."

"In the case of the White Sox, for example, the seven Negro players on the squad – Minnie Minoso, Al Smith, Juan Pizarro, Frank Barnes, Floyd Robinson, Stan Johnson and Winston Brown – live in an isolated world of second-class citizenship."[8] The Black players and many of their White teammates were opposed to the restrictions imposed upon them by segregation and discrimination in Florida. The Black players were also aware and appreciated the efforts by team owner Bill Veeck to effect change. The White Sox were under contract to train in Sarasota for three more years. As for lodging, the Negro members of the White Sox, as well as writer Smith, were refused accommodations at the Sarasota Terrace Hotel, the camp headquarters. The Sarasota Chamber of Commerce tried to persuade hotel owner James Ewell to accept all team members regardless of race. Ewell said to do so would be contrary to the customs of the community and furthermore jeopardize his position as one of the south's leading building contractors: "My clients throughout Florida and other sections of the south would reject my business, I believe."

Because Ewell refused to budge, Veeck moved the Black players to the DeSoto motel, located a mile from the Sarasota Terrace. The DeSoto was owned by a White, Jewish couple, Edward and Lillian Wachtel, liberals who lived in New York before moving to Florida in 1956. Unlike the flophouse conditions Black major leagues suffered for years or sometimes complained about, the DeSoto was comfortable. The teammates occupied four units, two men to a room. They were allowed to sleep and eat at the motel. The club provided a woman cook and maid service. Veeck rented two cars to transport the players to the ballpark each day.

The players' presence at the DeSoto integrated the motel, which was situated in a White neighborhood, two miles beyond the borderline of Sarasota's Black community. The Wachtels endured shunning and threats of violence from neighbors because of their choice. Edward Wachtel told Smith, "I accepted these young men because I do not believe in segregation. I am fighting it here in Sarasota in my own quiet way. I have lost some of my most intimate friends, but that is the price a man must pay sometimes for doing what he believes is right. The ball players were perfect gentlemen, and I was honored to have them as tenants. There isn't a neighbor around here who can point an accusing finger at them."[9] Still, people were furious that the Wachtels broke with the segregated customs: "People called us all hours of the day and demanded that we refuse them. They said that if we didn't, they would bomb us out. We also received calls from men who said they were members of the Ku Klux Klan, and they were going to kill us. Naturally, my wife and I were frightened, especially when they told us they were going to bomb the motel. But we decided that we would take the chance."[10]

No doubt, because of determined effort and sacrifices by some supportive Whites, some Black players were experiencing incremental, positive change at Florida spring training. Yet as veteran White Sox outfielder Al Smith explained, the lodging experience was surreal: "It's like living in an isolation booth. We can look out and see everybody, but we can't join them."[11]

In a few weeks, the White Sox moved north to Chicago and began the regular baseball season. Smith had made a pioneering career advancement as one of the first Blacks to work as beat writer for a major league team. The *Chicago American* assigned him to cover the Sox during the late 1950s and through the early 1960s.[12]

Two months after the 1961 season ended, on December 1, the *Chicago American* New York-based correspondent Milton Gross praised Wendell Smith's spring training series for producing the following changes:

- The expansion New York Mets, scheduled to debut in spring 1962, contracted to house and feed all of their players at the Colonial Inn in St. Petersburg Beach. The New York Yankees were expected to have a similar arrangement at the Yankee Clipper motel in Fort Lauderdale. The Yankees left their longtime St. Petersburg base;
- The St. Louis Cardinals arranged to have all of their players together at the Skyway motel in St. Petersburg. The Milwaukee Braves moved the team living quarters from Bradenton to Palmetto, a nearby town, where Hank Aaron would be as welcome as fellow slugger Eddie Matthews, reported Gross.[13]
- The Baltimore Orioles, credited last spring for working toward complete integration during spring training, were to return to the same facility in Miami.

With the addition of the Mets and the other expansion, the Houston Colt 45s (later renamed the Astros), Major League Baseball was a 20-team organization. In 1961 the American league added two teams – the California Angels of Anaheim and the new Washington Senators – as the old ones moved to Minneapolis. Gross cautioned that at spring training "there will be fewer teams still hidebound to archaic segregation than those who have agreed for one reason or another a Negro who does the hitting, fielding and pitching is entitled to equal facilities for rest and nourishment which are made available to others." Still, change was undeniable.

A week later on December 9, Wendell Smith reported the Chicago White Sox organization announced it would buy a Florida hotel and end the racial segregation of its team. The Sarasota Terrace hotel was purchased for $500,000, Ed Short, general manager of the team, told Smith. The 200-room hotel was adjacent to Payne Field where the White Sox train. Arthur C. Allyn, president of the White Sox, said, "We purchased the Sarasota Terrace because we desire to house all of our players, regardless of race, under one roof. This means that our Negro players will no longer be segregated from the rest of the team."[14]

Smith's report noted that most of the major league teams that trained in Florida succeeded in arranging accommodations that integrated its teams. The exceptions were the Washington Senators (Pompano Beach); Minnesota Twins (Orlando); Detroit Tigers (Lakeland), and Kansas City Athletics (West Palm Beach).

***

Like Wendell Smith, Sam Lacy of the Baltimore *Afro-American* was reporting on the spring training story and its civil rights flashpoints. Player Bob Boyd of the Kansas City Athletics was the lone Black player on that team and was separated from teammates for lodging. "I don't like it any more than they would in my place," he told Lacy.[15] In 1961, Baltimore Orioles executive Lee MacPhail arranged for the team to be lodged under the same roof in Miami. Earl Robinson, who was seeking to make the team, declined and said he would continue to stay at the Blacks-only St. John Hotel. Lacy criticized the player. Lacy told Earl, "Other colored players throughout Florida are protesting separate housing, not because they have any driving urge to live with other races, but because they think their contribution to the game and their citizenship entitle them to equal treatment. It is unfortunate that you didn't wish to make their aim logical and their road easier." Earl Robinson answered Lacy: "My first objective is to make the club. That is why I came to spring training. I am convinced that my best chance to win a job rests with my ability to relax, in an atmosphere in which I am completely at ease."[16]

In 1961, Lacy turned his attention to other major sports that were about to face lodging disputes because of race. When the American Football League launched in 1960 with eight teams, two of them, the Dallas Texans and Houston Oilers, were in the Jim Crow South. That year the National Football League added the Dallas Cowboys to its lineup. When Cleveland Browns running back Jim Brown learned his team was going to Dallas to play the Cowboys, he told Lacy in May that because hotel and motel operators were on record saying separation would be enforced, "You can be sure that we [Brown, Bob Mitchell, A.D. Williams, Prentice Gault, and John Wooten] have no intention of accepting it. It wouldn't be right for us to do so in the face of the daily sacrifice being made by students all over the South in their sit-in demonstrations. We're together on this thing and I'm sure [coach] Paul Brown understands that we mean business and will do something about it." The Browns beat the Cowboys at Cleveland, 25-7 on October 1, 1961. Jim Brown did play when the Cleveland visited the Cowboys in Dallas on December 3. Brown scored two touchdowns and gained 86 yards running and caught four passes for 51 yards. Cleveland won 38-17.[17]

Lacy reported that over in the NBA, Boston Celtics star Bill Russell and Elgin Baylor, star of the Los Angeles Lakers, received assurances of league action to protect Black players from Dixiecrat insults. In 1959 Baylor refused to play an exhibition game in Charleston, West Virginia because the team's hotel refused rooms to him and teammates Tom Hawkins and Alex Ellis. Meanwhile Russell and several teammates suffered humiliating racial bans three years earlier during an exhibition game in North Carolina. Russell told Lacy that Celtics owner Walter Brown issued strict orders that no game should be scheduled where assurance of equal treatment wasn't guaranteed.[18]

Lacy kept a sharp eye on the emerging AFL. A notable aspect about the audacious challenger to the NFL that it was welcomed many Black players, especially those who played at Historically Black Colleges and Universities.[19] In 1963 Lineman Buc Buchanan from Grambling was the first-round pick of the Kansas City Chiefs (which had moved from Dallas and changed its name to the Chiefs). Lacy warned that disaster awaited the AFL, and NFL, teams that ignored the horrible treatment Black players often received in the South. In a 1961 column, Lacy alleged that AFL commissioner Joe Foss and the expected owner of an assumed franchise in New Orleans could be expected of "winking" at the racial customs in the Crescent City while making statements that there would be no problems. Lacy noted the older, more established NFL had made progress in confronting Jim Crow, partly by abandoning New Orleans, Columbia, South Carolina, Jackson, Mississippi, and Birmingham, Alabama as preseason exhibition game sites. In 1963 Lacy repeated his AFL warning before the all-stars were scheduled to play in New Orleans. When the players arrived at the start of 1965, they found the doors on Bourbon Street closed to them, they were rejected by cabs, and received other racial insults.[20] The rejection seemed odd because, at the start of the new year, New Orleans hosted the first completely integrated collegiate Sugar Bowl game without incident. The Black AFL stars – 21 of them – refused to play. The commissioner responded to their legitimate protest by moving the game to Houston.[21] New Orleans would eventually receive an NFL team, the Saints, in 1967.

Lacy kept up his monitoring and sniping of football's Jim Crow resistance. When NBC decided not to telecast the December 28, 1963, collegiate Blue-Gray game in Alabama, the *Montgomery Advertiser* in an editorial blasted the network's decision calling it "a studied chastisement of the state of Alabama, a punitive expedition against a state's social order. NBC does not care if it destroys the institution of the Blue-Gray game if it cannot get a mixed roster of players in Montgomery, it does not hesitate to blight the game." Lacy blustered back that editorial page editor Grover C. Hall and his cronies, "appear to feel that NBC shouldn't create this sort of problem 'on account of a few colored football players,'" and added, "the arguments are so full of holes that anyone who takes him seriously would insult him ... Only die-hard local segregationists are expected to swallow it, I'm sure."[22]

At the time of that newspaper skirmish, civil rights activity and resistance to it were at fever pitches. That April, Martin Luther King Jr. opened an anti-segregation campaign in Birmingham, Alabama that resulted in the arrests of 2,000 demonstrators, including King. In June, an assassin murdered Medgar Evers, 37, NAACP field secretary in Mississippi, in front of his home in Jackson. In August an interracial mass of 250,000 participated in the March on Washington. Two weeks later four Black girls were murdered in the bombing of Sixteenth Street Baptist Church in Birmingham. And in January 1964, the 24th Amendment to the US Constitution eliminated poll tax requirements in federal elections.[23]

In the sports world, new professional franchises were opening in southern cities. Atlanta gained the NFL Falcons in 1966, the NBA Hawks in 1968, and the MLB Braves moved from Milwaukee. Miami acquired the AFL Dolphins in 1966, and New Orleans became the home of the NFL Saints in 1967. The three cities joined Dallas and Houston, which acquired big league sports teams in 1962 and 1960. Black athletes played on all of these teams. Working and being treated as first-class citizens were incrementally becoming socially acceptable.

***

In 1963, after 15 years at the *Chicago American*, Wendell Smith departed to work in television news. He joined WBBM-TV Chicago (CBS) to cover news and sports. The *American* printed a story in which Smith said, "I'm certainly sorry to leave *Chicago's American* where I've had many pleasant associations. This is an opportunity, though, which I could hardly afford to pass up. The *American* afforded me a wonderful opportunity. It was gratifying to be accepted as one of the staff right from the start — and that acceptance has never wavered through all the years I've been on the paper."[24] Nine days later sports editor Leo Fischer wrote, "No metropolitan daily had ever hired a Negro sportswriter before and it's no secret that one matter of concern was the kind of acceptance he'd [Smith] get on assignments. It turned out to be no problem. Not for Wendell Smith. Not for us."[25]

In February 1964 Smith interviewed Alabama Governor George Wallace for the WBBM panel show "Target: News." At his 1963 inauguration Wallace declared "segregation now, segregation tomorrow, segregation forever." Later that year he stood in from of the University of Alabama's Foster Auditorium in a failed attempt to stop the enrollment of two Black students. Smith maintained a professional demeanor while interviewing Wallace. After the show, the governor shook the newsman's hand and said, "When you come to Alabama, be sure to stop in and see me!"[26]

In June 1964, Smith moved on to WGN-Chicago, owned by the Tribune Company. The station call letters immodestly meant "World's Greatest Newspaper." Jack Brickhouse, the longtime WGN sportscaster, said, "Wendell was really the ideal addition to the staff at the time. The rest of us, it seemed, were always on the road with the Cubs, the [Black] Hawks [hockey], the Bears, or covering college football, or a basketball game. We needed someone who wasn't traveling to cover the sports scene in Chicago, someone who knew sports and knew how to communicate. At the same time, the WGN News staff needed about 'half' a reporter. So, initially, Wendell was shared between the sports and news departments."[27]

Chuck Shriver, who worked at WGN, said Smith successfully made the adjustment to writing for TV news: "He wrote most of his own scripts. He was an excellent writer. He picked it up very quickly." WGN producer Jack Rosenberg coached Smith on how to speak in front of a live camera. This mattered because, at WBBM, Smith at times did not appear on camera, and instead posed a question to a subject and positioned his microphone to record the answer. "It took him a little bit of time to get comfortable," said Shriver.[28]

Smith did catch on. Less than a month into his new job, WGN dispatched him to the federal courthouse in Chicago to cover jury deliberations for the trial of Jimmy Hoffa, president of the International Brotherhood of Teamsters, accused of misuse of the union's pension fund. The jury convicted Hoffa that July.

On March 13, 1965, Wendell Smith produced "Let Freedom Ring: The Negro in Chicago." The show presented the social and economic gains made by Blacks in Chicago. "Let Freedom Ring" included footage of the predominantly Black institutions Provident Hospital and Supreme Life Insurance Company. Smith interviewed *Chicago Defender* Publisher John Sengstacke, and Chicago Urban League Director Edwin C. "Bill"

Berry. The documentary showed Blacks working at Sears, Illinois Bell, and O'Hare Airport, examples of advancement in white-collar and semi-skilled employment.[29] A month later, on April 19, Smith was tasked to do the interviews for "Decade with Daley" commemorating the tenth anniversary of Chicago Mayor Richard J. Daley's election. Smith interviewed Daley and his wife Eleanor "Sis" Daley at their home. The special marked the first time the couple allowed TV cameras into their home. Smith also accompanied the mayor on a helicopter tour of the city. Bob Manewith, news director at that time, explained why Smith interviewed Daley: "Our City Hall reporter, Don Harris, did not get along with Mayor Daley. Wendell could put him at ease by talking sports, particularly White Sox baseball. Daley was a devoted fan. The mayor had a reputation for being no friend of African Americans and disdaining their abilities. Sending Wendell was sending a message."[30]

In 1967 Smith was the first WGN reporter, said Hogan, to cover the Richard Speck murder story. Between July 13 and 14, 1966, Speck killed eight student nurses by stabbing, strangling, or slashing them in their dormitory on Chicago's south side. A jury convicted Speck of murder the following year. He died in prison in 1991.[31] In early 1967 Smith became sports anchor of WGN's 10 p.m. broadcast. When John Drury was hired to anchor the newscast, the show expanded from 15 to 25 minutes. Paul Logan, a columnist for *The Herald*, a suburban Chicago daily, called Smith a terrible announcer:

> Wendell seems to mispronounce at least one sports name each night. And many times, he repeats the mistake on the same show which is uncalled for. Even if he gets the name right, his voice is atrocious. His style is as ragged as the day he began announcing, nearly seven years ago! The only good part of the show are the taped highlights, but he butchers them sometimes too.[32]

Brickhouse, Smith's colleague, offered an alternate take: "He didn't have the most professional broadcasting voice in history. You paid attention to the editorial content of what he was saying. And he was an excellent reporter. He knew how to report. If he said that 39 runs batted in, go to the bank and get a loan on it."[33]

***

Sam Lacy engaged in broadcasting too. He was a sports commentator on Baltimore's NBC affiliate, WBAL-TV from 1968 to 1978. Lacy was still writing his columns for the *Baltimore Afro-American*. He was in his mid-sixties when he began the part-time TV job. Jim Wittemore, a friend and co-worker at channel 11, expressed regret Lacy was handicapped as to what he could do in television because of a lack of opportunity. Lacy answered, not to worry. Lacy took the position to show people that Blacks could do the work, and there were Black people who knew about sports. At that time, few Blacks appeared on TV news, rarer still in on-air sports.

During the 1930s Lacy was on the radio, a commercial medium that was only a decade old. He did sports commentaries for WOL am radio station in Washington for a few months in 1935. People also heard Lacy's voice at the ballpark. He was a public address announcer for Homestead Grays games at Griffith Stadium. Lacy introduced the players, called the plays, and kept fans informed about what was going on. He mentored a young assistant, Harold Jackson. Lacy was credited with helping Jackson get hired at then WINX in Washington where he hosted a music and interview show. When the first play-by-play broadcasts of Negro League baseball occurred in August 1942, Jackson was one of the announcers. In 1944, Jackson and Lacy reunited on the WINX radio and collaborated on a weekly sports show where they interviewed Negro League players and recapped the week's games.[34] Jackson would go on to national fame as Black radio disc jockey and executive "Hal" Jackson.[35]

***

In 1967 Wendell Smith stopped writing his "Sports Beat" column for the *Pittsburgh Courier*, ending almost three decades with the Black weekly that began in 1937. Twenty years before – 1947 – when Smith left the *Courier* staff to work in Chicago for the daily *Herald American*, Smith continued to write a column for the *Courier* as a freelance correspondent. For most of the 1960s, Smith's primary focus was television news and sports, briefly with WBBM-TV, then with WGN-TV. In 1969, Smith returned to a newspaper writing routine with the *Chicago Sun-Times*, the city's second-largest circulated newspaper.[36]

In January 1971, Smith wrote about Jackie Robinson's visit to Chicago. Robinson spent a day with the Rev. Jesse Jackson, head of Operation Breadbasket, before municipal elections in the city. Robinson also spoke approvingly of Leo Durocher, his former Brooklyn Dodgers manager, and then adversary when Durocher moved on to manage the crosstown rival New York Giants. In 1971, Durocher was the beleaguered manager of the Chicago Cubs. Smith narrated in his column that there was a theory among baseball pundits that Durocher could not build a winning team. You must hand him a winner, said the pundits, because he does not have the patience to nurse and develop young players into stardom.

"I don't believe that" answered Robinson. "In 1951, he was fantastic with the [New York] Giants and he developed young guys like Willie

Mays, Monte Irvin, and others. He made that club a winner. Going into the last month of the season we [Brooklyn] were 13 games in front of the Giants, and he caught us and passed us. He was a great manager that year."[37] Robinson remembered the pain. That was the year of the tie-breaker one-game playoff, won by the Giants on a walk-off home run that sent them to World Series to play the New York Yankees.

Also, during an October interview with Robinson, he told Smith that Black baseball stars Frank Robinson (Baltimore Orioles) and Maury Wills (Los Angeles Dodgers) would make good major league managers.[38] Jackie's recommendation would prove prophetic. One year later October 15, 1972, he appeared at Game 2 of the World Series between the Oakland A's and the Cincinnati Reds. Robinson threw out the first pitch. Afterward, he said he wanted to live to see a Black manager in the major leagues. Nine days later, Jackie Robinson, 52, died from a heart attack. He did not get his wish to see the breakthrough in person; however, two years later Frank Robinson did become the first Black major league manager in 1974 with the Cleveland Indians.[39]

***

In 1968, Wendell Smith engaged in a writing project vastly different from sports or breaking news. He collaborated with Houston Branch on *The Unreasonable American*, a biography of Francis W. Davis, the inventor of power steering in automobiles. How Smith and Branch connected was not known. What both men had in common was they wrote for mass audiences. Branch wrote screenplays for Hollywood, 50 films from 1927 to 1958 that included "The Fighting Chance" (1955), "Girls of the Big House" (1945), and "West of Singapore" (1933).[40] Born March 5, 1899, in St. Paul, Minnesota, Branch began his career as a reporter for the *St. Paul Pioneer Press* and became a feature writer for the *San Antonio Express* and *Dallas News*. His papers are at the University of Oregon however the documents did not contain any information about *The Unreasonable American*.[41] The book publisher also left a few clues. Washington-based Acropolis Books published the Davis biography in 1968. By the early 1980s a major New York commercial publisher acquired Acropolis and provided no additional information.

Wendell Smith possibly connected with Branch because he had child-hood ties to Detroit and the automobile industry. Smith's father was the cook for magnate Henry Ford. Branch and Smith tackled this story of engineering because power steering, which meant the ease of turning an automotive wheel since the mid-1900s, took a long time to become a standard convenience. Their 216-page book contained 18 technical drawings;

however, the text did not feel as if it were written for a technical or scientific audience; it was meant for general readers. Also, neither Branch the co-author nor Davis the subject was Black. Smith was not only about race. He was about journalism, biography, and interesting people and events.

Davis owned a machine shop with George W. Jessup. They sought to solve the problem, the strenuous effort needed to maneuver eight-to-six-cylinder cars in parking and other tight spaces. Within a year, Davis and Jessup invented a hydraulic power steering system.[42] The design was accepted in 1926 by General Motors Corporation, known for Chevrolet, Cadillac, and other brands. GM sat on the plan for a few decades. Davis became caught between the tension of the inventor versus the modern, faceless corporation. That conundrum inspired Branch and Smith's book title, "The Unreasonable American." Francis Davis was not belligerent. He was patient and resolute. Davis continued to refine power steering. GM sought other engineers who could patent Davis' creation and cut the inventor out of receiving royalties.

After World War II, Detroit automakers were ready to install power steering in passenger cars. In 1950, the units were installed in 10,000 vehicles, then production leaped to 300,000 when GM entered the competition. By 1964 power steering was installed on three and a half million vehicles and then 50 million by all manufacturers in 1966.[43] Power steering became standard in automobiles at the end of the 20th century and Davis was responsible for the revolution in comfort and safety. Furthermore, he was compensated for his work.[44] Houston Branch and Wendell Smith were praised for chronicling Francis Davis for his solution to a problem and the creation of a system almost universally used in American automobiles today.[45]

***

In March 1971 about a month after Jackie Robinson's visit to Chicago, Wendell Smith wrote about the scene in Muhammad Ali's locker room after Joe Frazier beat him in what would be the first of three monumental heavyweight bouts. Smith depicted a battered Ali comforting a sobbing superstar singer Diana Ross, and his mother Odessa Grady Clay, who was watching over the boxer.[46] Smith's column was empathetic given that Smith scolded Ali in a 1965 *Pittsburgh Courier* "Sports Beat" piece: "He shouts to the housetops that he's the greatest, ignoring the fact that modesty is the mark of a champion, and that public esteem is a desirable goal for all athletes."[47]

That same year Smith was named to the Special Committee on the Negro Leagues for the Baseball Hall of Fame. Sam Lacy was also appointed to the committee.[48] That body named Satchel Paige as its first choice for induction into the Hall of Fame located in Cooperstown, New York. Wendell and Wyonella Smith took the trip to upstate New York.

Because Smith was a leader and expert in his field other appointments kept coming. In January 1972, he was installed as the first Black president of the Chicago Press Club, succeeding *Chicago Tribune* financial editor Nick Poulos.[49] Smith was unable to attend his installation with other new officers at the annual president's dinner at the Pick-Congress Hotel because he was hospitalized. Smith was battling cancer. Over some months Smith's condition worsened and he was forced back to the hospital. Jack Brickhouse later recalled: "When I saw that skeleton of a man lying there and realized what he had been compared to what he was, it grabbed you right in the heart."[50]

Smith's last column was an appreciation of Jackie Robinson, published shortly after the trailblazer died in October 1972. "He [Robinson] never backed down from a fight, never quit agitating for equality," Smith wrote. "He demanded respect too. Those who tangled with him always admitted that he was a man's man, a person who would not compromise his convictions." During that month's World Series, Smith returned to the hospital. He received a visit from Al Duckett who in 1972 collaborated with Robinson on the player's autobiography. Smith told Duckett he was thrilled that Robinson acknowledged him.

On November 26, 1972, Wendell Smith died, less than a month after Robinson's death on October 24, 1972. His wake took place on November 28 at Griffin Funeral Homes, located near Comiskey Park. "We have lost a great citizen, who was interested in the city and most of all the city's children," said Mayor Richard J. Daley who paid his respects.[51] The funeral was the following day at the funeral home. Two hundred people packed the facility and included Chicago Bears owner George Halas and local sports stars Gayle Sayers of the Bears and Billy Williams of the Cubs. Smith was buried at Burr Oak Cemetery in Alsip, Illinois, a suburb 15 miles southwest of Chicago.

Within a month of Smith's death, the Chicago Press Club renamed its scholarship fund the Wendell Smith-Chicago Press Club Scholarship Fund. Also, the *Chicago Sun-Times* donated $1,000 in Smith's memory to be awarded through the National Merit Scholarship Fund. In 1973, the Chicago Board of Education named an elementary school in honor of Wendell Smith and the building was dedicated in 1974. WGN created the Wendell Smith Memorial Award for baseball figures considered ambassadors of goodwill and presented by the Chicago chapter of the Baseball Writers Association of America at its annual dinners. In 1975 the Chicago Park District named a playground site after Smith. In 1982 he was elected posthumously to the Chicago Journalism Hall of Fame, and in 1983 to the Chicagoland Sports Hall of Fame.[52]

Wyonella Smith continued working for the Harlem Globetrotters after her husband's death. In 1976 the team was sold to Metromedia, and then the company moved the Globetrotters to Los Angeles. Wyonella remained in Chicago and found work in the public information office for the city Department of Aging. She also moved into a senior residence on Chicago's South Side. There Wyonella met resident Mary Frances Veeck, widow of former White Sox and Cleveland Indians owner Bill Veeck. The Smiths and Veecks had been good friends and both women maintained a strong relationship after the deaths of their husbands.[53] Wyonella donated Wendell's papers to the Baseball Hall of Fame. She died on Thanksgiving Day, November 26, 2020, at age 99. Wyonella Smith was buried at Burr Oak next to her husband.

Public interest and awareness of Wendell Smith cooled for 20 years after his death then revived. In 1993 the Baseball Writers of America J.G. Taylor Spink Award committee posthumously nominated Smith. The full membership approved the nomination, making Smith the first Black writer to receive the award. Jerome Holtzman of the *Chicago Tribune*, Smith's travel companion, campaigned for the writer.[54] Wyonella Smith accepted the award at the National Baseball Hall of Fame annual summer ceremonies.

Twenty years later Wendell Smith was among six inductees into the 2013 National Association of Black Journalists Hall of Fame.[55] Three months later in April, the movie "42" was released, starring Chadwick Bozeman as Jackie Robinson, Harrison Ford as Branch Rickey, and Andre Holland as Wendell Smith. Scenes depicted 30ish Wendell Smith as Robinson's chaperone, sounding board, and writer covering the trailblazer, manual typewriter in lap, while sitting in grandstands because he was barred from press boxes. "42" was a big-budget Hollywood movie, costing $40 million to make. It grossed $27.5 million in its opening week and $95 million overall in North America.[56]

Three months after the movie release, the Shirley Povich Center for Sports Journalism at the University of Maryland Philip Merrill College of Journalism created the Sam Lacy-Wendell Smith Award, which annually recognizes a sports journalist or broadcaster who has made significant contributions to racial and gender equality in sports. The following year, 2014, the Associated Press Sports Editors posthumously honored Smith with the Red Smith Award, named for the Pulitzer Prize-winning sportswriter, Walter "Red" Smith, who wrote for the New York *Herald Tribune* and the *New York Times*.[57]

***

Like Wendell Smith, Sam Lacy divorced and remarried. By his own admission, Lacy was not home much during his five-year marriage to Alberta plus he liked to gamble. They had two children together, and his son Samuel Howe "Tim" Lacy was also a columnist for the *Afro-American*. After his 1952 divorce, the next year Lacy married Barbara Robinson, a government worker who had the same last name as his previous wife but was unrelated to her. Lacy credited her as being a stabilizing force in his life and making him a more responsible person. Barbara's daughter Michaelyn, a teacher of dance in New York, became Sam's stepdaughter.[58] Barbara died in 1969. Sam was a widower for the rest of his life.

A decade after Jackie Robinson's arrival professional baseball was thoroughly integrated, Lacy's focus then was to advocate for more respect regarding Black athletes across multiple sports. He covered Olympic games, beginning with witnessing Jesse Owens' triumphs at the 1936 competitions in Berlin, and covering the summer games in Helsinki (1952), Melbourne (1956), Rome (1960), Barcelona (1992), and Atlanta (1996).

Lacy's long-distance career resulted in numerous honors. In 1985 he was inducted into the Maryland Sports Hall of Fame. In July 1991 Lacy received a lifetime achievement award from the National Association of Black Journalists.[59] On April 15, 1997, when MLB commemorated the 50th anniversary of Jack Robinson breaking baseball's color barrier, Lacy was invited to throw out the first pitch at the game between the Minnesota Twins and hometown Baltimore Orioles. That October, Lacy was named winner of the Baseball Writers Association of America Career Excellence Award (formerly the J.G. Taylor Spink Award, which Wendell Smith received posthumously in 1994). The next year, 1998, Lacy received the Red Smith Award from the Associated Press Sports Editors, for "major contributions to sports journalism."[60] That July, Lacy, was inducted into the Writers Wing (like Wendell Smith) of the Baseball Hall of Fame in Cooperstown, New York.

In a four-and-half-minute acceptance speech, he referenced what Ted Williams said during his Hall of Fame acceptance, hope that fine players in the Negro Leagues would be recognized (they were beginning in the 1970s), then added, "My presence here and Wendell Smith in 1993 should impress upon the American public that the Negro press had a role that should be recognized and honored." Lacy thanked friends and supporters who had come from Florida, Georgia, Texas, California, and Missouri. He thanked Boston Red Sox sportswriter Larry Whiteside for sponsoring his entry, Larry Doby who was entering the Hall of Fame too, and Wendell Smith, whose widow was at the ceremony.

Lacy ended by saying he was most thankful to Miss Carolyn Calloway. "You don't know who she is. She was my math teach. She taught algebra at Armstrong High School. I didn't understand algebra and algebra didn't understand me. We ignored each other. When Miss Calloway learned I was an integral part of the baseball and basketball teams, she went to coach Westmoreland and said I had to pick up in my algebra or not show up for her geometry class next year. I told coach Westmoreland she did not have that ladder to worry about; I certainly was not going to tackle geometry if I didn't know anything about algebra. Now, Miss Calloway gave me a passing grade that allowed me to play baseball and basketball and Armstrong won two championships thereafter. I was able to graduate. So as Jimmy Durante says, 'goodnight, Miss Calabash wherever you are.' I say thank you Miss Calloway wherever you are, for were it not for you, instead of standing here ready to enter this great edifice of history, I might still be a 94-year-old sophomore."[61]

***

In 1973, Sam Lacy, an octogenarian, left his Washington, DC home during the predawn hours and hour later arrived before sunrise at the *Afro-American* newspaper headquarters in Baltimore. New hire William Rhoden learned about Lacy's routine the hard way. Frances Murphy, an *Afro-American* executive, and adjunct instructor at Morgan State College, offered the graduate a writing job at the paper. Intending to make a good impression, Rhoden arrived at 7 a.m. and walked up the steep flight of steps to the newsroom. To his surprise he found Lacy at his desk. He had been in office since 5 a.m.

"That was lesson No. 1," said Rhoden.[62]

Lacy's usual dress was crisp white shirt and slacks. At his desk he worked with a notepad, little green portable manual typewriter, and landline telephone. Lacy worked the phone, calling numerous sources. Once he gathered the information he needed, Lacy tapped out his "A to Z" column, three to four items that added up to single-issue column length, about 700 words.

When Lacy did field reporting he would be welcomed like a visiting head of state, respectfully and even with a sense of awe. In 1986 Hamil Harris, a Florida State University graduate and varsity football lineman, worked as a young *Afro-American* reporter with Lacy. Harris said the elder was gentlemanly and humble. When Harris moved on to the *Washington Post* in 1992 and scored his first front-page story, he received a hand-written note from Lacy that said, "I'm proud of you." Said Harris, "Lacy had the respect of colleagues, Black and White. I was looking at history. You can't trade those memories."[63]

Ricky Clemons was another admirer. "I went to mlb.com because of Lacy," he said. "When I hesitated, Lacy said he was coming to my house in Northeast D.C. to break my arm if I did not take the job. Lacy was my guy. During the 1994 [baseball] strike season, I was a director, not a vice president, and was exposed to [possible] layoffs. Lacy wrote a column and called me 'a man for all seasons.' I kept my job."

In the newsroom Lacy routinely finished his writing then filed by about noon when many writers were just arriving. Lacy would drive home to Washington. During the last three years of his life, when Lacy was in his late nineties, his son Tim would drive him to and from work. Sam Lacy filed his last column several days before his death on May 8, 2003, at age 99.[64]

***

Decades of relentless crusading for professional baseball integration by Sam Lacy and Wendell Smith from the 1930s through the 1950s produced dramatic change in the 1960s and 1970s. Persuasion facilitated a new normalcy: it was no longer odd to see a Black man in a professional baseball uniform. Some change was revolutionary. In the October 1964 World Series, the American League champion Yankees, symbolized home run hitting and overwhelming Whiteness with stars Mickey Mantle, Roger Maris, and Joe Pepitone, plus pitcher Whitey Ford, faced the National League champion St. Louis Cardinals, which championed baserunning and fielding speed, plus power pitching among its Black stars, pitcher Bob Gibson, and outfielders Lou Brock, Curt Flood, and infielder Bill White.[65] Speed won, as the Cardinals beat the Yankees. After that year the Yankees slipped into a nearly decade-long decline as a second-division or basement-dwelling team of aging stars or mediocre newcomers until a new, bombastic owner – George Steinbrenner – arrived in the mid-1970s and restored the Yankees to pennant and World Series-winning expectations.[66] By then half the stars on the team were Black or Hispanic, and by 1978 the team's emerging home run leader was the African-American star Reggie Jackson.

In October 1969, swift St. Louis Cardinals centerfielder Curt Flood was traded to the Philadelphia Phillies. He balked. After 14 years of service Flood asserted, he was not property to be bought and sold. He challenged Baseball's Reserve Clause, which bounded players for life to the first team that signed them. That edict stood stonewall solid for most of the 20th century.[67] The Players Association unanimously (25-0) supported Flood's suit against MLB owners. When Flood filed his lawsuit on January 17, 1970, in US District Court in New York, he sought $4.1 million in damages, and his three goals were to invalidate the trade to Philadelphia, become a free agent, and end the reserve system. That August, the judge ruled against Flood's suit. Flood appealed and in April 1971 a three-judge US Appeals Court upheld the lower court decision.

Flood persisted. He took his battle to the US Supreme Court. On June 19, 1972, the high court ruled 5-3 against Flood, stating baseball could retain its unique status as exempt from federal antitrust legislation. Yet during the oral arguments that began in March, several justices did say Flood's case seemed better suited for labor-management negotiation and the Players Association should be the plaintiff.[68] In the end, Flood lost and exited baseball; however, he won a much bigger fight for his peers.

The reserve clause had been on Flood's mind since 1956 when he discussed the rule with Lacy at the Florida rooming house where they lived during spring training. Lacy talked again to Flood in the late 1970s at the ex-star's bar that Flood bought in Majorca in the Mediterranean. By that time, major league players were prospering.[69]

Emboldened before the Supreme Court decision, the Major League Players Association voted 663-10 to stage the first general strike. It lasted 13 days at the start of the season. The next year, 1973, two pitchers filed grievances against their respective teams. An arbitration panel ruled 2-1 in favor of Andy Messersmith of the Los Angeles Dodgers and Dave McAnally of the Montreal Expos. The first free-agent draft occurred the following year. As a result, the average MLB salary jumped from $29,303 in 1970 to $46,000 in 1975, then to $135,000 in 1980 and $329,000 in 1984.[70] Periodic labor versus management battles erupted. The owners locked the players out of spring training for thirteen days in 1976. On June 12, 1981, the players staged a 50-day strike, which involved the cancelation of 714 games. A strike in August 1994 canceled the final month of the season and eliminated the playoffs and World Series.[71] When the work stoppage ended in April 1995, teams played 144-game seasons instead of the customary 162 games. In the 21st century, journeymen players earn millions in salary, stars have multiyear contracts worth hundreds of millions, thanks to Curt Flood's challenge. Furthermore, Lacy wrote, Flood's crusade inspired NBA great Oscar Robertson to successfully press for the removal of restraints on the players under contract that led to free agency and increased salaries.[72]

***

On the playing field on September 1, 1971, a remarkable, reputedly accidental event occurred. The Pittsburgh Pirates started nine Black players in a regular season game. The lineup was a Western Hemisphere collection of players from the United States, the Caribbean, and Central America that included two future Hall of Famers, Willie Stargell and Roberto Clemente. When the Pirates' manager Danny Murtaugh posted the lineup he may not have realized he submitted an all-Black lineup. Thirteen members of the 25-player roster were Black. Once the game was underway, third baseman Dave Cash walked over to first baseman Al Oliver and said, "Hey Scoop, we've got all brothers out here."[73]

That day the Pirates beat the Philadelphia Phillies 10-7. There was no newspaper coverage of the home game because both Pittsburgh papers – the *Post-Gazette,* and *Press* – were on strike. *Philadelphia Daily News* columnist Bill Conlin, who was at the road game, noted Murtaugh's "all-soul lineup," but with no explanation. United Press International news service however did focus on the all-Black lineup and Murtaugh answered, "When it comes to making out the lineup, I'm colorblind, and my athletes know it. They don't know it because I told them. They know it because they're familiar with how I operate. The best men in our organization are the ones who are here. And the ones who are here all play, depending on when the circumstances present themselves."[74]

Twenty-five years after Jackie Robinson was the lone Black player in all of Major League Baseball, Black participation seemed normal. Black players were even oversubscribed, briefly, 18% in Major League Baseball compared to the 12% of the general African American population.[75] There were still challenges regarding the paucity of Black inclusion in the coaching boxes and front office. A notable exception was Bill White, who played for San Francisco Giants, St. Louis Cardinals, and Philadelphia Phillies. In 1989 he was elected president of the National League and served until 1994. Previously, White was a full-time sportscaster in 1969 and was play-by-play man and color analyst for New York Yankees television and radio broadcasts for 18 years.[76]

In the 1990s the Black players' share in baseball began to decline. There were multiple factors: Loss of interest by young Blacks in baseball; but high interest in football and basketball, abandonment by all forces of baseball in the rotting urban core cities. Some neighborhoods, notably Harlem, lost its Little League charter sometime in the late 1960s as families with means fled for the suburbs. Harlem did restore the charter in 1989 after a two-decade absence.[77] Major League Baseball reacted to the decline in 1990 by launching the Restoring Baseball in Inner Cities (RBI) program in the 1990s.

Overall, the percentage of Americans playing MLB dropped too because of the huge influx of Latin American players, and growing numbers from Japan and Korea.

***

The Sam Lacy and Wendell Smith legacy was transformative as civil rights facilitators; the two men were persuasive and activist sports journalists. By the 21st century Americans have witnessed milestones and feats not imaginable in the 20th century.

Baseball was transformed for the total American population, but not enough. In 1960 when the Gallop Organization asked Americans to name their favorite sport, 34% chose baseball, 21% football, and 10% basketball. That year, television saturation expanded to 85 of every 100 households, 52 million homes. Fans could watch baseball on their TV sets; they could watch NFL football too because the league inked a national broadcasting contract.

In 1972 Gallop's sports market share numbers reversed: 32% of poll respondents favored football, and 21% chose the National Pastime.[78]

Over the next 30 years baseball's relevance continued to slip. By 2007, Gallop reported football was favored by 43% of respondents, basketball was second at 12%, and baseball was third at 11%. Baseball's loss of substantial market share to football, and basketball did not have to be inevitable, yet was devastating because of a combination of stubborn fealty to tradition, greed, and blinders to gender and global changes in sports. From 1949 to 1958, New York was the capital of baseball. One, or sometimes two, teams from the city were in every World Series during that span, and a New York team won every year but 1957, when the Milwaukee Braves, led by Hank Aaron, beat the Yankees. Then the Dodgers and Giants left for California. But there would still be a New York team in every series for the next six years, except 1959.

As for styles, pro football and basketball made many rule changes to encourage speed and excitement. Baseball, however, slowed down, from two and half hours per average nine-inning game in 1960 to three hours, 10 minutes in 2021.[79] In 2023, MLB instituted timers that limited how long pitchers could wait to throw or how much time batters had to be ready to receive pitches. Pickoff throws were limited to two per base and the change encouraged stolen base attempts. Three months into the 2023 season, average games were still ending in three hours, and fans generally liked the changes.[80]

It remains to be seen if these innovations will ease baseball's decline. In 2022, a Washington Post-University of Maryland poll reported that 34% of all adults preferred football, and 11% each liked baseball or basketball. However, when young adults 18–29 from the sample answered, 7% chose baseball, 17% favored basketball, and 24% chose football.[81]

Yet Lacy and Smith's respective work was not in vain. They both planted the seeds and nourished the playing fields and stadiums for such bounties.

Johnny B. "Dusty" Baker, Jr., Black manager of the Houston Astros, led his American League team to win the 2022 World Series. Baker had excelled as a player, then as manager since 1993 in other cities.[82] Still, Baker lamented the lack of non-Hispanic Black players on his and the opposing team. That World Series marked the first time since Jackie Robinson desegregated baseball that no US-born Black player competed.[83]

In February 2023, two Black quarterbacks competed head-to-head in Super Bowl 57. In an epic wire-to-wire battle, Patrick Mahones of the Kansas City Chiefs edged Jalen Hurts and the Philadelphia Eagles 38-35, Mahones and Hurts played college ball at Southern universities – Texas Tech and Alabama – that two generations before they arrived were racially segregated until the late 1900s. Some sports analysts and historians concluded that the 2022 season and 2023 playoffs and Super Bowl revealed a new reality: the Black quarterback who could throw and run was the new model of the NFL quarterback, replacing the drop back, stationary style that was the pro standard for a half-century.[84]

A spotlight was also placed on America's premier 21st-century sport, NFL football, because of many owners' stubborn refusal to hire Black head coaches. One of those coaches, Brian Flores, sued his Miami Dolphins team owner, alleging that the boss asked him to deliberately lose games to improve chances of drafting top college stars. The coach refused and the owner was fined by the NFL.[85] Flores, who risked career advancement because of principle, landed a job at the Pittsburgh Steelers working under Black coach Mike Tomlin. A multipart *Washington Post* series noted that Black coaches often improved struggling teams yet were let go, kept on shorter contracts, or were employed only as assistant coaches amid an adversarial relationship among a few dozen billionaire owners and a few hundred millionaire players. By this time the NFL player membership is 70% Black.

In the NBA it was not unusual to find Black head coaches. Half of the thirty head coaches in 2022 were Black.[86] LeBron James followed the legacy of Ervin "Magic" Johnson in collaborating with management to shape his team's mission. James aspired to become a Billion-dollar brand and became so much more than a sports superstar. He achieved that billion-dollar goal in about a decade.[87]

Magic Johnson has been a part owner of the Los Angeles Dodgers since 2012. He also has ownership stakes in other major sports.[88] In 2023 there were six non-White NFL owners and one general manager. Derrick Jeter, the biracial superstar of the New York Yankees, was chief executive officer and part owner of the Miami Marlins baseball team from 2017 to 2022. Yankee Aaron Judge in fall 2022 signed a monster contract to stay with the team after eclipsing his team's single-season home run record. The Yankees' hostility to Black players was clearly a relic of the past.

From the 1930s to the 1950s Sam Lacy and Wendell Smith scolded, satirized, and cajoled White owners, fans, and players to include Black talent, often to be told Blacks were not good enough, or simply NO because social mores prevented such interaction. By the end of the 20th century and beyond America was transformed when it came to race and sports and is slowly changing with regard to gender and sports. What does the future project?

When Joe Louis retired from boxing in 1948, he wanted to own and operate a Ford Dealership in Chicago where he was living at the time. Louis' family migrated from Alabama to Michigan because Henry Ford Sr. made a $5-a-day promise to his workers, and furthermore paid White and Black employees the same. Young Louis worked briefly as a stockboy at the River Rouge, Michigan plant. CEO Henry Ford II considered brand-loyal Louis' bid. Ford Jr. tasked his general sales manager to get reactions of dealers and general managers. A file obtained from the Benson Ford Research Center revealed 32 memos expressing overwhelming rejection of Louis the universal American hero, or any Black person selling Ford products. Louis did not get the dealership, nor any other Black person before the Civil Rights Act of 1964 became law.[89]

***

Wendell Smith lived to see Black baseball players who were previously shut out of America's National Pastime become accepted, then thrive professionally, and then be adored by fans in the 1970s. Sam Lacy meanwhile lived much longer and witnessed Black professional athletes expand their footprints into coaching, management, and ownership in the 21st century. "One day I would witness Black athletes holding six of ten top spots for endorsement income," said Lacy five years before his passing in 2003. "In 1998, those athletes were Michael Jordan, Tiger Woods, Shaquille O'Neal, Grant Hill, Ken Griffey Jr., and Deion Sanders."[90] Over time Black sports professionals did not have to pretend to be perfect angels to be respected or liked by fans and the media. Still, late in his 60-plus year journalism career, Lacy was there as the conscience of modern athletes, warning them in print to protect their reputations and steer clear of drugs and avoid dangerous liaisons.[91]

Together, Lacy and Smith were towering influences on American sport and society.

***

EPILOGUE

The start of the 1974 baseball season was tense. It was as if most fans collectively woke up from a decade-long slumber and were shocked. Henry Aaron of the Atlanta Braves crossed the once unbreakable home run barrier owned by Babe Ruth (714) and was on the verge of passing the immortal. How could this happen? Aaron was remarkably consistent and low-key. He averaged 30 to 40 home runs annually during his long career with the Braves as the team relocated from Boston to Milwaukee, and then Atlanta. For some White fans accustomed to or even OK with seeing Blacks play well in professional baseball, the possibility of a Black man owning the ultimate status of baseball power was a bridge too far. In 1973, Aaron reached the 700-home run milestone on July 21. He ended the season one home run shy of tying Ruth's record.

At the start of the 1974 season Aaron received repeated death threats, mostly via menacing letters.[92] On opening day April 4, Aaron tied Ruth at 714 against the Cincinnati Reds. On April 8, the Atlanta Braves hosted the Los Angeles Dodgers. In his first at-bat Aaron sent the ball over the left-center field fence for the record-breaking 715th home run. As Aaron rounded the bases, two 17-year-old White boys bolted onto the field and ran toward Aaron. Aaron did not flinch from his trot; the teenagers patted Aaron on the back before security escorted them off the field. Aaron's teammates – and his mother and father – met him at home plates and took turns hugging him. Fireworks exploded at Fulton County Stadium.

"What a marvelous moment for baseball. What marvelous moment for Atlanta and the state of Georgia. What a marvelous moment for the country and the world. A Black man from the deep South is getting a standing ovation for breaking the record of an all-time baseball idol," said play-by-play announcer Vin Scully. Aaron would finish his career in Milwaukee with the AL Brewers and 755 home runs. He held many other lifetime records as well. Aaron was inducted into the Hall of Fame Class of 1982.

***

Some Black major league stars were multigenerational, including Ken Griffey, Sr. and Ken Griffey, Jr., and Vlad Guerrero senior and junior. This most famous father-son duo was also the most tragic. Bobby Bonds of the San Francisco Giants hit for power and played right field across from Willie Mays. Bonds' son Barry was a longtime star at the Pittsburgh Pirates, then joined his father's former team. As a Giant, Barry Bonds broke the single season (73) and Aaron's lifetime home run record (762). However, because Bonds was allegedly bulked up on performance-enhancing drugs late in his career, numerous sportswriters and fans view his statistics as tainted. These opinions matter because it is unlikely that Bonds will be enshrined in the Hall of Fame, joining other Black and White castaway steroid users, Sammy Sosa, Mark McGuire, and Roger Clemens, and two White stars who were banned from Major League Baseball for gambling, Pete Rose, and "Shoeless" Joe Jackson.

***

At this writing in 2023, baseball and sports journalism are thoroughly integrated and international. Shohei Ohtani of the Los Angeles Angels is a leading home run hitter, winning pitcher, and presumptive Most Valuable Player. Ichiro Suzuki of the Seattle Mariners, New York Yankees, and Miami Marlins was an American League Rookie of the Year, 2001 American League Most Valuable Player, and winner of multiple Gold Glove and Silver Slugger awards. Top Korean MLB stars include outfielder Shin-Soo Choo, who signed with the Seattle Mariners and played from 2005 to 2020, and pitcher Chan Ho Park, who signed with the Los Angeles Dodgers and played from 1994 to 2010.

Black TV sports commentators are visible everywhere in baseball, football, and basketball, and in other print and broadcast journalism. Carl Rowan was a barrier breaker at the *Minneapolis Tribune* in the 1950s, and later became a syndicated columnist. Charlayne Hunter-Gault, who integrated the University of Georgia in 1961, was a multimedia journalist before such nomenclature was created, having a career at *The New Yorker* magazine, the *New York Times*, PBS, and NPR. Contemporary talent includes anchor Lester Holt of "NBC Nightly News," Abby Phillip and Audie Cornish of CNN, Gayle King, and Nate Burleson of "CBS Mornings." Finally, leading sports journalists who follow in the footsteps of pioneers Sam Lacy and Wendell Smith include Michael Wilbon of ESPN/ABC and the *Washington Post*, William C. Rhoden of the *New York Times*, Stephen A. Smith of ESPN, and James Brown of CBS Sports.

Notes

1. Smith, "Negro Ball Players Want Rights in South," Chicago's American, January 23, 1961, p 1.
2. Davis, Jack E., "Baseball's Reluctant Challenge: Desegregating Major League Training Sites, 1961–1964," Journal of Sport History, Summer 1992, Volume 19, No. 2, pp 114–162, University of Illinois Press.
3. Smith, Chicago's American, January 23, 1961.
4. Bennett, "Before the Mayflower," pp 597–599.
5. Smith, "Negro Players Gain in Equality Bid," Chicago's American, February 6, 1961, p 16.
6. Smith, Chicago's American, February 6, 1961.
7. Smith, Chicago's American, February 6, 1961.
8. Smith, "What a Negro Ballplayer Faces Today in Training," Chicago's American, April 3, 1961.
9. Smith, "Sports Beat," *Pittsburgh Courier*, April 15, 1961, p 38.

10. Smith, "Taking a Stand and Paying a Price," *Chicago's American*, April 5, 1961. Thestacksreader.com.

11. Smith, *Chicago's American*, April 3, 1961.

12. Marsh, "The Wendell Smith Reader," p 31.

13. Third baseman Matthews played 17 seasons for the Braves and hit 512 home runs. He was a 12-time all-star and two-time World Series champion. Matthews was inducted into the Baseball Hall of Fame in 1978.

14. Smith, "Sox Buy Hotel to End Race Ban: American's Campaign Succeeding in Florida," *Chicago's American*, December 9, 1961. The $500,000 purchase was worth $4,955,000 in 2022 dollars according to calculator.net.

15. "Lacy says Orioles would lower bar," *Baltimore Afro-American*, March 18, 1961, p 1.

16. Lacy, "A to Z," *Baltimore Afro-American*, March 21, 1961. Lacy, "Fighting for Fairness," p 95. Earl Robinson physically resembled Jackie Robinson, Wendell Smith wrote: "Jackie Robinson fought for everything ... not only equality on the field, but also in hotels and restaurants, on trains and planes ... everything. His namesake, Earl Robinson fights for nothing. He submits to segregation and discrimination willingly. The Dodgers signed him and gave him a fat bonus because Buzzie Bavasi, the general manager of Los Angeles, visualized another Jackie Robinson in the making. But Earl didn't have it. They sent him to Baltimore last December." Smith, "What a Difference a Name Makes!" Pittsburgh Courier, June 3, 1961, p 34.

17. Pro-football-reference.com https://www.pro-football-reference.com/boxscores/196112030dal.htm

18. Lacy, "Big leagues zero in on Jim Crow," *Baltimore Afro-American*, August 12, 1961, p 13.

19. Clay, Gregory, "New Book Tells Story of HBCU Legends of the American Football League," andscape.com, July 5, 2016. Ross, Charles K., "Mavericks, Money, and Men: The AFL, Black Players, and the Evolution of Modern Football," Sporting, 2016. "Minority Players and the American Football League," remembertheafl.com

20. The discriminatory acts in New Orleans occurred five months after the 1964 Civil Rights Act became law.

21. Farrar, Doug, "How the 1964 AFL All-Star Game Player Boycott Struck a Blow for Civil Rights," August 26, 2020. touchdownwire.usatoday.com

22. Lacy, "Fighting for Fairness," pp 104–105. (*Baltimore Afro-American* column on January 8, 1964.)

23. Bennett, "Before the Mayflower," pp 607–609.

24. "Smith to Enter TV, Radio Field," Chicago's American, February 9, 1963. Indeed, Smith left the daily newspaper for a new and rapidly growing medium. WBBM was a CBS owned-and-operated station since 1953. Chicago at the time was the nation's second biggest TV market.

25. Fischer, Leo, *Chicago's American*, February 18, 1963, p 15. Fischer was sports editor from 1943 to 1969.

26. Lyons, Herb, "Tower Ticker," *Chicago Tribune*, February 21, 1964, p 16.

27. Brickhouse, Jack, "Wendell Smith Rates a 'Hey Hey!' as a Natural for Newscaster," Overset: News Bulletin of the Chicago Press Club, January–February 1972; 1, 3. Courtesy of the Chicago Public Library's Special Collections Division. Brickhouse (1916–1998) was known for his play-by-play coverage of Chicago Cubs games on WGN-TV.

28. Pifer and Marsh, "The Wendell Smith Reader," p 33.

29. "WGN sports anchor Wendell Smith, responsible for Jackie Robinson's rise, broke barriers in baseball." In March 2023 during WGN-TV's 75th anniversary the station aired a 10 minute, 40 second tribute to Smith. Sources interviewed included Fred Mitchell, a DePaul University professor identified as the first Black Journalist at the Chicago Tribune, and biographer Michael Marsh, co-author of "The Wendell Smith Reader." During the segment about Smith's documentary "Let Freedom Ring," as students walked the crowded halls of

DuSable High School, the voiceover said many of the 4,000 were children of southern field workers. https://www.youtube.com/watch?v=Zr02Q_2pkcs

30. Pifer and Marsh, "The Wendell Smith Reader," pp 33–34.
31. Gilligan, Matt, "Born to Raise Hell: 5 Things to Know About Richard Speck & the Chicago Nurse Murders," investigationdiscovery.com, July 12, 2019.
32. Logan, Paul, *The Herald*, April 22, 1971, section two, p 8.
33. Pifer and Marsh, "The Wendell Smith Reader," p 34.
34. Halper, Donna L., "Missed Opportunity: Radio and Black Baseball," radioworld.com October 22, 2021.
35. Jackson, Hal, Haskins, James, "Hal Jackson: The House that Jack Built," New York, Amistad Press, 2001, pp 24–25. Jackson (1915–2012) joined New York radio station WLIB. By 1954 he became the first radio personality to broadcast three daily shows at three different New York stations. In 1971 Jackson and Percy Sutton co-founded Inner City Broadcasting Corporation, which acquired WLIB and made it the first African American owned and operated station in New York.
36. The *Sun-Times'* peer newspapers included the New York *Daily News*, *Philadelphia Daily News*, *Boston Herald-American*, and Denver *Rocky Mountain News.*
37. Smith, "Jackie Robinson Discusses Old Adversary Leo," *Chicago Sun-Times,* p 72.
38. Smith, "Jackie Robinson Tabs Black Managers," *Chicago Sun-Times,* October 5, 1971, p 75.
39. Cleveland's front office insisted that Frank Robinson serve as player-manager. In 1976 the Indians had its first winning record in eight years. Robinson managed the San Francisco Giants from 1981 to 1984. In 1988 he was named manager of the Baltimore Orioles, and the next year was awarded American League Manager of the Year for leading the team to an 87-75 record after a previous 54-107 season. Robinson's last assignment was manager of the Montreal Expos/Washington Nationals from 2002 to 2006.
40. Internet Movie Database, imdb.com https://www.imdb.com/name/nm0104355/ Houston Branch movies
41. Lauren Goss, public services librarian, Special Collections and University (of Oregon) Archives, said the Houston "Bill" Branch Papers had a small amount of correspondence, none of it related to the Francis Davis biography. Also, there were no materials related to the book in the collection finding aid. *The Unreasonable American* was discovered during a search of the Library of Congress database. The author purchased a used copy of the book.
42. Davis studied engineering at Harvard College. His freshman classmates in 1906 included T.S. Elliot; John Reed; Walter Lippman, and Heywood Broun. Davis graduated in 1910. That year Davis was hired by Pierce-Arrow motor company. While test driving a large truck he realized power-assisted steering would be necessary in order for such vehicles to be practical (Branch, Smith, "The Unreasonable American," pp 38–39).
43. Branch, Smith, "The Unreasonable American," p 155.
44. Branch, Smith, "The Unreasonable American," p 153.
   The GM negotiating team initially balked at paying royalties to Francis W. Davis. There was an impasse and the negotiating team sought advice from Lewis M. Spencer, former head of the patent department. The exchange went like this with Spencer initiating the questions:

   "Is the manufacturing arrangement satisfactory?"
   "Well, yes, it is."
   "Is the Bendix unit price, OK?"
   "Yes, there isn't any problem there."
   "And the royalty schedule to Davis, is that a fair royalty for a thing like this?"
   "The schedule would be all right ordinarily, but we think under the circumstances ..."
   [Lewis M. Spencer cut off the man in mid-sentence, then said,]
   "I consider that General Motors has a moral obligation to respect the Davis patents."

45. J.W.R., Business History Review, Cambridge University Press, June 11, 2012 cambridge.org

46. Smith, "Ali Tells Diana Ross: I Ain't No Champ," *Chicago Sun-Times*, March 9, 1971, p 83.

47. Smith, "Sports Beat," *Pittsburgh Courier*, January 16, 1965, p 15.

48. Lacy complained about how his proxy vote was used. He approved of Paige and Gibson, but not the third and fourth players inducted, Buck Leonard and Monte Irvin. "In my judgment, Oscar Charleston, the old outfielder-first baseman; Martin Dihigo, the old all-rounder; Rube Foster, the old pitcher who contributed also as an organizer, owner and promoter; and Bingo DeMoss, perhaps the most eye-catching second baseman of the second decade, pared out to equal status in the grouping behind Paige and Gibson." Lacy resigned from the committee in 1974 (Lacy, Newson, "Fighting for Fairness," pp 164–165).

49. It should also be noted that Smith was elected president of the Chicago Boxing Writers and Broadcasters Association in 1953. Furthermore in 1958 Smith was part of an unusual championship boxing radio commentary team, he, Dr. Joyce Brothers, and Jack Drees, for the bout between Sugar Ray Robinson and Carmen Basilio.

50. "The Wendell Smith Reader." Interview with author Michael Marsh, March 3, 1996, p 36. Smith in good health was described as a big man, at least six feet tall and about 200 pounds. He walked with a shuffle, a limp left over from his athletic days at West Virginia State College, said colleague Irv Kupcinet of the *Chicago Sun-Times*.

51. "Daley: He Loved Our City and Its Children," Chicago Defender, November 29, 1972, p 4.

52. Pifer, Marsh, "The Wendell Smith Reader," p 40.

53. Strauss, Ben, "Friendship as Priceless as the National Pastime," *New York Times*, August 22, 2012.

54. Gross, Larry, "Smith: A Trailblazing Sportswriter," *Chicago Defender*, February 19, 1994, p 46. Holtzman was a Spink award winner. As competing baseball beat writers in the late 1950s and early 1960s, both men faced Jim Crow. During spring training, once Holtzman bought Smith a sandwich at a Tampa, Florida restaurant because the establishment would not serve Smith because of his skin color. Holtzman told the story during the February 20, 1994, broadcast of WGN's "People to People."

55. Program guide, January 17, 2013, pp 22–23. The other inductees were Betty Baye; Simeon Booker; Alice Dunnigan (like Smith, posthumous); Sue Simmons, and Cynthia Tucker.

56. Imdb.com internet Movie Database. Other key cast members were Nicole Beharie as Rachel Robinson, Christopher Meloni as Leo Durocher, and Lucas Black as Pee Wee Reese.
   Sam Lacy's son, Samuel Howe "Tim" Lacy, condemned the "42" movie, alleging that scenes depicting Wendell Smith's actions sometimes were actions done by his father. However consistent with Hollywood-style filmmaking, characters often are composites of multiple people to streamline storytelling. (Cowherd, Kevin, "Sam Lacy's Son Upset by Snub of Dad in New Movie '42,'" Baltimore Sun, April 15, 2013.)

57. Walker, Rhiannon, "Wendell Smith Honored with Red Smith Award," University of Maryland Sports Journalism Institute, May 21, 2014. During a boxing match at Chicago Stadium in the 1950s, Wendell Smith told his co-workers about the famous reporters who covered the fight. He listed the names then concluded, "There was Red Smith (New York Times), and then there was Black Smith." Bill Gleason interview with Michael Marsh, July 22, 1995.

58. Lacy, Newson, "Fighting for Fairness," p 27.

59. Dominguez, Alex, "Pioneer Black Sportswriter Cleared a Path for Others," *Baltimore Sun*, August 26, 1991, p 4B.

60. "Afro-American's Lacy Presented Smith Award for Sports Journalism," *Baltimore Sun*, April 19, 1998, pp 2C.

61. Hall of Fame acceptance speech https://www.youtube.com/watch?v=rNTjbLIlLWg
   Larry Whiteside (1937–2007) joined the *Boston Globe* staff in 1973 and was the only Black at that time covering major league baseball daily for a major newspaper. Whiteside

previously covered the Milwaukee Braves and civil rights for the *Milwaukee Journal.* "Larry Whiteside, 69, Black Journalist," *Houston Chronicle* via Associated Press, June 15, 2007.

62. Rhoden was the third winner of Sam Lacy-Wendell Smith Award. https://www.youtube.com/watch?v=J-3FTftf9Gc&t=30s Rhoden worked 33 years at the *New York Times* as a sports journalist, 26 of those years writing the "Sports of the Times" column.

63. February 22, 2023, interview with Harris at Howard University, Washington, D.C. In addition to the Washington Post, Harris has written for USA Today, the Christian Chronicle, Religion Unplugged, and the Washington Informer.

64. Klingaman, Mike, "Pioneering Sportswriter Fearless," *Chicago Tribune*, May 11, 2003, section 3:1.

65. The Yankees' rare Black star was Elston Howard, the team's first, who the previous year was the American League Most Valuable Player.

66. Hensler, Paul, "The American League in Transition, 1965–1975: How Competition Thrived When the Yankees Didn't." Jefferson, North Carolina, McFarland & Company, Publishers, 2013, pp 10, 230.

67. Ufberg, Ross, "How Much Longer Can Baseball's 100-Year Monopoly Last," *Wall Street Journal*, April 2-2, 2022, p C-4.

68. Ashe, "A Hard Road to Glory," pp 30–31.

69. Lacy, "Fighting for Fairness," pp 113–134.

70. Ashe, "A Hard Road to Glory," pp 33–34.

71. Chass, Murray, "BASEBALL: THE SEASON; Owners Terminate Season, Without the World Series," *New York Times*, September 15, 1994, p 1.

72. Lacy, "Fighting for Fairness," pp 133–134.

73. Oliver, Al, O'Toole, Andrew, "Baseball's Best Kept Secret: Al Oliver and His Time in Baseball," Pittsburgh, City of Champions Publishing, 1997, p 51.

74. Pirates Field First All-Black Starting Team," Tyrone (Pennsylvania) *Daily Herald*, September 2, 1971, p 5.

75. Mehtha, Jonaki, "At the HBCU Swingman Classic, pro baseball confronts its decline in Black players," npr.org, July 15, 2023. The year 1991 was the first year that data was collected about Black MLB participation.

76. Siegel, Robert, "Blazing Baseball Trails from Field to Executive Suite," NPR All Things Considered, April 14, 2011. White, Bill, "Uppity: My Untold Story About the Games People Play," Grand Central Publishing, 2011.

77. "After a Two-Decade Hiatus, Little League is Back in Harlem, *New York Times*, February 16, 1989. Gibbons, William, "Harlem Little League is Still Going Strong After 30 Years," andscape.com, August 25, 2019.

78. Shapiro, Michael, "Bottom of the Ninth: Branch Rickey, Casey Stengel, and the Daring Scheme to Save Baseball from Itself," New York, Times Books, 2009, p 2.

79. Enten, Harry, "Why is Baseball No Longer America's Game?" cnn.com, April 7, 2022.

80. "Baseball is Speeding Up: 62% of MLB Fans Like the Pitch Clock," Gaming Today, May 10, 2023.

81. Enten, "Why Is Baseball No Longer America's Game?" cnn.com

82. Brown, Tim, "Dusty Backer Finally Gets a Fairy-Tail Ending in the World Series," *Wall Street Journal*, November 8, 2022, p A14. Newberry, Paul, "Baker chasing elusive crown," Associated Press/*The Virginian-Pilot* (Norfolk), October 23, 2022. Baker was 73 and had managed nearly 4,000 games over three decades before winning the ultimate championship. As a player, Baker was kneeling in the on-deck circle when Henry Aaron hit his 715th home run in 1974. Baseball-reference.com

83. Mehtha, Jonaki, "At the HBCU Swingman Classic, pro baseball confronts its decline in Black players," npr.org, July 15, 2023.

84. Brewer, jerry, "Long Maligned, the Black Quarterback Emerges as an NFL Standard," *Washington Post,* February 11, 2023.
85. Louis-Jacques, Marcel, "Brian Flores Sues NFL, Three Teams as Former Miami Dolphins Coach Alleges Racism in Hiring Practices," espn.com, February 1, 2022.
86. Reynolds, Tim, "Half of the NBA's Franchises Now Have Black Coaches," Associated Press, June 2, 2022. Clough, Christina, "Head coaches in the NBA 2010-2022, by ethnicity," October 27, 2022. In 2010, there were 21 White, eight Black, and one Asian NBA coaches. In 2022, the breakdown was 14 White, 15 Black, one Asian. The Asian [Filipino descent] was Eric Spoelstra, head coach of the two-time champion Miami Heat.
87. Peterson-Withorn, Chase, "Lebron James is officially a billionaire," *Forbes,* June 2, 2022
88. Williams, Madison, "Magic Johnson Shares Emotional Statement After Owners' Vote on Commanders Sale," July 20, 2023, *Sports Illustrated.* si.com
89. Weineck, Slike-Maria, Szymanski, "City of Champions: A History of Triumph and Defeat in Detroit." Also "Freakonomics," NPR, December 18, 2022, https://freakonomics.com/podcast/how-much-does-discrimination-hurt-the-economy/
90. Lacy "Fighting for Fairness," p 147. Furthermore, in chapter 12, "1990s Stats Show Progress Made, Needed," pp 188, Lacy marveled at the following: "In the 1994–1995 sports year, Felipe Alou [Montreal Expos] was Major League and National League Manager of the Year, and Lenny Wilkens [Atlanta Hawks] surpassed Red Auerbach as the winningest NBA coach of all time. And this followed 1993-1994, when Blacks were Coach of the Year in college basketball [Nolan Richardson of the Arkansas Razorbacks], the NBA [Lenny Wilkens of the Atlanta Hawks], and the National League [Dusty Baker of the San Francisco Giants]. Also, Cito Gaston, later dropped by Toronto, had become the first Black manager to win consecutive World Series championships."
91. Lacy, "Fighting for Fairness," pp 152–154. Lacy also issued cautions about what kinds of women Black athletes could see – or be seen with – or otherwise face scandal mongering or condemnation in the general media. Cy Young Award-winning pitcher Vida Blue confided that he dated women of different ethnicities and clammed up when he received constant inquiries about his love life. Also, Los Angeles Dodgers base stealing champ Maury Wills was mum after rumors floated, he was romantically linked to actress-singer Doris Day. Wills called the story "ridiculous." Gertrude Wills, Maury's wife, told Lacy, "If my husband says that it is good enough for me."
92. Pasquini, Maria, "Hank Aaron Used Record-Setting Hate Mail for Inspiration Before Breaking Babe Ruth Record," People magazine, January 22, 2021.

PART **II**

Documents

The Unreasonable American Title Page

Wendell Smith grew up in Detroit, and his father J.W. Smith was Henry Ford's cook. These connections partially explain why Wendell Smith co-authored a 1968 biography of Francis W. Davis, inventor of power steering.

DOI: 10.4324/9781003283928-10

SOURCE

Acropolis Books, Washington, D.C., 1968. Wayne Dawkins's collection.

THE UNREASONABLE AMERICAN
MECHANICAL DRAWING

Smith co-wrote *The Unreasonable American* with Houston Branch, who wrote Hollywood screenplays. The book contained two-dozen mechanical drawings; however, the written narrative revealed the writers appealed to mass audiences.

———————

DOI: 10.4324/9781003283928-11

reached the demonstration stage. Although they attacked the steering problem along similar lines, Vickers
and Davis were only in indirect competition. Vickers
concentrated on heavy vehicles, while Davis was mainly
interested in the larger passenger car market.

The Vickers gear was a linkage type, so it would
be adaptable to many different installations. Since he
was a supplier to several truck manufacturers this
flexibility was mandatory. On the other hand, Davis
could design more compact integral gears since they
were going to be used in vehicles produced by one
company.

On the Vickers gear the valve and power cylinder
were located in one housing between the Pitman arm
and the frame. Vickers also used spring centering
against stops and adopted the open center valve prin-

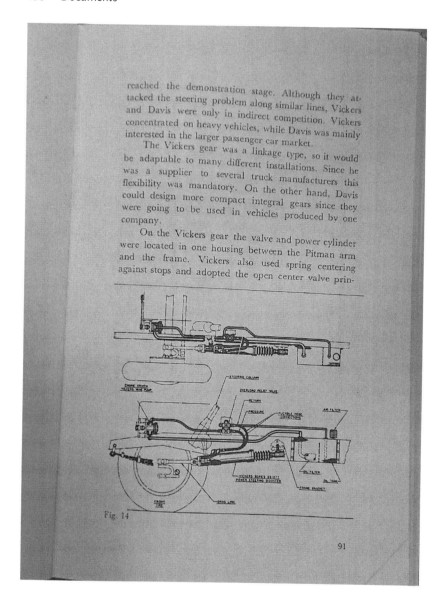

Fig. 14

91

SOURCE

Acropolis Books, Washington, D.C., 1968. Wayne Dawkins's collection.

SAM LACY'S LETTER TO THE NEGRO NATIONAL LEAGUE

After abruptly quitting the Baltimore Afro-American in 1943 and moving to Chicago, Sam Lacy rejoined the Afro in 1945. In 1945, he pitched a news bureau idea to the Negro National League owners.

———————————

DOI: 10.4324/9781003283928-12

COMBINED CIRCULATION OVER 200,000

The Afro-American Newspaper Chain

EXECUTIVE OFFICES: 628 N. EUTAW STREET, BALTIMORE 1, MD.

Baltimore
Washington
Philadelphia

National
Newark
Richmond

January 29, 1946

Baseball Owners,
Negro National League

Dear Member:

The anticipated sports boom, already begun and sure to embrace professional baseball as well as any other activity, demands that a progressive organization such as yours, give more thought to the setting up of a bona-fide press relations office.

I am writing this letter in carbon so that a copy may be forwarded to each of you for consideration prior to the proposed meeting of the league, February 20.

I could set up a bureau which would be held responsible for the dissemination of news on any player in the organization for the coming year. What I have in mind is a central office from which newspapers throughout the country could obtain pictures and news notes on any player on any team in the circuit. All they would have to do wouldbe to ask for them.

In addition, this office could provide daily and weekly papers with game results, standings of teams, personal sketches, etc.

My suggestion is that the league give this idea a one-year trial. The cost would be no more than would be spent on another player, say $125 per month for each team while the experiment was on.

Sam

(L a c y,
722 Park Road, N. W., Washington, D. C.

LETTERHEADS ARE PRINTED ON NEWSPRINT T O CONSERVE PAPER DURING THE WAR PERIOD.

SOURCE

Newark Eagles Collection, Newark Public Library.

Wendell Smith's Letter to Effa Manley

By writing this spring 1944 letter to the Newark Eagles co-owner, Wendell Smith served as an emissary for Manley's former employee Willie Wells. Smith relayed word that Wells was doing well in the Mexican baseball league. Wells told Smith he left Newark of a lucrative salary south of the border.

DOI: 10.4324/9781003283928-13

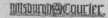

Pittsburgh Courier

2628 CENTRE AVENUE
PITTSBURGH, PA.
MAYFOWER 1401

EDITORIAL ROOMS

May 8, 1944

Mrs. Effa Manley
71 Crawford Street
Newark (2) New Jersey

Dear M,s. Manley:

This is to thank you for your quick response to my appeal
for coverage on the game scheduled in Newark last Sunday. I am sorry you
were rained out, but that is baseball.

As you know, I was in Mexico for a month and while there
saw Willie Wells. He is getting along fine and sent his regards. He seems
to be very fond of you and Mr. Manley. Said the only reason that he left
was because of the big salary they offered him in Mexico.

I have before me a letter you wrote on May 23 regarding
an article concerning your team which was not published in The Courier.
I left here on that date and therefore was unable to answer. I do not
recall off hand just how that story missed the paper, and am sorry that
it did. However, I want you to know that it was not intentional and that
I will do my best to see that the Newark team gets every consideration
the rest of the season. As you know we have be cut down considerably
with regard to space because of the paper shortage, however I'll do everything possible to see that you get a square deal in The Courier.

If you don't mind, please instruct your publicity man to
wire me Sunday night a 150 word story and include one complete boxscore
and one running score of your games Sunday with the Philadelphia Stars
in Newark. Tell him I shall expect him to service me that way on all
Sunday games at home. Games (league games) played on week days can be
mailed. It will only be necessary to wire the Sunday games. We are trying to maintain our complete coverage of Negro baseball and if your man
will cooperate as he has in the past we shall be able to do another good
job this season.

If there is anything I can do to help you out please do
not hesitate to call upon me. I am always at your service.

Sincerely yours,

Wendell Smith

MEMBER AUDIT BUREAU OF CIRCULATIONS

SOURCE

Newark Eagles Collection, Newark Public Library.

Jackie Robinson's Letter to Branch Rickey, Page 1

In 1950, Jackie Robinson spent of his Dodgers spring training in the Dominican Republic. There he learned Branch Rickey, his mentor and friend, was forced out of the Dodgers organization.

———

DOI: 10.4324/9781003283928-14

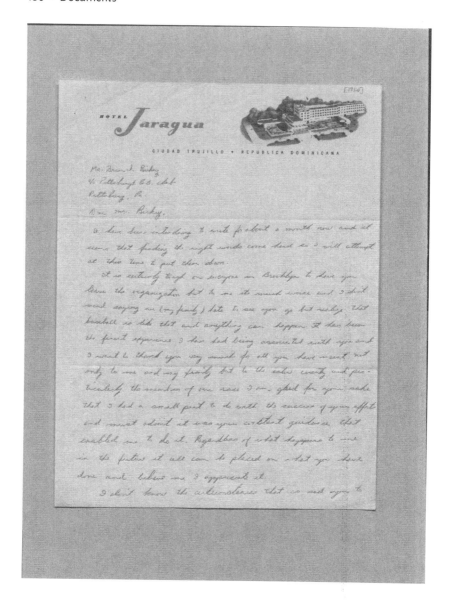

SOURCE

Branch Rickey papers, box 24, Library of Congress.

Jackie Robinson's Letter to Branch Rickey, Page 2

Page 2 of Robinson's hand-written letter to Rickey, who was now an executive with the Pittsburgh Pirates club.

_____

DOI: 10.4324/9781003283928-15

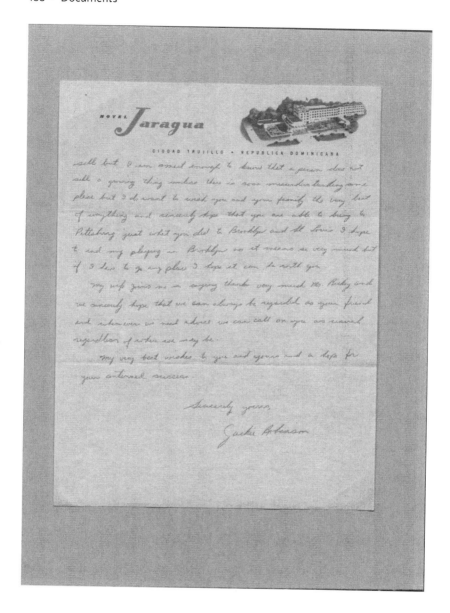

SOURCE

Branch Rickey papers, box 24, Library of Congress.

BIBLIOGRAPHY

Anderson, Stefan, "Jackie Robinson's Special Cap to 'Protect His Head from Beanballs' Up for Auction By Lelands," New York Daily News, September 27, 2017.

Araton, Harvey, "The Dixie Walker She Knew," New York Times, April 10, 2010.

Athans, Drew, "Red Sox Could Have Signed Willie Mays Before Anyone Else," May 15, 2020, bosoxinjection.com.

Brioso, Cesar, "Groundbreaking Started in Cuba," USA Today, April 15, 2022, pp C 3.

Bristol, Douglas Jr., "What We Can Learn About World War II From Black Quartermasters?" August 27, 2021, nationalww2museum.org.

Butler, Kirstin, "The Blinding of Isaac Woodard," American Experience, March 25, 2021, Pbs. org.

Cahan, Richard, "A Court that Shaped America: Chicago's Federal District Court, from Abe Lincoln to Abbie Hoffman," Evanston, Illinois, Northwestern University Press, 2002.

Cosgrove, Stuart, "Sonny Liston – The Santa that Scared America," December 19, 2019, bigissue.com.

Davis, Jack E., "Baseball's Reluctant Challenge: Desegregating Major League Training Sites, 1961–1964," Journal of Sport History, Summer 1992, Volume 19, No. 2, pps 114–162, University of Illinois Press, www.jstor.org/stable/43610537.

DeFord, Frank, "The Boxer and the Blonde: Billy Conn Won the Girl but Lost the Fight," Sports Illustrated, February 13, 2015.

The Quinn-Ives Act, May 13, 2010, Dodgersblueheaven.com.

Doutrich, Paul E., "Carlos Paula Integrates the Washington Senators," Society for American Baseball Research, September 6, 1954, https://sabr.org/gamesproj/game/september-6-1954-carlos-paula-integrates-the-washington-senators/.

Eisentadt, Peter, "Racial Integration and Opening Day," March 31, 2008, greaterny.blogspot. com.

English, J. Douglas, Johns Hopkins University, "Sam Lacy, 23 October 23, 1903, MSU

Fimrite, Ron, "Sam Lacy: Black Crusader: Resolute Writer Helped Bring Change to Sports," Sports Illustrated, October 29, 1990, vault.si.com.

Finkelman, Paul, "Baseball and the Rule of Law Revisited," Thomas Jefferson Law Review, 2002, Volume 25, pps 17–52.

Finkelman, Paul, Dawkins, Wayne, "Before the NBA Coped with Kyrie Irving's Anti-Semitism, Baseball Faced a Similar Dilemma," Washington Monthly, November 23, 2022.

Fortenberry, Lawrence, 1974, "Freedom's Journal: The First Medium," The Black Scholar, November 1974, Volume 6, No. 3.

Frommer, Frederic J., "Nervy jurist tapped as first MLB commissioner," Washington Post,

Futterman, Allison, "5 Interesting Facts About Chemist Percy Julian: Julian Isn't a Household Name, but He Should Be," Discover Magazine, February 1, 2023.

Ghent, Henri, "Oral History Interview with Romare Bearden," June 29, 1968, Smithsonian Magazine. Archives of American Art, aaa.si.edu.

Haupert, Michael, "MLB's salary leaders since 1974," Outside the Lines, Fall 2012. Baseball Almanac, Year in Review.

Halper, Donna L., "Sam Lacy," Society for American Baseball Research

Holt, Alex, Tim Lacy audio files [six]

Holtzman, Jerome, "How Wendell Smith Helped Robinson's Cause," Chicago Tribune, March 31, 1997, pps 7, 3:1.

"Irving Ives Dead; Ex-U.S. Sen., 66; New York Republican was a specialist in civil rights and labor legislation defeated Lehman in '46," New York Times, February 25, 1962.

Jeansonne, John, "One man's Righteous Wrath: As Early as 1937, in the Pages of the Pittsburgh Courier and in Personal Letters to Bigwigs, Wendell Smith Campaigned Against Segregation in Professional Sports," Newsday, Long Island, New York, March 26, 1997, pp B 4 (50th anniversary, Jackie Robinson)

Lengel, Ed, "The Black Panthers Enter Combat: The 761st Tank Battalion," The National WWII Museum-New Orleans, June 18, 2020, https://www.nationalww2museum.org/war/articles/black-panthers-761st-tank-battalion.

Los Angeles Times, "Hank Greenberg, First $100,000 Player, Dies," September 5, 1986.

Manley, Effa, 2006, Eagles, Newark, "Effa Manley, Executive, Class of 2006," National Baseball Hall of Fame, https://baseballhall.org/hall-of-famers/manley-effa.

Marlett, Jeffrey, "1947 Dodgers: The Suspension of Leo Durocher," Society for American Baseball Research, https://sabr.org/journal/article/1947-dodgers-the-suspension-of-leo-durocher/.

Marsh, Michael, 2020, "Wendell Smith," Society for American Baseball Research

McCaffrey, Raymond, "From Baseball Icon to Crusading Columnist: How Jackie Robinson Used His Column in the African American Press to Continue His Fight for Civil Rights in Sports," Journalism History, 2020, Volume 46, No. 3, pps 185–207.

McCormick, Mark, "KU Journalism Professor Led with Love Amid Hate," May 15, 2019, klcjournal.com.

McCue, Andy, "Branch Rickey," Society for American Baseball Research https://sabr.org/bioproj/person/branch-rickey/.

Michigan Advance, "U of M Celebrates Athlete Willis Ward, Who Was Benched for His Race in the 1930s," February 1, 2016, footballfoundation.org.

Nussbaum, Eric, "The Story Behind Jackie Robinson's Moving Testimony Before the House Un-American Activities Committee," Time Magazine, March 24, 2000.

Negro League Baseball Museum, 2024, "Carlos Paula – Barrier Breakers Integration Pioneer," barrierbreakers.nlbm.com

Odzer, Tim, 2006, "Rube Foster," Society for American Baseball Research, https://sabr.org/bioproj/person/andrew-rube-foster/

Parham, Jason, "The Man Who Spurned a Baseball Career to Become a Renowned Artist," The Atlantic, March 14, 2012

Journalism.org, 2005, After 1950, US newspaper circulation did not keep pace with the population and stagnated, then declined. As for radio, much of its content was appropriated from television when the latter medium became dominant in the late 1950s to 1960s.

Randle, Quint, 2001, "A Historical Overview of the Effects of New Mass Media Influence on Magazine Publishing During the 20th Century," firstmonday.org

Reisner, Alex, "Baseball Geography and Transportation," Baseball Research Journal, 2006, Vol. 35.

Frommer, Frederic J., "A Half-century Ago, Hall of Fame Wanted Separate Wing for Negro League Stars," Retropolis, Washington Post, January 22, 2023, pp D8.

Frommer, Frederic J., "50 Years Ago Today, Former Negro Leaguers Gibson and Leonard Made History," Retropolis, Washington Post, August 7, 2022, pp D8.

Frommer, Frederic J., "Nervy Jurist Tapped as First MLB Commissioner," Retropolis, Washington Post, April 10, 2022, pp C8.

Richardson, Haley, "Freedom's Ladder: WNYC and New York's Anti-discrimination Law," [Annotations: the NEH Preservation Project] Retrieved June 21, 2022, WNYC.org.

Rutland, Robert Allen, editor, "Clio's Favorites: Leading Historians of the United States 1945–2000," University of Missouri Press, 2000, Finkelman, Paul, pps 49–67.

Smith, Wyonella, "Wendell Smith Papers/Cooperstown," 1997.

Sandomir, Richard, "In Print, Cheerleading and Indifference," New York Times, April 13, 1997.

Schall, Andrew, "Wendell Smith: The Pittsburgh Journalist Who Made Jackie Robinson Mainstream" (Andrew Schall tells the story of the writer whose careful coverage of Jackie Robinson created the media strategy for the civil rights movement. Wendell Smith's secret weapon? Exerting soft power over public opinion.) Pittsburgh Post-Gazette, June 5, 2011, pp B7.

Smith, Wendell, "Major Taylor: Record Breaker on a Bike," (Black Heroes in Sports History, Number Five) August 24, 1971 (Cleveland Plain Dealer).

Spink, J.G. Taylor, "Judge Landis and 25 Years of Baseball," St. Louis, the Sporting News Publishing Company, 1974. Stahl, John, Society for American Baseball Research.

Thornton, Jerry, "'Bernie' Jefferson, NU Star, School Principal," Chicago Tribune, August 19, 1991.

Tokumatsu, Gordon, "Daughter Honors Kenny Washington, Who Broke NFL's Color Barrier," February 10, 2022, nbclosangeles.com.

Tygiel, Jules, "The Court Martial of Jackie Robinson," American Heritage, August/September 1974, Volume 35, Issue 5, pp 33–37.

Ufberg, Ross, "How Much Longer Can Baseball's 100-year Monopoly Last?" Wall Street Journal (WSJ), April 23, 2022, pp C-4.

Wolinsky, Russell, 2004, "Vic Power: 'Power to the People,'" baseballhalloffame.org/library/columns/rw_040707.htm.historicball.com

BIBLIOGRAPHY, BOOKS

Ashe, Arthur R. Jr, with Branch, Kip, Chalk, Ocania, Harris, Francis, "A Hard Road to Glory," Volume I (1619–1919), Volume II (1919–1945) & Volume III (1946–1988), New York, Warner Books, 1988.

Barone, Michael, "The New Americans: How the Melting Pot Can Work Again," Regenery Publishing, Inc., 2001.

Booker, Simeon, Booker, Carol McCabe, "Shocking the Conscience: A Reporter's Account of the Civil Rights Movement," Jackson, Mississippi, University Press of Mississippi, 2013.

Boyd, Herb, "Black Detroit: A People's History of Self-Determination," New York, Amistad, 2017.

Branch, Houston, and Smith, Wendell, "The Unreasonable American: Francis W. Davis, Inventor of Power Steering," Washington, D.C., Acropolis Books, 1968.

Branson, Douglas M., "Greatness in the Shadows: Larry Doby and the Integration of the American League," Lincoln, Nebraska, University of Nebraska Press, 2016.

Brown, Ashley, "Serving Herself: The Life and Times of Althea Gibson," New York, Oxford University Press, 2023.

Buni, Andrew, "Robert L. Vann of the Pittsburgh Courier: Politics and Black Journalism," University of Pittsburgh Press, 1974.

Cottrell, Robert Charles, "The Best Pitcher in Baseball: The Life of Rube Foster, Negro League Giant," NYU Press, 2001.

Campanella, Roy, "It's Good to Be Alive," Lincoln, Nebraska, University of Nebraska Press, 1995.

Carter, Dan T., "Scottsboro: A Tragedy of the American South," Baton Rouge, LSU Press, 2007.

Dickson, Paul, "Bill Veeck: Baseball's Greatest Maverick," New York, Walker Publishing Company, Inc., 2012.

Dorinson, Joseph, "The Black Athlete a Hero: American Barrier Breakers from Nine Sports," Jefferson, North Carolina, McFarland & Company, 2022.

Durocher, Leo, and Linn, Ed, "Nice Guys Finish Last," Chicago, University of Chicago Press, 2009.

Falkner, David, "Great Time Coming: The Life of Jackie Robinson from Baseball to Birmingham," New York, Simon & Schuster, 1995.

Farrar, Hayward, "The Baltimore Afro-American, 1892–1950," Westport, Connecticut, Greenwood Press, 1998.

Forde, Kathy Roberts, Bedingfield, Sid, "Journalism and Jim Crow: White Supremacy and the Black Struggle for a New America," University of Illinois Press, 2021.

French, Howard W. "Born in Blackness: Africa, Africans, and the Making of the Modern World, 1471 to the Second World War," New York, Liveright, 2021.

Gates, Henry Louis Jr., "Black in Latin America," New York, New York University Press, 2011.

Halberstam, David, "October 1964," New York, Random House, 1994.

Hauser, Thomas, "Sugar Ray Robinson Revisited," Muhammad Ali: His Life and Times, New York, Touchsone, 1991.

Haskins, Jim, Mitgang, N.R., "Mr. Bojangles: The Biography of Bill Robinson," New York, William Morrow and Company, Inc., 1988.

Hensler, Paul, "The American League in Transition, 1965–1975, How Competition Thrived When the Yankees Didn't," Jefferson, North Carolina, McFarland & Company, 2013.

Herbers, John N., Rosen, Anne Farris, "Deep South Dispatch: Memoir of a Civil Rights Journalist," Jackson, Mississippi, University Press of Mississippi, 2018, pps 95, 239.

Holway, John B., "Blackball Stars: Negro League Pioneers," New York, Mecklermedia, 1988.

Holway, John B., "Voices from the Great Negro Baseball Leagues," New York, Dodd, Mead, 1975.

Howell, Ronald, "The Boss of Black Brooklyn," New York, Empire State Editions, Fordham University Press, 2019.

Irvin, Monte, and Riley, James A., "Nice Guys Finish First," New York, Carroll & Graf Publishers, 1996.

Kashatus, William C., "Jackie & Campy: The Untold Story of Their Rocky Relationship and the Breaking of Baseball's Color Line," Lincoln, University of Nebraska Press, 2014.

Kendi, Ibram X, Blain, Keisha N., "Four Hundred Souls: A Community History of African America, 1619–2019," New York, One World, 2019.

Kennedy, Kostra, "True: The Four Seasons of Jackie Robinson," New York, St. Martins, 2002.

Lacy, Sam, Newson, Moses J., "Fighting for Fairness: The Life Story of Hall of Fame Sportswriter Sam Lacy," Centreville, Maryland, Tidewater Publishers, 1998.

Lamb, Chris, "Conspiracy of Silence: Sportswriters and the Long Campaign to Desegregate Baseball," Lincoln, University of Nebraska Press, 2012.

Lanctot, Neil, "Negro League Baseball: The Rise and Ruin of a Black Institution," Philadelphia, University of Pennsylvania Press, 2004.

Lessenberry, Jack, "Reason vs. Racism: A Newspaper Family, Race and Justice," Toledo. Ohio, Block Communications Inc. Press, 2020.

Lieb, Fred, "Baseball as I Have Known It," New York, Coward, McCann & Geoghegan, 1977.

Lowenfish, Lee, "Branch Rickey: Baseball's Ferocious Gentleman," New York, Bison Books, 2009.

Lowenfish, Lee, "The Imperfect Diamond: A History of Baseball's Labor Wars," New York, Bison Books, 2010.

Lowenfish, Lee, "Baseball's Endangered Species," Lincoln, University of Nebraska, 2023.

Madden, Bill, "1954: The Year Willie Mays and the First Generation of Black Superstars Changed Major League Baseball Forever," New York, Da Capo Press, 2014.

Marsh, Michael, Pifer, Michael Scott, "The Wendell Smith Reader," Jefferson, North Carolina, McFarland & Company, Inc, Publishers, 2023.

Michaeli, Ethan, "The Defender: How the Legendary Black Newspaper Changed America," New York, Houghton Mifflin Harcourt, 2016.

Parmer, Charles, "For Gold and Glory," New York, Carrick, and Evans, 1939, pp 50.

Peterson, Robert, "Only the Ball was White: A History of Legendary Black Players and All-Black Professional Teams," New York, Oxford University Press, 1992 (1970 Prentis-Hall).

Pietrusza, David, "Judge and Jury: The Life and Times of Kenesaw Mountain Landis," South Bend, Indiana, Diamond Communications, Inc., 1998.

Pride, Armistead, Wilson, Clint, "A History of the Black Press," Washington, Howard University Press, 1997.

Rampersad, Arnold, "Jackie Robinson, A Biography," New York, Knopf, 1997.

Reisler, Jim, "Black Writers/Black Baseball: An Anthology of Articles from Black Sportswriters Who Covered the Negro Leagues," Jefferson, North Carolina, McFarland & Company, 2007 (1991 First Edition).

Rhoden, William, "Forty Million Dollar Slaves," New York, Crown Publishers, 2006.

Ribowsky, Mark, "A Complete History of the Negro Leagues, 1884 to 1955," Secaucus, New Jersey, Carol Publishing Group, A Citadel Press Book, 1995, 1997.

Rickford, Russell, "1944–1949: The Black Left," from "Four Hundred Souls: A Community History of African America, 1619–2019," New York, One World, 2021.

Riley, James A., "The Biographical Encyclopedia of the Negro Leagues," New York, Carroll & Graf Publishers, 1994.

Roberts, Gene, Klibanoff, Hank, "The Race Beat: The Press, the Civil Rights Struggle, and the Awakening of a Nation," New York, Albert E. Knopf, 2006.

Robinson, Jackie, Duckett, Al, "I Never Had it Made," New York, G.P. Putnam's Sons, 1972.

Robinson, Jackie, Smith, Wendell, "Jackie Robinson: My Own Story," Greenburg Corporation/ Allegro Editions, 1948.

Ruck, Rob, "Sandlot Seasons: Sport in Black Pittsburgh," Urbana, Illinois, University of Illinois Press, 1987, 1993.

Rust, Art Rust Jr., "Get that Nigger Off the Field! A Sparkling, Informal History of the Black Man in Baseball," New York, Delacourte Press, 1976.

Rutland, Robert Allen, editor, "Clio's Favorites: Leading Historians of the United States 1945–2000," University of Missouri Press, 2000, Finkelman, Paul, pps 49–67.

Schlesinger, Arthur M. Jr., "The Almanac of American History," New York, G.P. Putnam's Sons, 1983.

Shapiro, Michael, "Bottom of the Ninth: Branch Rickey, Casey Stengel and the Daring Scheme to Save Baseball from Itself," New York, Times Books, 2009.

Snyder, Brad, "Beyond the Shadow of the Senators: The Untold Story of the Homestead Grays and the Integration of Baseball," New York, Contemporary Books, 2003.

Sokol, Jason, "All Eyes Are Upon Us: Race and Politics from Boston to Brooklyn; the Conflicted Soul of the Northeast," New York, Basic Books, 2014.

Spivey, Donald, "If You Were Only White: The Life of Leroy 'Satchel' Paige," University of Missouri Press, 2012.

Talmage, Lake, "1939 – Baseball's Tipping Point," Albany, Texas, Bright Sky Press, 2005.

Tsoukas, Liann, Ruck, Rob, "Mal Goode Reporting: The Life and Work of a Black Broadcast Trailblazer," Pittsburgh, University of Pittsburgh Press, June 2024.

Veeck, Bill, "Veeck – As in Wreck: The Autobiography of Bill Veeck," New York, Ballentine, 1976.

Ward, Geoffrey C., Burns, Ken, "The War: An Intimate History 1941–1945," New York, Knopf, 2007.

Washburn, Patrick, Lamb, Chris, "Sports Journalism: A History of Glory, Fame, and Technology," Lincoln, University of Nebraska Press, 2020.

Weiss, Nancy J., "Farewell to the Party of Lincoln: Black Politics in the Age of FDR," Princeton, New Jersey, Princeton University Press, 1983.

Whitaker, Mark, "The Untold Story of Smoketown: The Other Great Black Renaissance," New York, Simon & Schuster, 2018.

Wilkerson, Isabel, "The Warmth of Other Suns: The Epic Story of America's Great Migration," New York, Vintage, 2011.

Wolseley, Roland E., "The Black Press," U.S.A., Ames, Iowa, Iowa University Press, 1990.

NEWSPAPERS

Baltimore Afro-American.
Baltimore Sun.
Chicago American.
Chicago Tribune.
Chicago Defender.
Los Angeles Times.
New York Daily News.
New York Times.
Pittsburgh Courier.
Pittsburgh Post-Gazette.
USA Today.
Wall Street Journal.
Washington Post.

INDEX